REIMAGINING ACADEMIC STUDIES

RUDOLF STEINER (1923)

REIMAGINING ACADEMIC STUDIES

Science, Philosophy, Education, Social Science, Theology, Theory of Language

Seven lectures given during the Anthroposophic College Course in Berlin, March 6–11, 1922
with a report about the College Course read in Dornach, March 18, 1922

Translated by Judith Wermuth-Atkinson

Introduction by Christopher Bamford

RUDOLF STEINER

SteinerBooks

CW 81

Publication of this volume was made possible by a grant from the
Waldorf Curriculum Fund.

* * *

SteinerBooks
Anthroposophic Press

610 Main Street
Great Barrington, Massachusetts 01230
www.steinerbooks.org

Original translation from the German by Judith Wermuth-Atkinson.

This volume comprises volume 81 in the Collected Works (CW) of Rudolf Steiner, published by SteinerBooks, 2015. This is a translation of the German edition *Erneurungs-Impulse für Kultur und Wissenschaft – Berliner Hochschulkurs*, published by Rudolf Steiner Verlag, Dornach, Switzerland, 1994.

ISBN Print: 978-1-62148-126-3
ISBN eBook: 978-1-62148-079-2

CONTENTS

3.
Anthropoposophy and Philosophy

BERLIN, MARCH 7, 1922

Different experiences of philosophy, earlier and today. Differentiating philosophy of the West, the Center, and the East today. West: Herbert Spencer. Orientation according to natural science. Strict separation between science and the religious belief of the individual. Center: Hegel. The uniting of the spiritual and the sense-perceptible world, of belief and knowledge. Hegel's remaining stuck in abstraction was a tragedy; his logic as the first beginnings toward being able to experience thought as reality. East: Vladimir Soloviov. Experience of the spiritual. Use of Western concepts as illustration of mystical experience. East: philosopher as priest; West: philosopher as sophisticated, experienced person of the world; Center: philosopher as teacher. Unconscious taking on of Western natural-scientific thinking in Central Europe in the nineteenth century. No further forming or building of concepts in the West, resulting in loss of concepts in the Center. West: natural-scientific results as world question/problem. Center: breakthrough to thought by Hegel. East: looking to what lives above the thought. Building a bridge between the West and the East through anthroposophy.

pages 28–41

4.
Anthroposophy and Education

BERLIN, MARCH 8, 1922

Effect of anthroposophic ideas on the entire human being. Speculations in psychology on the connection between the psychic-spiritual nature and the physical-bodily nature of the human being. The application of metamorphosed natural-scientific principles in the anthroposophic observation of the human being. Relationship between the psychic-spiritual and the physical-bodily natures in the child. The impulse of imitation in the first phase of life; the principle of authority in the second. Unsatisfactory educational methods as the result of abstract intellectualism. Determining the educational program and goal in Waldorf education based on the development of the child. Intellectualism in the third epoch of life, after puberty. Importance of art, music, and movement in child development. The intellectual-cultural impulse in our times; the resulting problems in understanding children and youth. Anthroposophy as a bridge between the world of the child and the adult. Artistic and intellectual approaches in Waldorf pedagogy. The attitude of the teacher.

pages 42 – 55

5.
Anthropsophy and Social Science

BERLIN, MARCH 9, 1922

Core Points of the Social Question: the requirement for a threefold formation of the social organism; impulses instead of utopian ideas. Misinterpretations of the book by theorists of social science and practitioners of economy. Ancient cultures' instinctive regulation of economic life and its penetration by intellectual thought since the fifteenth century. Two schools of thought: theorists with no influence on practice; practitioners of economics remaining in the realm of instinct. A kind of synthesis of the two in today's realism of social science and the resulting socio-political legislation. Woodrow Wilson as an abstract theorist. The difference between abstract thoughts and living impulses. Turning to vital social impulses through anthroposophy instead of to abstractions.

pages 56–69

6.
Anthroposophy and Theology

BERLIN, MARCH 10, 1922

Discussion of a note published in a theological journal. Basic principles of the relationship between anthroposophy, theology, and religion. Anthroposophy as a field of study and a research method. The Father-experience; atheism is a disease. The understanding of the Christ-phenomenon and guidance to the Christ-experience through anthroposophy. The inability to find Christ is fatal misfortune; the inability to find the Spirit is spiritual narrow-mindedness.

pages 70–83

7.
Anthroposophy and Theory of Language

BERLIN, MARCH 11, 1922

The conscious and the unconscious in language. Language as an object of scientific observation. On a lecture given to an English speaking audience, as well as to people from other countries. Emotional nuances regarding the words *Pflicht* and *duty.* Language as a nuance of the spirit of the people.

APPENDIX

INTRODUCTION

CHRISTOPHER BAMFORD

With the end of the First World War, anthroposophy, like Germany (and Western civilization as a whole), stood at a watershed moment. Those who were aware of what had happened realized that the social, political, economic, and human catastrophe they had just lived through demanded radical spiritual-cultural transformation: away from a materialistic worldview of egotism, fear, greed, and violence and toward a renewed, unified vision of a spiritual earth and cosmos, and within it, a dynamic, participatory culture of free, creative individuals. Sadly, however, their numbers were not sufficient to effect the great changes that the times required. Yet, despite overwhelming odds, they, and above all Rudolf Steiner, gave the moment everything they had.

Thus, beginning in 1917, Rudolf Steiner—as always in response both to requests and questions from concerned individuals and the evident needs of the times—attempted to bring the accumulated and ever increasing teachings of spiritual science to bear upon the actual conditions on the ground. This meant a significant shift of approach for anthroposophy: in a word, outward, toward the world. This was not the first time that he had tried to do so. Early (1905-7) in the life of the then German Section of the Theosophical Society, he had tried to interest his students in social issues (questions of economics, education, natural science), but without luck. As he put it, "Theosophists would rather hear of devachan than Ricardo's economic law of rent." This being the case, after the Munich Congress of 1907 and the turn to a more explicitly esoteric Christian and Rosicrucian "Theosophy," he initiated a new artistic framework (painting, architecture, eurythmy, the mystery dramas) for working spiritual insights into the social fabric. Now, however, in the face of the calamity of the Great War, not only impelled by love of humanity and the earth but also called by the spiritual world, he felt he had no choice. In this way, the multiple epochal initiatives—the "movements" by which anthroposophy is largely known today—arose: Social Threefolding, Waldorf Education, Anthroposophical Medicine, The Christian Community, and Biodynamic Agriculture.

Undertaking these ventures—especially social threefolding to which he dedicated five tireless years of issuing books and pamphlets, while giving countless lectures (both public and to Society members), working intensely with businessmen as well as factory workers, and starting businesses on threefold principles, which eventually had to declare bankruptcy—was an enormous anxiety-provoking, energy-draining, time-consuming business: a struggle. What was worse—and perhaps caused Rudolf Steiner even greater pain and suffering—was that this effort continually risked causing a serious rift between older and younger members in the Anthroposophical Society. For older members, it was as if, without warning, what they knew and loved as more or less an "esoteric school" with its roots in nineteenth-century occultism and Theosophy was being transformed before their eyes into a broader spiritual, social, and cultural movement. The implication, as they saw it, was a sea change in anthroposophy itself, experienced especially in how it was expressed, which was less "Theosophical" and much more direct and in ordinary, phenomenological and experiential language. Thus they found themselves being forced to change: to become representatives of anthroposophy in the world, to translate what they had thought of as their spiritual path into a more public, accessible discourse—and to do so out of their own experience.

At the same time, this change required a renewed intensity and deepening, a new dedication, indeed, a veritable transformation of inner, spiritual work—which had become habitual and dulled by routine. With the end of the Kali Yuga in 1899 and the beginning of the Michael Age (fully present since 1879), the spiritual world clearly called for spiritual renewal: a living commitment to spiritual practice in keeping with the times was now demanded. All this was psychologically difficult—and often impossible—for the older members. After all, they were comfortable and happy with the old model. They had grown up with it. It fitted them. Thus, from the beginning, a tension arose between the old and the new.

The "new" was present, most evidently, in the larger numbers of young people who now, really for the first time, were coming to anthroposophy, seeking meaning and authenticity in a world that seemed to them desperately intent on falsity and lies. On the cusp of their adult lives, they had just witnessed and endured the apparent collapse of Western civilization in the bloodiest conflict and then the most duplicitous peace the world had yet seen. Wide-awake, energetic, committed to the recovery of spiritual meaning in human life, they wanted to do something about it.

Unlike those who joined Steiner in 1900 when he started teaching, most of whom were mature and already set in their ways, the new generation came to anthroposophy out of their hearts' needs, without any connection either to traditional esotericism or to the remarkable spiritual happenings of the last third of the nineteenth century. They knew little if anything about Spiritualism, Theosophy, Masonry or any of the other movements from which the first theosophists/anthroposophists were drawn. They did not think of themselves as aspirant occultists, but saw themselves as spiritually open activists, true philosophers, who sought to become spiritual, social, scientific, and philosophical pioneers. They wanted to change the world as well as themselves. They saw that if it were allowed to continue unchecked, "life as usual" would result only in the progressive dehumanization of humanity, the gradual destruction of the earth, and the alienation of the gods and consequent loss of any and all transcendent purpose to life. They understood—as we do still today—that a radical change in the human "being" is necessary. The older generation of anthroposophists seemed to them from another world, another culture, with which they could find little shared ground—and the feeling was mutual. On the other hand, Rudolf Steiner could not but welcome the opportunity to speak to such a group. He had been waiting all his life for these young people, who like him had had no patience for conventional values and conventional thinking. Conventionality—synonymous with being "asleep"—was one of the few things that irritated him. He saw it as a symptom of a potentially fatal disease, one carried preeminently by the bourgeoisie, whose unthinking espousal of egotism, utility, and comfort as primary virtues dominated not only social and cultural life, but also all academic, artistic, scientific, and even religious life.

What is remarkable is that from Steiner's beginning to teach in 1900, it took more or less twenty years for a new generation of young people to be drawn to him. Put another way, those who came to him when they did (1918–1922) were born at about the time that he began to teach. As Steiner saw it, this was not a coincidence. For him, the year 1900 marked an important moment in human evolution: the end of the Kali Yuga. Those born after that date would necessarily be different from those born before it. To be able to grasp his teaching in the truly new way he intended it to be understood, a person would have to have grown to maturity in the post-Kali Yuga period. Therefore, when those whose destiny it was to do so stood before him, he understood with perfect clarity that here were people truly prepared to receive his teaching.

These were young people who wished to make a difference with their lives. They wanted to develop spiritually as well as intellectually. They yearned to overcome the separation between everyday life and the disciplines of science, art, history, psychology, religion, and so on. They wanted spiritual life, professional life, and personal life to be a continuum, lived from the same source. On this basis, they wished to change the world. They envisioned anthroposophy as a way of life—self- and world-transformation in one.

*

Suddenly, then, in the universities and colleges in Germany, Switzerland, and Austria, anthroposophic student groups came into being. In the summer of 1920 the Union for Anthroposophical College Work was founded. It was focused on college students and kept contact with the anthroposophic student groups that formed on various campuses. Steiner encouraged the participants to practice an open mind. As he told those attending the Youth Course (*Becoming Michael's Companions*, CW 217), "I wish to ask that you do not undertake these things in a separatist or sectarian manner, but with largesse. Do not turn anyone away; include everyone who wants to participate. The only determining factor should be the will to honestly engage in the kind of work we want to do."

All this youthful "academic" activity was not well received by the older members, who felt the foundations of their world and their understanding of anthroposophy shaking. Steiner, for his part, was delighted with the enthusiasm and epistemological clarity of the younger generation. They were friends indeed. At the same time, he had his reservations. There was, after all, a difference between exoteric and esoteric work—between the esoteric mission of anthroposophy and its exoteric or outer mission. Clearly, these were related. But equally clearly the exoteric mission could not thrive or even function without the solid, initiatory—holy—foundation of the esoteric mission. And it was not clear to him that this had been established. Increasingly, spiritual work seemed to lag behind the "activism." The Goetheanum had been built, but it had not yet been truly consecrated. Thus, sometimes, as Christoph Lindenberg, author of a comprehensive biography of Rudolf Steiner, points out, Rudolf Steiner felt himself swept up in events with which he could not fully concur. This was certainly the case with many of the business decisions. Whether it was equally so with regard to the "College Courses"—the first of which took place at the Goetheanum in September 1920—is less clear, as Lindenberg points out: "...The fact is that Rudolf Steiner let himself be convinced by Roman Boos to open the Goetheanum and begin the 'college' courses, and gave him a free hand in planning the festive program. On the evening before the ceremonies to open the Goetheanum, September 25, 1920, Rudolf Steiner gave a talk during which he spoke not only of the history of the anthroposophic work, but also about Roman Boos, praising his work":

> Dr. Boos, the founder and leader of the Swiss Threefold Committee, is more than anyone else the one who had the strength and initiative to bring about the work we will begin tomorrow.
>
> In a certain way, one would have to be completely convinced of the necessity of enriching all scientific, all artistic and social

life out of anthroposophy. One would have to be armed with the ingenuity to wed absolutely clear, crisp thinking with the intuitive sense that what flows through the stream of anthroposophy can truly bring to science what is needed. Then one must have the kind of holy fire that enables one to serve such an undertaking. This has happened in a manner (for which we cannot thank him enough) through our friend Dr. Roman Boos, and we have him to thank for these anthroposophic college courses, which we will begin tomorrow.

Naturally it would not do to forget all those who have contributed richly to this venture and worked to make it possible, but a driving force must be present in everything. And this driving force, I'd like to say, must be a social impetus. This is what we have had with this undertaking, and I could only wish that we could have many more initiatives with Dr. Boos; then we would certainly make some progress!"

Lindenberg comments:

When one reads these words today, spoken as they were without the slightest restraint, it is difficult to imagine that Steiner was not in agreement with Boos' actions at the time they were spoken. But whoever is familiar with Steiner's inner posture knows that it was less important for him to be in complete agreement with everything his colleagues were doing; he focused on the enthusiasm, the intention, and initiative, which was for him something sacred. He supported the initiatives of his students even if he was not completely in agreement with them. Already in *The Philosophy of Freedom* [*Intuitive Thinking as a Spiritual Path*], we find the maxim: "To live in the love of action and to let live in understanding of the will of another is the fundamental maxim of the free individual."

It is also possible to assume that Rudolf Steiner had also in some ways become resigned. He pointed out clearly that the Goetheanum had not been consecrated, merely opened, because the work done in the college courses did not reflect its true

> intention. He resisted ceremoniously opening the Goetheanum. But one thing is certain: He did not try to block Roman Boos' activities. Those who heard him speak must have had the impression that he completely supported Boos' work.

Whatever misgivings Rudolf Steiner might have had, the course was, in a certain way, a success. It marked the opening of the Goetheanum. Steiner began with the words: "My heart is moved to speak these first words in this Goetheanum. For the solemn goal that this still unfinished building will serve in the future stands before my soul." There were more than thirty speakers, each addressing their own particular field. It was a new generation of anthroposophists—only three older, original members (Elizabeth Vreede, Adolf Arenson, and Carl Unger) participated. Many represented the middle generation, and there were also many young speakers such as Eugen Kolisko, then twenty-seven years old. Rudolf Steiner gave the opening address in which he wove together the unity of science, art, and religion. And yet, in spite of everything, Steiner would later confess to a feeling of disharmony: he felt that the lectures "did not arise out of the same source as the building. It was something brought into the purely anthroposophic space." Elsewhere, he spoke of the need to create buildings appropriate for "specialized studies and presentations."

Clearly, there is a conundrum here—what philosophers call an *aporia*, a philosophical puzzle or a seemingly insoluble impasse. It is one that still haunts us. Namely, how to reconcile or integrate esotericism and exotericism: how to bring the insights (spiritual, ethical, developmental, theological, and cosmological, and so on) of "Initiation Science" into the exoteric-cultural world. Anyone working in anthroposophy must wrestle with this question, which cuts both ways, for, as Rudolf Steiner himself experienced, the young people whom he hoped would be able to transform "college studies," and who came to him for advice as to how to do so, often seemed less interested in their chosen fields of study than in hearing from him about the "secrets of the cosmos"—that is, they really wanted to hear about anthroposophy rather than science or philosophy. Interestingly, too, most of those drawn to anthroposophy did not end up working in the world—for instance, as academics in their chosen fields—but working in anthroposophy as Christian Community priests or Waldorf teachers. This is to say that the problem cuts very deep. Though the incarnation of Christ happened two thousand years ago, when "the veil of the Temple was rent"—dissolving the distinction between esoteric and exoteric—we have still not realized the unity of esoteric and exoteric or found a single experiential, phenomenological language. Thus we continue to be crucified on two kinds of discourse, two ways of speaking, two ways of living. Nevertheless, Steiner was convinced that "in the course of human development, humanity has reached the point where it needs .... a science of initiation." By this he meant, as he put it in 1920:

> It is necessary that the academic branches of human cultural life become permeated by this spiritual science, and, secondly, that the way we think and feel about the nature of being social becomes permeated by the feelings and emotions that arise in the human soul out of a consciousness that there is spiritual revelation, supersensible revelation—one needs but to turn toward it. (CW 196)

Therefore, despite these irreducible paradoxes, Rudolf Steiner threw himself wholeheartedly behind the youth movement, and continued to support it and participate wholeheartedly in the College Courses. To begin with he spoke mostly on science, to science-oriented students. Simultaneously, however, we see him giving the first medical courses for doctors, and the theological courses for those who would become priests of The Christian Community, as well as the "economics course" for economics students— all these initiatives essentially drawing on the same student movement. No wonder, then, during the first members' meeting of the Anthroposophical Society after World War I—held on September 4, 1921, in Stuttgart—following a motion by a student from Tübingen University, he exclaimed:

> Here a representative of the youth movement has spoken! Here sit a whole number of student representatives! My dear friends:

> That members of such an organization have come to our Anthroposophical Society is something that we must look on as *epochmaking* in the history of our anthroposophic movement.

*

The College Course that makes up this volume, the 1922 Berlin Course, lasted a full week and focused on science, philosophy, education, social science, theology, and language. Besides Rudolf Steiner himself, there were seventeen other speakers. In addition, there were evening events with further lectures by Steiner, as well as eurythmy and recitation performances. This extraordinarily full program was not organized by Rudolf Steiner, who of course was consulted, but left the organizers free to do what they wished. Under the general leadership of Friedrich Rittelmeyer of The Christian Community, this large-scale public presentation of anthroposophy was put together by four Berlin anthroposophic groups (the Association of Anthroposophical Work in Academia, The Berlin Section of the Society, The Association for a Threefold Social Organism, and The Union for Educational Reforms on the Basis of Anthroposophy). There is much material related to the organization and the speakers, as well as various reports on the gathering, in the appendix to this volume.

In other words, it was a program Rudolf Steiner had to fit into. His presence there was above all an act of service and support. Asked to set the tone, to lay the groundwork for an anthroposophic approach to the different fields to be explored on each day, he did so and willingly. And yet it must have been with some trepidation that he accepted the invitation, knowing that, in a way, he was stepping into a potential hornets' nest. Berlin, after all, was the capital city. The event as planned was highly publicized. The fields that were to be addressed were in many cases fiercely defended and ideologized fiefdoms. He would have to tread lightly to avoid controversy. As always, however, despite his myriad other concerns and commitments (and whatever misgivings he might have had about the organization of the event), he took his task with great seriousness. Thus, the lectures he gave are dense, and require close and repeated readings. Moreover, though they appear to deal with quite separate topics—what we are used to thinking of as separate fields—the lectures are intimately connected with, and build upon, each other.

The first lectures deal with science. By the end of the nineteenth century, as a result of the rise of experimental science, science was beginning to experience a crisis— which is still ongoing—with regard to the nature of scientific knowledge itself. Gradually, the idea of science as process was replacing science as system. The dominant mechanical view, which hoped to be able to reduce all phenomena to their smallest parts and the forces acting between them, was crumbling. At the same time, the idea of a single science was giving way slowly to the idea of many sciences, not reducible to each other. This was reflected in a shift from considering the relationship between concept and object from the point of view of the knowing subject to considering the relationship between object and concept from the point of view of the object. Two figures, often noted by Steiner, were symptomatic of these changes: the electro-physiologist Emil du Bois-Reymond and the physicist and philosopher Ernst Mach. Du Bois-Reymond, in his famous *Ignorabimus* speech of 1872, claimed the mechanical view (which he endorsed) was faced by two insurmountable barriers to complete success. It would never be able to account for its own basic concepts (matter, force, movement) according to its own inductive method. At the same time, it was powerless to explain the phenomena of perception and consciousness mechanically in terms of matter. What was left therefore was a kind of dualism and science, as du Bois-Raymond called it, as an "extremely useful fiction." Mach, on the other hand, saw science as, in principle, impossible to complete, and developed an approach, a form of empiricism, that he called "phenomenalism," which would later lead to logical positivism. In this view, sensory phenomena were simply "pure data," prior to any distinction between mental and physical phenomena, and "objects" were logical constructions built from sense data. Steiner's approach, from the beginning, was different. As he wrote in 1894 in *The Philosophy of Freedom*:

> Thinking is beyond subject and object. It produces these two concepts just as it produces all others. And therefore, when, as

> thinking subjects we refer a concept to an object, we must not regard this as a merely subjective activity. It is not the subject that makes the reference, it is thinking. The subject does not think because it is a subject, rather, it appears to itself as a subject because it can think. Thus the activity that a human being performs as a thinking being is not merely subjective, neither is it objective: it transcends both...

And the same holds, in different ways and at a different level, for feeling and willing.

Against this background, Steiner begins his two lectures on the anthroposophic approach by first noting the surprising resistance to anthroposophy demonstrated especially by those working (or interested) in science and philosophy. Rather than attending with an open mind to what anthroposophy *does*, they simply assumed that its method contradicts "scientific method." In reality, the opposite is the case: Anthroposophy actually develops precisely the method, phenomenology, that has proved most productive for science. Communicating this is the hardest task anthroposophy has.

Several things contribute to this difficulty. Above all, there is a confusion between what amounts to the analogical application of "theory" and what is scientific method itself. The "development" of scientific method is confused with transferring concepts of thinking theoretically developed in one area, say, physics, to another, say, biology. On the assumption, for instance, that the kind of causality that works in one area will work in another—that the causality that works in the inorganic world is universal—the same system of thinking, the same system of ideas, is transferred from the inorganic world to the organic world, rather than allowing the thinking, the ideas, to metamorphose in accordance with the phenomena.

Anthroposophy sees things quite differently. It sees them "phenomenologically." Rather than a linear transference of ideas, it seeks to develop "a certain independent growth or self-metamorphosis" in the movement from one order of phenomena to another. What remains the same—i.e., what is developed—is the experiential, cognitive consciousness of "certainty" given by sticking closely to the phenomena in question. For this reason, anthroposophy begins with Goethe's "phenomenological understanding of nature," namely, that the world of phenomena is in itself already theory.

This Goethean approach stands in stark contrast to a science, which, almost without exceptions, depends on the application of mathematics. However, though Kant proclaimed that in any science there is only as much certainty as there is mathematics, mathematics is not applicable everywhere. In fact, there is an inherent danger in its utilitarian, calculative aspect: namely, the danger facing us in the reduction of science to technology. To view mathematics solely in its calculative aspect is only another face of reductionism. However, if mathematics is viewed from a process, rather than a calculative, perspective, the situation is different. Then, as Steiner remarks, "Goethe was in a way more of a mathematical brain than many mathematicians, for he had a fine sense of mathematical processes, of nature producing mathematical concepts." What Steiner means is that Goethe saw mathematics as exemplary of inner soul and imagination processes, in which the primary proof or confirmation is inner. That is why, when describing the "archetypal plant" (*Urpflanz*) for Schiller, and being told it was just an idea, he replied, "In that case, I see my ideas with my eyes." As Steiner puts it: "[Goethe] was talking about an image that could be created internally, but that could nevertheless be verified anywhere in the external world."

Goethe's shortcoming, as Steiner sees it, is that he restricted his phenomenological approach to the sensory world. While this had the benefit that it stopped him from stepping behind phenomena into a rationalized "atomic" world, it can also be seen as "unproductive" or "unfulfilled," for it failed to realize that the results of phenomenological apprehension of the sensory world—understandings or concepts—could themselves be approached phenomenologically. In other words, he failed to fully grasp that for its practice to be virtually indefinitely extendable the phenomenological approach must be understood as a kind of "reading" in which *all* phenomena potentially, and with enormous implications, can open to infinite depth by means of a kind of meditative "receptivity," thus avoiding the rationalistic temptation to construct some hypothetical (mathematical) ground:

> The laws of nature will be the content of such a manner of speaking, but the phenomena themselves will always be at the foundation of the forms of expression. *This is how we can achieve what I would like to call a natural science immanent in the phenomena.* This is the kind of science Goethe was seeking. His methods, however, will have to be changed in the face of the progress achieved today. Nevertheless, the basic principles could be preserved.

With this as an introduction, Steiner turns to the relation between inorganic and organic phenomena. Present natural science rests on concepts derived from inorganic phenomena, which are relatively simple. These may be followed into the organic realm of the higher natural kingdoms, say plants. However they are changed thereby; they metamorphose. But the temptation is to disregard this: to remain at the level of mathematics—of a mechanical, calculative approach. What is lost is the *qualitative* difference that arises with the phenomenon of life. To recover it requires that "reading" becomes the goal of looking at phenomena:

> Reading is the goal of looking at phenomena. In other words, what I see as the essence of natural laws is already in the phenomena, in the same way as the meaning I discover in a word is already in the letters. If I remain within the phenomena, lovingly, and I do not attempt to infiltrate reality with some kind of hypothetical thought system, then my sense of science will be free to develop new concepts. This ability to remain free is what we need to establish.

A pure phenomenology, then, gives rise to a new system of concepts, rather than the re-application of those established for the inorganic world: *different worlds giving rise to different concepts.* The key here is that "we can develop a completely different relationship to thinking if we establish a pure phenomenology." This is because by keeping our thinking within the phenomena at whatever their level we can begin to experience that the natural laws (concepts, understandings) that appear in our thinking are already present in the phenomena. It other words, it makes no sense to separate subject and object: we are dealing with one world.

It is this approach, then, that allows us to move from the inorganic to the organic world and "see" it in its own right. If we allow the new phenomena—say the color of animals—to speak to us as phenomena in their own, living context—then we will no longer be living in a dualized world of rationalistic abstraction on the one hand and materialistically-conceived processes on the other. We will discover the one in the other. Moreover, we will discover, too, that it has ever been so. The so-called phenomenal and the so-called spiritual have always been completely interwoven: reflected in one another. It is always the sensory cosmos that we discover within us. In this way, not only cosmology, but also medicine and many other human-oriented sciences could be renewed.

*

In his second lecture—filling in for Eugen Kolisko—Rudolf Steiner turned to the relationship between humans and animals, beginning again with Goethe, whose discovery of the intermaxillary bone proved to his satisfaction that humans and animals exist on a continuum in which the human organization is able to manifest the whole human being not through something in the structure or morphology of humans but rather through a higher transformation of the animal organization: that the individual organs are somehow transformed so as to express the human being as a whole. In other words, as Steiner observes, the true differences between humans and animals will be "biological"—in the processes of life—rather than "morphological," for instance, in the bones. This is to suggest, for instance, that since sensory functions are vital in both animal and human life we should assume that some form of sensory functioning occurs throughout such organisms—for instance, the experience of taste as paralleling the purely chemical processes of metabolism. In other words, "if we analyze animal organization objectively we will never find anything that does not involve some form of sensory experience."

From this point of view, Steiner continues, something like the life of the senses will best lead to an understanding of the difference between the biological organization of humans and animals. After describing the anthroposophic twelvefold human sensory organization (the five senses of sight, smell, hearing, taste, touch; plus seven further senses: a motion-sense, a balance-sense, a warmth- or temperature-sense, a life-sense, a speech- or language-sense, a concept–sense, and an "I"-sense,) he establishes a contextual framework that separates humans and animals—the upright, vertical spine thanks to which "humans live a completely different life compared to that of animals "who stand on four legs." He then considers sensory processes in this light.

Visual processes, which are dominant in human life, manifest a duality: there is the sense perception that disappears into the nervous system and there is the imaginative, nuanced, qualitative remnant, the image, which we can see and which can be stored in memory. And so Steiner asks: Can we see this duality in all the senses, even the more inner, hidden ones, like the sense of balance? Does imagination play a role here also? In answer, Steiner points to the way through our sense of balance by which we "construct" an internal "geometry" that corresponds to the one outside us in the time-space of the external world. In fact, he says, it is through such internal "constructing" that we were able to come to mathematics or mechanics at all. In other words, there is a phenomenologically apprehensible polarity in all the senses between an inner and an outer, and the shape of that polarity would be different in animals: we live in three dimensions precisely because we are vertical. This begins in the first years of life. Our verticality separates us from animals; the fact that we have imagination, thoughts, makes us specifically human. In this way, extending this approach, Rudolf Steiner clearly articulates the anthroposophic approach to science.

*

Turning next to philosophy, Steiner begins by placing it under the sign of the *logos* (word, reason), as a special kind of thinking. He points to the fact that, initially, in pre-Socratic Greece, it must have referred to a particular human inner experience of wisdom or Sophia. Today, however, we no longer have the same deep relation to the wisdom in what we can know. Therefore, the "inner feeling" of what we are talking about when we speak of "philosophy" (love of wisdom) is unclear. Moreover, to do so, requires exploring the evolution of consciousness or, as he puts it, "the human experience of philosophy in the course of our historical development," which in itself is not an easy thing to do.

Added to this is the reality—at least in the minds of non-philosophers—that philosophy has been eclipsed by natural science, a situation which led some philosophers more or less unsuccessfully to found a "new" philosophy based on "matter and force." As a result of this loss of vision, philosophy since the middle of the nineteenth century was no longer held in the high regard it was in the age of Kant, Fichte, Hegel, and Schelling. Despite this, certain philosophers continued to confront the "big" questions—but only to be led back to the safe haven of Kant. In other words, courage was lacking. Here it should be noted that Steiner makes no reference to Nietzsche, Bergson, or Husserl, the consequences of whose thinking reaches through the twentieth and into the twenty-first centuries. Instead he takes three philosophers, Spencer, Hegel, and Soloviov—one from the West, one from the Central Europe, one from the East—to characterize the situation of philosophy.

Spencer (behind whom lie Bacon, Locke, Hume, and Mill) is taken as symptomatic of the Western approach in its then present form, that is, Spencer sought to create a philosophy based on the concepts of natural science. In other words, philosophy for Spencer exists as a conclusion to and justification of the natural-scientific view. Behind it, according to Rudolf Steiner, lies a "fear" of considering any more inclusive, non-sensory world. Now, a large part of human life is not sensory. Therefore Spencer must draw a strict distinction—an impenetrable barrier—between science-based philosophy and everything else of a non-sensory nature. His philosophy is reductionist by definition.

Hegel, the Central European, takes a contrary path. He cannot stand Newton and has no sympathy for any mechanical view. At the same time, he seeks to rehabilitate Kepler, because Kepler's theory of planetary motions originated in spiritual experience. Kepler in other words was able to penetrate spirit with thinking and thus build a bridge between knowledge and what was previously thought of as the province of faith. Hegel, for his part, possessed the great gift of being able to live within thought. As Steiner puts it: "His life, so to speak, was entirely within the realm of thought." For Hegel, if a higher spiritual world existed, it was only because it was reflected in thought. Indeed, Hegel experienced thought itself as spiritual. He could not experience natural phenomena in their elementary presence, but only experienced them as reflected in the soul in the form of thought. His task, then, was to unite the sensory and spiritual worlds—knowledge and faith—through thought. His tragedy was that he could not experience the inner, living, spiritual power within thought. Therefore his philosophy remains abstract. Yet these abstractions can come alive through anthroposophic research, which can show that Hegel's abstractions can be experienced as realities.

In the East, Soloviov comes closer to anthroposophy. He sought a real experience of the spiritual, but he did so unconsciously, atavistically, almost as a dream. Yet he does not get stuck in "foggy mysticism." He treated religion as science, looked for it everywhere, and developed it philosophically, almost in the same way that the great Greek Church Fathers did. Yet he was not able to fully conceptualize it in the modern sense.

Something else is needed, Steiner concludes, something that goes beyond these three approaches.

In Soloviov, we have someone like an old priest; in Spencer, a man of the world, seeking a practical foundation for life; in Hegel, a teacher, "the pedagogue of the people." What is needed, as in science, is a truly phenomenological approach: a phenomenology that unveils concepts. Therefore, as Steiner puts it, "Here in Central Europe, we have the task to observe what exactly a naturalistic way of thinking really is." This depends on understanding phenomena as *questions*: "To the unbiased thinker, all of natural science becomes gradually a great universal question, rather than an answer to our questions."

Hegel understood this character of "questioning" and tried to approach it through thought. Soloviov grasped that there was something beyond thought, but was not able to fully awaken to it. To fill the gap, Soloviov adopted concepts from the West. His philosophy therefore has a kind of "shadow" nature; it lacks a skeleton. What philosophy needs to do is develop a skeletal structure for spiritual experience that would build a bridge both between nature and spirit and between East and West. This is what anthroposophy seeks to do: to give substance to its own experience of thought. If it does so, then it can also allow for experiencing natural reality in a fully materialistic way, as it is experienced in the West, and build a bridge between faith and knowledge, cognition and subjective certainty, scientifically, but with abstract concepts.

In other words, for anthroposophy, philosophy has the primary task of building a bridge between "truth" and "science" in full accord with contemporary consciousness and thinking.

*

After these two introductory lectures, which lay the ground for everything to follow, Rudolf Steiner turns to the applications of anthroposophy to real world tasks: education and social issues, that is, Waldorf education and threefolding.

In the case of education, his task was to show that anthroposophy, far from being "mystically" or "Platonically" mistaken for an abstract, theoretical, and fantastic account of spiritual realities, was rather a profoundly fruitful source of living ideas with real human power that affect the whole human being. This was demonstrated by the Waldorf School in Stuttgart, a school whose success or failure depended entirely upon its pedagogy, as in its creation there was no choice about its location or its students—the school was located in the factory of its initiator, Emil Molt, who owned the Waldorf Cigarette Company, and the students were the children of the factory workers.

At the end of the day, however, as Steiner says, "education and teaching are based on the understanding of the nature of the human being as this is demonstrated in the relationship between the teacher, who is the educator, and the one who changes, the growing human being, the child." "Therefore," he adds, "our Waldorf pedagogical system is established on the immediate basis of anthropogenesis, the child"—that is, on what we would call today child "development." As Steiner says, most approaches to this question flounder because they lack an adequate understanding of the complex interactions of psychic-spiritual and physical-bodily components in human unfolding.

With this, Steiner turns to the significant moment of the change of teeth, which changes the whole psychic life of children, who begin to live in themselves. Before the change of teeth, children live their surroundings, which means that their relationship to the world is mediated through imitation. Learning occurs through imitation. As the teeth change, this changes. Children begin to create independent images and, with this, develop an incipient inwardness and an initial capacity for abstract thinking. At the same time, imitation becomes something more subtle: cognitive, soul capacities begin to form through the growing predisposition to attend to the world and adults as "authorities." Thus, between the change of teeth and puberty (seven to fourteen), forces previously within and contributing to the physical, bodily being of the child are increasingly freed to become soul capacities. Here, again, Rudolf Steiner shows—giving many more examples—the profound phenomenological basis of anthroposophy, something that both in its practice and application runs counter to the dominant "intellectual" paradigm.

In the following lecture, he then shows how the same holds true when one seeks to understand social issues: the practical, phenomenological approach continuously runs up against abstract intellectualism that almost wilfully resists understanding the anthroposophic approach.

*

Following this, Steiner turns next to the perhaps thornier issue of theology. He begins by noting that this particular lecture was announced in a Christian newspaper as "obviously a challenge to the theologians..." To this, he objects almost angrily (giving away in the process some of his general misgivings):

> Most honored participants, the lecture today may be anything but a challenge. If that is the general belief, it is a profound misunderstanding; this lecture is certainly not a challenge to

> theologians. I did not initiate these lectures, and I have never been involved in them in any other way except that I was asked whether I wanted to participate in this college course by giving lectures and making some introductory remarks. I am least involved with today's lecture in the sense that it was not my decision to include this particular topic in the college course, and it never crossed my mind that what we will be discussing here today could be interpreted as "an obvious challenge to contemporary theologians." Therefore, dear participants, in order to avoid any further misunderstandings, repeated or new, of the few introductory words that I will say, today I will limit myself to the topic "the relationship between anthroposophy and theology." So that there are no further misunderstandings, I will give up some of the points I was going to make, because I do not wish to see my intentions misinterpreted again.

Given this situation, Rudolf Steiner begins by making certain things clear. Anthroposophy has never sought to challenge or argue with modern theology. The contrary impression is due simply to the fact that theologians have often attacked it, despite the fact that anthroposophy sought to remain "completely neutral" with regard to theology. Its intention was to work "in the spirit of contemporary science," though naturally not in its footsteps. Science itself, after all, while achieving great technological triumphs, had done so by largely sacrificing much of its observation-based, phenomenological openness to the undeniable power and efficacy of a mathematized, reductive materialism. This, in turn, had led philosophy—epistemology—into confusion as to its relation to this new turn in the scientific method. Experimental psychology likewise suffered essentially from the same problem, namely, the problem of materialism. Anthroposophy therefore had to develop its own approach, while remaining true to what it held to be the essence of the scientific method. Steiner puts the difference beautifully:

> The question is what do we actually experience through the scientific methods of observation and through the fact that we

> are trained in scientific precision and attitudes? In other words, what ideas and concepts can we form when we simply need to work with natural science? There is one thing that remains true for all methods of observation: (because of insufficient time I cannot prove this here) if the statement that "nothing is in the mind that is not first in the senses" is true for external observation through the senses, then Leibniz's addition to that statement—"nothing...except the mind itself" is also true....
>
> Once we have fully comprehended this, nothing will prevent us from observing what we see internally, and from further developing the categories of the mind through an inner psychic and spiritual process, through a process that represents internally something similar to the external processes of growth in a plant or an animal.

It is through this "meditative-phenomenological" method, then, that anthroposophy or spiritual science is able to develop the cognitive processes of imagination, inspiration, and intuition, upon which its research is based. It is precisely in this sense that anthroposophy is a field of study or research to which people from all walks of life and of all religious denominations and theologies—Catholics, Protestants, Jews, and others—are drawn, freely, of their own will. Within this situation, then, the need to discuss Christianity and its renewal arose in the same way as any other subject—to be explored (researched) as everything else through its own methods.

He begins with the "Father-idea." In earthly life, as human beings, our lives are founded in the body and its senses. These form the basis of our spiritual and psychic lives. Initially at least, we are bound to this body for our thinking, feeling, and willing: through it we process and act in the world through our senses and psychically-spiritually. Reflecting, meditating, on this, provided we are able to close out the world in our reflection, we can come to realize, on the one hand, that our mind, which is "intrinsically spiritual," is able to do this on its own: to put the world together and act in it. On the other hand, engaging our minds—analyzing and meditating the process both whereby we put the world together and how the world is put together

—can culminate in an idea, a "spiritual content." This idea, which synthesizes and contains how we put the world together, its coherence, represents, as Steiner puts it, "the divine- or the Father-idea, if I may phrase it this way." This, the intuition that there is something divine about how the outer world is put together and constituted, comes, as it were, as a natural process. It is the "healthy" thing to happen. If it does not happen, Steiner continues, then something is wrong, or unhealthy. Those who do not have—or refuse—this experience actually suffer from a sickness: the sickness of atheism. Those who are atheists cannot be healthy.

And if we are healthy, we realize we must go beyond this idea of the divine coherence of the phenomena of nature: we must come to the idea, the experience, of the Christ. For this we must analyze our own human development on a deeper level. We must internalize the outer world in our soul. Living with that process, however inchoate and unformed it may initially be, we will come to the "Christ-experience."

One way to this experience is to contemplate the deed of Christ's coming, the Mystery of Golgotha, in the context of the evolution of consciousness. This clearly reveals that, before the Mystery of Golgotha, the Christ-spirit was not united with the earth and human beings. Examining human evolution, we see preceding Christ's coming a gradual diminution of the capacity for the spiritual. This event is at once human, earthly, cosmic, and divine:

> Anthroposophy sees in it how the Spirit (which before could have been searched for only in the supra-terrestrial) now flows into a human body, how Christ flows into the human body of Jesus.... [It] shows that, from that moment on, from the moment of the Mystery of Golgotha, a new era began, an era that all the older religions mention. Christ, who went through the Mystery of Golgotha, Christ whom Paul saw on the road to Damascus, this Christ remained on earth among human beings. This is the meaning of the words: "I am always with you until the end of time." He lives among us; he can be found again.... If we take this road to Christ, who has been present on earth since the event of Golgotha, we will experience him through

> contemplation, by looking at our own inner development. We will find Christ through an inner experience, as we find the Father-God through experiencing the outer world, unless we are sick with atheism.

Through its research, then, anthroposophy tries to present the Mystery of Golgotha in all its details and thereby rediscover the path to Christianity, to Christ. For anthroposophy, not to find God is a disease. Not to find the Christ is a fatal misfortune—for he is there to be found—on the other hand, not to find the Spirit is but a limitation of the soul. But whoever finds Christ becomes part of the spiritual world.

All this is to say, Steiner concludes, that anthroposophy does not deal with theology but only with religion. People who have "religious needs," whatever their denomination, can find them fulfilled by anthroposophy. At the same time, anthroposophy is not a religion. It respects the denominations, the different religions. As for the different theological orientations, it has only sought to make them understandable in their differences. Yet, as Steiner stresses: "In all of them—in all religions—there is a certain kind of person who, through life, is able to experience in the soul the real Christ—an idea that I believe to be Christian." The Christ-experience is a universal-human one.

*

The series of lectures then ends with a lecture on "Language"—not language in the sense of a universal linguistics (the nature of grammar, syntax, etc.), but "spoken language," speech, the nature of different languages. Language is a difficult topic, because it arises deep within the soul, the unconscious, and is deeply interconnected with many other living psycho-spiritual elements. Words uttered are only the tip of an iceberg. As an example, Steiner recounts how he had to give the same lecture to several different groups—some were German, some English. To each group, he gave the lectures in German. At one point, he was addressing the question of "duty"—in German, *Pflicht*, which he associates psychologically with *pflegen*, to care for or look after. *Pflicht*, that is, has "soul" tone. The English word "duty," however, he says, "refers to the intellect, to the spirit that guides us internally." Thus, though the dictionary tells us that the meaning of duty and *Pflicht* is the same, in a way it is not. (These are complex matters: duty, derives from Old French, meaning due, owed, proper, just; while *Pflicht* derives from Old High German *Pfliht*, meaning plight, but also danger, risk. Furthermore, Steiner adds, these two nuances refer back to "the soul of the nation, the national spirit."

These different connotations emerge from deep levels, which makes the scientific study of these inner unconscious substances, which are "only partially expressed in the conscious process of speech," different from, and trickier than, other areas that science studies. However, as Owen Barfield, among others, recognized, being aware of such dimensions gives great insight, not only into different languages and dialects, but also into the consciousness of those who use them. Thus, Ancient Greeks used the word *logos* to refer both to language or word and reason:

> There was a very good reason for why the Greeks felt essentially the same way when they spoke the word *language* and when they spoke the word *reason*, and why they combined these two concepts into one word. This was because the experience within the word and the experience within the thought, within the idea, were to a certain extent still indistinguishable and overlapping for the Greeks, while in our modern epoch there are distinctions in this respect. When Ancient Greeks spoke, they felt that the thought was transformed into word.... Today, if we become conscious of this process, we may feel when we pronounce a word, on the one hand, as if the word floats away while we pronounce it; and on the other hand, as if the thought somehow swims on top of the stream of words. However, the thought is again clearly distinguishable from the stream of words.

Sanskrit, which is more ancient, challenges us all the more. It comes from a time when the meaning of sounds was experienced with great intensity. Vowels and consonants had profound effects both on the speaker and the listener. With consonants, for instance, the ancient Sanskrit speaker (and listener) was immersed in the outer world. Consonants created a metamorphosed imitation of the outer world. Vowels, on the other hand, articulated an inner relationship to that outer world. During that ancient time, giving a context to the language, "dream-like imagination was still alive in the human soul." People lived and saw life in images—not sharply defined images, but "dreamlike instinctive images," experienced as living forces. These, too, were expressed as vowels. To regain something of these insights today, one needs to, and still can, experience the sounds imaginatively.

Returning then to our contemporary languages—English and German in this case—Steiner then shows how a similar way of looking yields interesting results. Thus, as he concludes, the anthroposophic approach is both serious—not just "sticking its nose into things"—and extraordinarily fertile.

*

Steiner was undoubtedly relieved when the week was over. As he said in his report (see the extensive Appendix): "It was an exhausting program." "These days were extremely busy." Nevertheless, he deemed the event a success. He was very pleased with what had been accomplished. The event not only spoke to the spirit of the times, but also fully expressed the spirit of anthroposophy, as did the many other speakers and all the artistic events.

As for Steiner's own lectures: at first reading, when taken separately, they might seem introductory, "aphoristic,"—as it were, improvised and lightly skimming over vast and deep topics. However, the range and cumulative effect of the lectures, covering such disparate topics, when taken together, as a whole, give a quite different impression. Here one feels that the anthroposophic approach—how anthroposophy approaches questions of science and life—has been demonstrated as both unified and unifying. Gradually, as we read and reflect, we begin to see the "wholeness" of life, and we witness how spiritual, psychological, and physical worlds are interconnected in complex ways that the refined phenomenology of spiritual science—its many levels reciprocally related through metamorphosis—is in a unique position to reveal.

REIMAGINING ACADEMIC STUDIES

Rudolf Steiner

1.
Anthropposophy and Natural Science

BERLIN, MARCH 6, 1922

MOST HONORED PARTICIPANTS: the committee for this Academic Week has requested that each day I give an introduction to the topic that will be discussed later from a scholarly perspective during the course of the same day. This decision was based on the view, perhaps, that the various branches of science and of life could be enriched by the perspective of anthroposophy. In that sense, I would like to ask you to take these first lectures of mine only as introductory comments to the discussions of each particular day.

With regard to the perception of anthroposophic research methods, it has always been most astonishing to me to realize the resistance demonstrated toward anthroposophy, especially on the part of philosophy and natural science, although I am not saying only on the part of natural science. The reason for that resistance is apparently the belief that in some implausible confrontational way anthroposophy contradicts the methods of natural science, which have been established as extremely productive in the course of the last few centuries, particularly during the nineteenth century. This belief seems to me one of the things concerning anthroposophy that is most difficult to understand in our times. It is precisely those productive methods of research established in natural science that anthroposophy wants to develop further. However, if we want to understand anthroposophy, we should be able to assume that in the idea of "further development" there is something more than what, today, people usually call further development of theoretical views.

Development of theoretical views means to most contemporary people that the specific way of analogical thinking (particularly with regard to theoretical paradigms themselves, if I may put it this way) remains the same, even if the respective systems of thinking are transferred to other areas of universal phenomena. For example, when we are confronted with inanimate inorganic nature, we need to establish certain analogies, particular frameworks of thought, a sum of interconnected thoughts as a basis for defining theories of these inorganic or inanimate phenomena in nature. Then, when we are trying to understand a different set of phenomena, for instance organic natural phenomena, we assume that we can simply expand that very same system of thoughts. We try to use the same causal understanding that is so productive in the area of inorganic matter, in the realm of living beings, and to explain them with the very same concepts. Hence, from a conceptual point of view, we are trying to turn the area of living beings into the same functional system of causalities that we are forced to establish when dealing with inanimate or inorganic nature. We simply carry the paradigm we have adopted from inanimate nature over to organic nature. This is what we usually understand today under the expression *expansion of ideas or of theories.*

What anthroposophy means by *expansion of ideas*, however, is quite the opposite. Anthroposophy should support a certain independent growth or metamorphosis of ideas when we move from one area of universal phenomena into another, so that we do not simply transfer to living nature what we have learned only from inorganic phenomena, even though it may seem logical. Thoughts concerning one particular area have to take different forms when they appear in another area as, comparably, things in the living world change when they grow, or when they go through metamorphosis, and often become unrecognizable in the new form that they have taken. What remains always the same throughout all areas, giving the entire scholarly worldview a monistic character, is the way we relate to what we could call *scholarly certainty*, a concept fundamental for scholarly beliefs. Only those who are able to test why they cannot come to any satisfaction of causal human needs (if I may repeat the phrase of du Bois-Reymond†) if they use the same concepts they apply to inanimate nature, only those who really come to know this inwardly, would be able to transfer their experience to a different way of making arguments about the living world while using completely different concepts, even if these are only metamorphoses of earlier concepts. The position the human being takes within the world of scholarship and science is definitely monistic throughout the entire scientific worldview. Misunderstanding this usually leads to the fact that people tend to ascribe a dualistic rather than a monistic character to the scientific-anthroposophic worldview.

The second reason for misinterpretations is phenomenology, which anthroposophy must acknowledge, particularly with respect to natural science. Precisely in the era of such productive scientific developments, at the time when the great natural scientist Virchow[†] gave a speech about replacing the philosophical worldview with a scientific one, we learned that the productive concepts of inorganic matter (which, looking from a historical perspective, we have rightfully established) have in fact substantiated a certain rationalism in natural science. So, the era that on the one hand, with regard to the external world of facts, was strongly focusing on empiricism, ended on the other hand with a powerful rationalism when scientists moved from observation to explaining the facts of nature they discovered through experience.

In contrast, anthroposophy represents a viewpoint that (at least for me, if I may make this personal remark) is based on Goethe's understanding of nature. Anthroposophy is established on the foundation of a phenomenological understanding of nature. In modern times, this phenomenology was in a way explained again by Ernst Mach.[†] The way he explains it makes it look as if it provides very productive viewpoints, as long as we stay within its parameters. We can find Goethe's explanation in his statement that "the world of phenomena is a theory in itself, and we do not need to take another step toward creating artificial theories."[†] The blue of the sky is a phenomenon in which we do not have to look first for hypothetical, assumed explanations of the meta-phenomena in a rationalistic way through simple thoughts. This is how Goethe came to the realization of what he calls the *original phenomenon.*[†]

Many of Goethe's ideas concerning natural science have certainly been outdated in the very creative nineteenth century. Nevertheless, we could say that the methodology or the way of thinking that Goethe introduced into natural science is not only still relevant now, but it also, in my view, is not yet fully understood. I do realize that many or almost all the *details* of Goethe's explanations about natural science were outdated in the course of the nineteenth century. And yet, I would like to refer to something I said before the end of the last century about Goethe's view of nature: that Goethe is both a Copernicus and a Kepler for natural science.[†] I still repeat that statement today because I believe that the statements that follow are justifiable.

How do we eventually come to a view of nature in the particular area in which the nineteenth century achieved so much? (I am not able to give other outlines for the things I mean to explain, except those of history.) All the achievements of the nineteenth century in natural science led back to the application of mathematical methods, with almost no exception. A mathematical way of thinking was fundamental even in those cases that did not directly concern mathematical methods, but where other kinds of causal thinking were used instead, and where other theories were established.

The following facts are indicative. We have seen that during the nineteenth century certain branches of natural science were explained in a rationalistic way by using mathematics. We all know Kant's statement that in each science there is only as much certainty as there is mathematics.[†] Now, we certainly cannot bring in mathematics everywhere. Causal explanations offer more possibilities than the producing of mathematical concepts. However, explanations based on causality do follow the patterns employed in mathematical concepts. When Ernst Mach aimed at an overview of this system of concepts from a phenomenological viewpoint, he had to look back at the concept of causality as well, and at the way this concept had developed in natural science during the nineteenth century, to find the particular content of this concept. Finally, he concluded that if he could think of some effect and its cause in connection to each other, then this thought would represent nothing but the concept of a mathematical function.† For example, if I said *x* equals *y*, having in mind that *x* is the cause and *y* the effect, then I have brought everything down to the concepts I use in mathematics when I produce a function. Thus, we can see from the history of science how we have transferred the concepts of mathematics into natural science.

Goethe, of course, is rightfully seen as a non-mathematician; after all, he defined himself as such.† However, considering him simply as a non-mathematician will lead to new misunderstandings. We would then assume that Goethe could not achieve a lot in the area of mathematics, and that he was not particularly capable of solving the mathematical problems that existed at the time. And, in fact, we should admit this. I even believe that as a person Goethe would have not had much patience for solving particular mathematical problems, especially if they were about algebra. We should admit this too. Nevertheless, as paradoxical as it may sound, Goethe was in a way more of a mathematical thinker than many mathematicians. He had a fine sense of the nature of mathematical *processes*, of the nature of *producing* mathematical concepts. He appreciated the kind of thinking that remains hidden in the inner soul-process and in the content of imagination when concepts are constructed.

When we construct mathematical concepts, we overlook our own internal process. A simple example would be the common proof from Euclidean geometry of the three angles of a triangle, which add up to 180 degrees. If we draw a line across the top parallel to the baseline, and we observe the newly created angles, whose total as alternate angles is equal to the total of the other two angles of the triangle—the one in between remains the same—we can see that those three angles at the top add up to 180 degrees, or that their total equals the total of the three angles within the triangle. In case we overlook this fact, we still have mathematical proof, but at the same time we have something that shows that we could be completely independent from external observation and could fail to see things in our internal process of constructing. Then, if we have an external triangle, we realize that we can prove through external facts the same thing that we previously failed to see internally. This is true for mathematics in general. Everything appears in a way that does not require sense perception for us to come to what we call *proof.* At the same time, everything that we have figured out internally could always be proven, bit by bit, externally too.

Goethe thought that what this special quality of mathematics represents is eminently scientific in character, and in that sense he really did have a mathematical mind. This view was also the basis of the famous conversation about the method of scientific observation that Goethe and Schiller once had at the height of their friendship.[†] They were both listening to a talk given by the natural scientist Batsch[†] at the Jena Society of Natural Science.[†] When they were leaving, Schiller made a comment about what they had just heard. He said to Goethe that this was a way of looking at nature in which one only takes things apart, and that it would never lead to anything that is whole. We can imagine that Batsch had simply examined natural objects individually, one after the other. As was typical for the scientists of the time, he had failed to produce an argument that could have led to an overall view of nature. To Schiller, such an approach was unsatisfactory, and he expressed his disappointment to Goethe. Goethe told him that he knew how to bring some unity, some wholeness, into the way we look at nature. And, with a few brief strokes, as he himself describes it, he began to outline the *original plant* in the way we could imagine it internally—not as it is manifested in a specific plant that has roots and stem, leaves, blossoms, and fruit.[†]

In my introduction to Goethe's *Naturwissenschaftliche Schriften* (Works concerning natural science),[†] which I wrote in the 1880s, I tried to repeat the drawing that Goethe had sketched for Schiller on a piece of paper at the time.[†] Back then, Schiller looked at the drawing and said something based on his own way of thinking. "This is not an experience, this is an idea." What Schiller meant by this was that one could draw something like that only if it comes out of one's own imagination. This was something great as an idea—as a thought—but it had generally no physically existing source. But Goethe did not understand what Schiller meant and ended the conversation summarizing what they had said so far: "If that's so, then I see my ideas with my eyes."[†]

What did Goethe mean by that? He did not spell this out, but he meant that if he tried to draw a triangle, its angles would naturally add up to 180 degrees. No matter how many triangles he looked at, what he had constructed internally in this one triangle would apply to *all* triangles. Hence, he made a conclusion based on something that came from inside himself, and which now fully applies to his experience. This is how Goethe wanted to draw the *original plant*, in a way similar to the *original triangle*, and this plant was supposed to show what we could find in any specific plant. In the same way that the angles of any triangle add up to 180 degrees, given that we have the original triangle, the ideal form of the original plant should be found in any particular plant throughout the full range of all plants.

Goethe meant to shape science entirely in accordance with such a perception. In essence, though he never succeeded, he wanted to shape organic science using the same way of thinking that had proved to be productive in inorganic science. This became particularly clear when he wrote from Italy that he kept developing the idea of the original plant further and further.[†] In this context he said that looking at the plants in Southern Italy and Sicily, at the variety of the flora there, he came to realize better and better what the original plant is.[†] He thought that there must be some species that carries in itself the potential of all actual plants; a species that could vary in its form, that could adopt a variety of shapes (an elongated leaf or a leaf with a different form); a species in which either the blossoms or the fruit would develop more; and so forth—as a triangle could be obtuse or acute. Goethe wanted to find a species that was a model for all plants.

It is completely wrong to insist, as Schleiden later did, that with his "original plant," Goethe meant an actual specific plant.[†] This was absolutely untrue—as untrue as it would be to insist that a mathematician who speaks of "a triangle" has a certain physically existing triangle in mind. Goethe was talking about an image that could be created internally, but which could nevertheless be verified anywhere in the external world.

This is why I see Goethe generally as being mathematically-minded. He was more mathematically inclined than the astronomers. And this is what really matters. This is what made Goethe say to

Schiller: "In that case, I see my ideas with my eyes." He saw them with his eyes because he could find them everywhere, in all phenomena. He did not quite understand why some things are perceived only as *ideas,* because when he was producing ideas he was in complete harmony with experience, exactly as the mathematician feels that he is in harmony with experience when producing mathematical ideas. However, I have to say that consequently, through an internal logic, this led Goethe to a mere phenomenology. In other words, he was not looking for anything else beyond appearance, and most important, he was not trying to create a rationalistic world of atoms.

Now, in mentioning phenomenology, we come to a subject that has had many arguments directed against it. To me, the arguments are all based on misinterpretations. We are talking primarily about the fact that we consider a *phenomenon* to be anything that the external world offers to the senses, or anything that is part of experience or of an experiment. Goethe—and with him the entire scientific phenomenology—is trying not to jump from the sensory phenomenon directly to some atomic process hidden behind it. Rather, Goethe focuses primarily on the purely sensory phenomena and on the unique elements of sensory facts, without drawing a connection to anything behind them. What he searches for are simply elements in the phenomenal world that are related to each other, and he tries to find the connections between them.

I can fully understand where the respective misinterpretations come from, and how easy it is to see such phenomenology as unproductive. For example, one could say that if we limit ourselves to simply describing the interconnections between sensory phenomena, if we look only for the simplest phenomena in which the processes are most easily comprehensible (and which Goethe calls *original* phenomena), then our approach will never lead us to understanding the very productive discoveries of modern chemistry. One could ask how we could deal with atomic weight relationships without any understanding of the world of atoms. In this case, one might want to ask a counter-question: if we become aware of a given phenomenon, would it be necessary to distance ourselves from it? We certainly would not have to do this. Even when we compute atomic weight relationships, we still have to deal with a phenomenon, namely with weight relationships. Would it bring us any further to try to explain the same weight relationships, which are expressed in numbers, in a purely rational intellectual way through the fact that from the atomic weights we produce certain molecular structures? We could ask that question, couldn't we? To summarize: from Goethe's perspective, this is all about the fact that we should stay within the realm of phenomena.

Here, I would like to give a very simple example. Let us assume that we are given a written word to look at. What do we do? Well, if we have never learned how to read, we will stare at it as if it is something inexplicable. But if we have learned how to read, then, unconsciously, we will put together the different forms of the letters and we will experience the meaning of the word in our soul. One thing we certainly would not do is try to explain the meaning of the word on the basis of the form, say of *W*, considering the beginning of the upward stroke and then the one going downward, thinking that in this way we will discover something profoundly significant about that letter. In other words, we will be reading, rather than trying to explain things through assumptions. This is how phenomenology wants to *read*. It wants to stay within the context of phenomena and it wants to learn how to read, and, if it has to deal with a complex of phenomena, it does not want to go back from that complex to the small atomic structures.

Hence, this is all about accepting the realm of the phenomenal, and about learning how to read its own internal meaning. Such an approach will bring us to a kind of natural science that will contain nothing rationalistic constructed beyond the phenomena. Instead, simply by the way it views phenomena, this science will find certain regular structures. This kind of natural science will always represent the sum of the phenomena themselves. People will speak in a very particular *manner* about nature. The laws of nature will be the content of such a *manner* of speaking, but the phenomena themselves will always be at the foundation of the forms of expression. This is how we can achieve what I would like to call a natural science immanent in the phenomena. This is the kind of science Goethe was seeking. His methods, however, will have to be updated in the light of the progress achieved today. Nevertheless, the basic principle could be preserved. And if we do preserve this basic principle, we cannot but discover something important about our human perception of nature that I would like to characterize as follows.

It is understandable that contemporary humanity has established its concepts of natural science primarily on the basis of inorganic nature. The reason is that inorganic natural phenomena are relatively simple. In addition, there are processes of the inanimate world that certainly continue to act when we move up into the realm of organic matter. When we move from the kingdom of minerals to the vegetable kingdom, we cannot say that there are no inanimate processes in the plant; they are included in a higher principle, but they persist in the plant. We are right to explore physical and chemical processes in the plant organism as we would explore them in inorganic nature. In this case, however, we should be able to accept modified, metamorphosed concepts in our paradigms. We should follow how the same processes found in inanimate nature are extended to plants too. Scientists are tempted, however, to follow only those processes that originate in the kingdom of minerals and extend to plants and animals, while failing to consider what else is happening in the higher natural kingdoms. This temptation became extremely strong because of particular circumstances over the course of the nineteenth century.

This is how that happened. When we observe inanimate nature, we feel deeply satisfied in a way, because we can follow the phenomena with a mathematical kind of thinking. I would say that it was completely understandable when, in his speech "On the Limits of our Cognition of Nature,"du Bois-Reymond celebrated Laplace's worldview,[†] which, in splendid and rich language, he called "the astronomic conception" of the entire existence of nature.[†] According to this astronomic conception, with the help of mathematical thinking, we can grasp not only the various phenomena of the firmament and construct with them, as much as possible, one undivided whole, but we can also try to dive deep down into the constitution of matter. We are trying to construct a small universal system in the molecule, where the atoms move and relate to each other as do the stars in the universe. In this way, we construct the smallest universal systems in our small scale world, and we are satisfied because in this small scale world we find the same laws that apply to the large scale universe. We know, for example, that the atoms and molecules represent a system of moving particles like the system of fixed stars and planets out there in the universe.

This example is characteristic primarily of the intellectual quests of the nineteenth century, and of the way in which the human need for causality is satisfied, as du Bois Reymond says. This is simply the result of the desire to apply certain productive methods from the area of mathematics to all natural phenomena. It is also the basis of the temptation to remain at the level of mathematics when we observe all sorts of different phenomena in nature. Unless we speak about those things like amateurs, no one, not even an anthroposophist, would deny that there are logical explanations of all those facts when we look from within the phenomena, and when we try to understand the details, say about astronomy, in this context. No one will disagree with such explanations.

What happened during the nineteenth century, however, was a failure to see the *qualitative* elements in what the world offers. Rather, people saw only what was manifested, what could be comprehended with the help of mathematics, even though that was all part of the *qualitative* too. We have to make a distinction. We can certainly admit that this mechanical explanation of the world is completely plausible—no objections; but it makes a difference whether we declare a mechanical explanation to be reasonable in certain areas, or whether we want to present it as the only possible system of concepts, using it to explain every single thing in the world.

This is the point where opinions differ. Anthroposophists do not deny or fight against the things that are legitimate. In fact, it is interesting to observe how, in discussions, anthroposophy accepts everything that is within legitimate limits. The goal of anthroposophy is certainly not to deny what natural science asserts. The question is whether it is legitimate to try to explain the entire world of phenomena through mathematical thinking. Should we take from the sum of phenomena only the mathematical, causal abstraction and treat it as an *imagined* universal content, as, for example, the former atomism did? Today, atomism has become to a certain degree phenomenological, and up to a point, anthroposophy agrees with it. The problem is that today's atomism is affected by the ghost of the nineteenth century, and it is in complete contradiction to Goethe, who was not limited to phenomena, but established a paradigm beyond them. If we are not clear about the fact that science now uses only one paradigm, one system of concepts, to express the world beyond appearance, and if in confusion we adopt the false view that with this system of concepts we have captured something real, then this very system will actually mislead us. Because of it, we will become dogmatists. We will say that although there are people who want to explain the world of organic nature with completely different concepts, there are no such concepts. We will think we have already established paradigms that cover the world beyond the phenomena. We will think that the world of our concepts is the only one, and it must work somehow with regard to the organic too. In this way, however, we would apply everything that we have established regarding inorganic matter to the observation of organic matter. We would begin to look at the organic in nature as if it came to be in the same way as the inorganic.

Here, we have to be very clear. Without complete clarity, we will never be able to establish the foundation for a real discussion. Anthroposophy has no desire to commit the sin of superficiality against any legitimate methods; it does not want to sin against what is legitimate in atomism. However, anthroposophy wants to clear the way for the establishing of thought systems similar to those established earlier in the study of inorganic matter, systems that should now be established in other areas of nature too. This could happen only if we say to ourselves, *reading* is the goal of looking at phenomena. In other words, what I see as the essence of natural laws is already in the phenomena, in the same way that the meaning I discover when I read a word is already in the letters. If I remain within the phenomena, lovingly, and I do not attempt to impose some kind of hypothetical thought system on reality, then my sense of science will be free to develop new concepts. This ability to remain free is what we need to establish.

We should not restrict ourselves to the use of one paradigm when we shift to examining a different area of nature, even if the first one was rightfully established. We can develop a completely different relationship to thinking if we establish a pure phenomenology—something that would certainly be possible only if we come to the natural laws by interspersing the phenomena that we look at (or that we present through experiments) with thoughts, and if we make connections between them. In other words only by remaining within the phenomena can we experience how natural laws that appear in our thoughts are already present in the phenomena themselves. If we accept this idea, it will make no sense to speak about an "opposition" between subjective thoughts and natural phenomena, at least not insofar as we remain within the phenomena. We simply submerge ourselves in the phenomena and then, in the essence of natural laws, the essence of thoughts is given to us, coming directly from the phenomena. This is why Goethe remarked naively, "Then I see my ideas," (which were actually natural laws, in nature) "with my eyes."[†]

If this is our approach to the phenomena in inorganic nature, then it will be possible to transfer it to organic nature, including the scientific study of organic nature. And if we see then that a horse is brown or white, we are not going to ascribe this phenomenon to inorganic colors. Instead, we will see it in relation to something that lives as a spiritual or a soul being in an organism. The created inner organization will teach us to understand that animals, as well as plants, give themselves a color. In that case, we should certainly be able to observe internally all the details—how metabolism works, for example. But then, we do not simply transfer to the organic what we have found in the inorganic. We do not restrict ourselves to one particular paradigm, and we do not rigidly carry our attitudes from one particular area into all others. We keep thinking in a more *mathematical* way than those who do not want to see concepts metamorphosed into qualitative categories. This is how we validate inner seeing when it comes to the higher realms of natural existence, how we validate inner seeing when it comes to inanimate mathematical constructs.

This is only a brief outline of all these things. Further development would show that anthroposophy is really capable of accounting to anyone, including the strongest mathematician, as Goethe put it.[†]

This was Goethe's goal when he formulated his idea of the original plant, or with his idea of the original animal (which, however, he did not develop further).† This is also the goal of anthroposophy: to take from Goethe's views everything that concerned phenomena in nature, and to move from the understanding of what lives in our imagination to the type of the plant or the type of the animal. I demonstrated already in the 1880s that we should metamorphose the concepts that we apply to inorganic nature, and in that way adapt them to organic nature.† I will be discussing this further in the next few days. In this way, however, we also begin to see what the real driving or creating principle of organic nature is. To this observation, I would like to add something that will show that anthroposophy does not underestimate the materialistic phase in the development of natural science, a statement I will comment on again in the next few days.

Anthroposophy should see this materialistic phase of natural science as a transition, as a method of learning how to yield to the pure sensory experience. This phase was highly educational for human civilization. We can have a clear overview of certain things only after we have experienced this kind of learning. Only one who is armed with such a sense of science can observe the external material world and see how the external material world *mirrors* itself within us, if I may use this expression.

The world, as we experience it in ourselves, is more or less an abstraction, an image of the external material world, interwoven with our senses and impulses of will. Thus, when we move from observing the external material world to observing the spiritual world, we come to the purely imagined. Let us hold on to this point: externally, we have all the material phenomena that we observe in a phenomenological sense; internally, we have the spiritual, the psychic, in a certain abstract form, in the form of an image. If, however, we observe with an anthroposophic worldview the things that spiritually are at the foundation of the external material world—if we enter the spirit that is active in the motion of the stars and in the formation of the minerals and plants and animals—then we enter the spiritual in the very coming into being of the external world. We come to know it through imagination, inspiration, and intuition, which also give us an inner image of the human. But what is this inner image of the human? These are our physical organs. They now correspond to what we had learned before as the nature of the sun, the moon, minerals, plants, animals, and of other things; this is what the internal human organs correspond to. We can get to know our own human organism only if we get to know the external world. The material world *outside us* is reflected in the spiritual and the psychic *within us*, and the spiritual world *outside us* is reflected *within us* in the forms of lungs, of liver, of heart, and so forth. If we look at our internal organs, we will see that they are in the same relationship to the external spiritual world as our thoughts and feelings are to the external material world.

This demonstrates that anthroposophy is not overeager to reject materialism. But, let us look at the entire range of sciences. We will not be satisfied with the results of thousands of them using the traditional methods. By contrast, anthroposophy will achieve a worldview through its methods that does not leave us unsatisfied. It recognizes the physical/material both in the inner organization of the human being and in the phenomenology of the surrounding world. At the same time, anthroposophy has to recognize that this inner organization is a result, a consequence, of the spiritual in the cosmos. Therefore, it wants to complete what astrophysics, physics, or chemistry have achieved through mathematics alone. Anthroposophy will do this in the form of an organic cosmology, and it will continue to search until it brings us to a better understanding of the material aspect of the human being. Such methods are fundamental to the understanding that anthroposophy can develop also in service to medicine, biology, and so forth.

I hope that with these brief comments, I have pointed out why anthroposophy, if we understand it correctly, is not in opposition to contemporary science. Instead, it seems to me that contemporary scientists have not found the bridge that shows that anthroposophy strives to be strictly scientific with regard to natural phenomena.

2.
On the Organization of Humans and of Animals

BERLIN, MARCH 6, 1922

Most honored participants: I would like to ask you to keep in mind that until last night I was assuming that today I would attend this lecture given by Dr. Kolisko, rather than give it myself. Thus, in the short time I had, it was impossible to prepare properly what I am going to say, and I can only hope that by and large I will be able to present the points that Dr. Kolisko wanted to talk to you about.[†]

When we speak about the relationship of the animal world to the world of the human being from an anthroposophic perspective, we should emphasize that historically there is a connection between present anthroposophic ideas and Goethe's worldview—a fact I have already mentioned twice. Regarding the topic in question, we should consider most of all one of Goethe's first achievements in the area of science, his treatise titled "Humans as Well as Animals Have an Intermaxillary Bone in the Upper Jaw."[†] We have to imagine all the circumstances that led Goethe to write this treatise, which is based on his extensive studies in the areas of anatomy and physiology, and on some embryological studies.

Goethe became involved with these questions first as a young student, and then later as a friend of the Jena University institutes, (which to a certain degree depended on him). When he started dealing with the question of the main difference between human and animal, Goethe realized that everyone was eager to find something in the structure or the morphology of humans and of animals that would point to a strict distinction between the animal world and the human being—the crowning glory of creation. People believed they had found a profound difference between human and animal precisely in the structure of the head, in the fact that the so-called intermaxillary bone, which in animals is clearly separated from all other jawbones, is not a separate bone in the human being.

Goethe did not pay attention to that. Since human and animal have in general an analogous structure, he was convinced that such a detail could not express differentiation. Since in adult individuals the intermaxillary bone has grown together with the rest of the jawbones, Goethe was trying to prove that this is the result of a later development, and that the human embryo has the same intermaxillary bone structure as the animals.

We should observe the enthusiasm with which Goethe points out that he had succeeded in demonstrating that both humans and animals have an intermaxillary bone, and that consequently there is no profound difference between them to be found in details of their structure or morphology. Thus, we cannot say that Goethe shared the view of the strict separation of the human from the animal world that was characteristic of the eighteenth century, and anthroposophy does not share this view either.

Goethe did assume a transformation in the process of development from the organization of animals to the higher organization of humans; the individual organs that are already present in the animal are transformed.[†] Once the organs are transformed, they can manifest, in this transformed animal organization, the inner world of the human, the human being as a whole. Goethe thought only of an ascending metamorphosis of the animal world into the human, and not of an independent human morphology.

This viewpoint should also be the basis of our anthroposophic search for the differentiation between the animal and the human organism. If the forms of organization are based simply on the metamorphosis of the animal and of the human, then looking for the differentiation, we should observe particularly the processes of life in humans and in animals, how the organs of humans and of animals function. In other words, we should look for a biological rather than for a morphological difference.

The idea that there is a biological difference anticipates future scientific developments by examining the foundation of the functioning in animals or that which is related to the sensory organs in both humans and animals. Sensory organs, or rather their functions, are vital for more or less everything that is happening in both animal and human organisms. We should assume that some functions of a primitive form of the senses occur even in the simplest nutritional processes, in the metabolism, of the lower rank of animals. This would mean that, for example, the experience of taste occurs parallel to the more or less purely chemical process of metabolism. These processes become more and more differentiated as we follow the development of higher animals up to the human being. However, if we analyze animal organization objectively, we will never find anything that does not involve some form of sensory experience. We can certainly ask how this sensory experience relates to the formation of lymph or of blood, and so forth.

Currently, science that is not influenced by anthroposophy speaks of the unconscious processes of the human psyche. Even though I can mention this only briefly because of insufficient time, I would say that it is plausible to ask why we assume that the experience of taste in the mouth and at the gum (the experience of taste that occurs under the influence and because of the function of ptyalin or pepsin, and so forth), is not brought to the unconscious? Why should the experience of taste (and I am saying this as a postulate of sorts) not expand throughout the entire organism? Why do we not think that unconscious experiences of taste might be occurring parallel with the formation of lymph and blood, and all other processes in the organs of which we are not conscious? Once we begin to observe the life of the senses, we will certainly be able to analyze human and animal organization from a biological perspective.

As I have been telling some of you for years, and as natural science already accepts, the life of the senses occurs in more than the five senses usually mentioned.[†] There are actually twelve clearly distinguished human senses. This applies only to the human being. Those who recognize the possibility of more than the five or six senses (seeing, hearing, smelling, tasting, feeling, touching) will accept that it is justifiable to speak, for example, of a sense of balance. This sense allows us to recognize internally whether we stand on two feet or only on one, whether we perform a movement with one or the other arm, and so forth. When we place ourselves in the world as human beings, we take a position of balance. We perceive our own position of balance with our senses, just as we perceive what occurs in the process of seeing, though in a somewhat more obscure way. Hence, we can talk about a sense of balance as surely as we talk about a sense of sight. We should be clear that when we use the sense of balance we are focusing on our own organization: in a way, we look inward; while using our eyes, we look outward. Nevertheless, the basis of our experience of balance is certainly some function of the senses.

We could expand the number of senses in another direction too. When we simply hear a noise, the functional processes of the human organism are substantially different from the processes of listening to speech, which is a different kind of hearing. In hearing speech we perceive, again directly through our ears, but we focus also on what we perceive indirectly through language. When we follow the words, the sentences, of another person, using our inner understanding, then we are dealing with more than our judgment. The process of judgment is preceded by a sensory process of perception. Therefore, we should speak of having a "sense of speech," or rather a sense of language or of words, like our sense of hearing. Put in another way, if we look at words from a more anatomical or physiological viewpoint, we should assume that within the organization of the human there exists a special organization of the senses that corresponds with listening to what is said, just as the organization of the hearing sense corresponds with listening to unarticulated sounds. Consequently, we should assume the existence of a special organization of the sense of speech that is similar to any other sense organization, such as the senses of sight or hearing.

If we approach this objectively, we should not say that we recognize another human being because we see things like a nose, two eyes, and so forth. We should not make an assumption, based on analogy, that in this thing that stands before us, there is a human being simply because in ourselves, there is a human being that reveals itself in the outer world through a nose, through eyes, and so forth. In fact, such an unconscious conclusion is not the basis of recognizing another human. Rather, there is an immediate grasping of the other human that must correspond with something special in the human organization, something that can be compared only to the organization of senses. In fact, we could speak of a sense of the Self that helps us recognize ourselves in the other. If we understand the functioning of the human being completely objectively, we will be as justified to speak of sensory organizations for the perception of words, of thoughts, and of the Self (not of one's own Self, however, which is based on something totally different), as we are in speaking of the sensory organization of hearing, of speaking, and so forth. Furthermore, we should be able to speak of a sense of movement, since it is one thing to move and another to stand still, and we perceive the difference. Similarly, we should speak of a sense of life—natural science already speaks of it, to a degree.

If we define in this way the number of sense-organization systems, we will come up with twelve human senses. Some of them, however, are inner senses, since we perceive our inner organism as well—we perceive how we feel with regard to our sense of balance or to our sense of movement. Nevertheless, the quality of our experience of the inner organization is absolutely the same as the quality of the processes of seeing, hearing, or tasting. Thus, it is all about looking at things in the right context.

If we take as a starting point an integral physiology of human senses, we will see certain significant biological phenomena both in humans and in animals. The significance of these phenomena will remain the same, even if we completely agree with the new theories of the relationship between the morphological and physiological organization of humans and that of animals, including with Haeckel's theory.[†] Here, however, we can observe the most impossible misunderstandings. For example, it is believed that anthroposophy must be opposed to Haeckel's theory simply because anthroposophy is trying to progress from observation through sense perception to the higher level of empirical observation of the spiritual. It is believed that, based on this background, anthroposophy must change something in

Haeckel's theory. No! If there is anything to be corrected in Haeckel's theory, it should be done using the methods of natural science, and anthroposophy has nothing to say about it. Natural scientists can argue with Haeckel themselves.

What anthroposophy has to say relates to a completely different area. We have the right to emphasize that if we count the bones of the higher animals, the number will be the same as that in humans. The same applies to the number of muscles; but this is not the way to differentiate between human and animal organization. However, if we approach the issue from the viewpoint of biology, then we see a real differentiation. Then, we come to appreciate the fact that the human organization has an essentially different place in the universe from that of animals.

When we observe the higher animals, we have to say that an important element of their development is the position of their spinal axis, which is parallel to the surface of the ground, while in humans it is just the opposite. In the process of human development the horizontal position of the spine has changed into a vertical one, and, thus, one of the most important functions of humans is to stand in an upright position. I realize that people could object and point out that there are also animals that have a more or less vertical spinal axis. The question, however, is not how a species appears in relation to an external morphology, but what the nature of its entire organization is. In particular animals, such as some birds, or even mammals, the possibility that their spines could be brought more or less to an upright position is an assumption. In fact, an upright position would be a sign of degeneration, considering the nature of the animals' organization. By contrast, for humans to have an upright position of the spine is precisely in the nature of their organization.

Once, years ago, when I mentioned this at a lecture in Munich, an educated natural scientist came up to me and said something I could understand very well.† "But when we sleep, the spine is nevertheless in a horizontal position." I told him that this is not what matters. What is important is how the spine is positioned in relation to, say, the bones of the legs or the feet in relation to the rest of the body, considering the entire cosmic context of the human being and also how this positioning affects the human or the animal. Our spine is certainly in a horizontal position when we sleep, but this horizontal position is external. The inner dynamics of our body are organized in a way that allows us to take an upright position of balance in which the spinal axis is vertical. When animals bring themselves to such a position of balance, they are either degenerated to a certain degree or they develop some humanlike functions—a fact that only proves what I would like to explain next.

We could say that already in the first years of life, human beings find for themselves their own position in the balance of the universe. They form the vertical position of their spine—a position that is different from that of the animals—for purely functional reasons, because of the entire dynamics of their being. At the same time, each being is formed as part of the entire universe, and one could say that beings adjust to the universe. I will not elaborate on this right now.

Observe further the structure of particular bones in the human being, such as the ribs or the skull. We see in the forms of the ribs or the skull of a human or of a dog that from a morphological point of view it is possible to find signs of adjustment to the vertical or horizontal position of the spine. By positioning themselves vertically, humans live a completely different life compared to that of animals standing on four legs; they live in a different position of balance, and thus in a different cosmic context. Now, let us try to approach the problem from a different angle and clarify what is really happening in the human being in terms of sensory processes, and what is happening as a consequence of those sensory processes. All this could be translated into a very precise biological or physiological terminology, but because of insufficient time, here I will only outline what I want to discuss.

Let us consider the visual process. We could subdivide it into the specific functions of the visual organ and into the processes that occur further as a continuation on the physical level. What I want to stress here, as analogy, is the fact that the optic nerve begins in the eye and then disappears in the rest of the system of nerves. Hence, we can distinguish between the visual process itself and what follows in the whole process of life. The imaginative element is also inherent in the immediate visual process; that is, when we look at something, we do not separate the imaginative element from the visual process. If we turn our eyes away from the object we are looking at, we still retain its image, an image that is clearly related to the object perceived in the visual process. Those who analyze this correctly would see how different the imaginative result of a visual process is from that of an auditory process. Within ourselves, I want to stress, we experience the visual process in a dualistic form: on the one hand, there is something related to the real sense perception, and on the other hand, there is something that is like an imaginative remnant and that stays with us more or less as a formed memory.

Take now everything that lives in the human imagination but that is based on the five senses. Most of what is in the psychic life of the human is based on the visual process; we perceive very few imaginations through the auditory process in comparison to the number of things we perceive in the visual process. If we observe the inner life of our psyche, we will find even fewer things that are based entirely on it alone than the things that are based on the processes of seeing, hearing, and so forth. We do know that the imaginative element, which leads to lasting memories, plays some role in the life of our psyche, but this role is much less significant than the role of the visual and auditory processes.

We can now pose the question: does this duality exist also in the cases of the more hidden senses, such as the sense of balance or of motion? Is it the same duality we see in the visual sense—between the element of perception and the element of imagination? To a really objective physiology or psychology this duality should exist in the case of the sense of balance too, but we usually fail to see the connection. In the previous lecture I just gave, I discussed mathematics, and the ability to find one's way in spatial relations where the mathematical element is used for the purposes of geometry.† What is it really that we are doing when we construct spatial relations? With respect to the human being as a whole, we do exactly the same as when we clearly separate perception from imagination in the visual process by retaining the image internally. [We perceive a color not only externally]; we also experience the qualitative element of the color, the nuance, and we even have the feeling of a warm or of a cool color, a feeling that persists internally.

Thus, we could take as a task at some point, in an extensive inspection of the psyche, to collect all the images that we have established in life because of our ability to see. Then we could achieve an inner visual system in our psyche; we would have built a reconstruction of the external visual process. If you consider the same possibility with regard to the sense of balance, you will come to the realization that through everything you have experienced in your organism because of your sense of balance, you have reconstructed internally something that corresponds to the geometry of the external world.

We did not discover mathematics or mechanics from [external experience].[†] We discovered these [laws] through [internal constructing]. If you imagine certain mechanical [laws] you have [discovered them] on the basis of the imaginative element of your sense of balance. In this case, our entire being becomes a sensory organ and we construct [internally] the other pole, the opposite of [perception]. For example, we create mathematics and believe that, in it, we have a pure *a priori* science. But mathematics is not a pure *a priori* science. We simply fail to see that we transform the experience of our sense of balance into [mathematical and geometrical images] in the same way visual perception is transformed into visual images. Without our noticing this bridge, the perceptions of our sense of balance are transformed into mathematics and mechanics.

If we keep this in mind, we will understand the inner connection between the complex human organism and its position of balance in the universe. Then we will realize that the particular experience of balance reflected internally in animals, who stand on their four legs and whose position affects the very content of their sense of balance, must be very different from the human experience of balance that is reflected in mathematics. We will consider mathematics to be the result of our specific upright position in the universe.

We speak of three dimensions because we are positioned in three dimensions in the universe. However, we have reached the vertical dimension thanks only to our own effort in the course of our life. We had to position ourselves in the vertical dimension. Our experience from early childhood is reflected later in mathematics, but this process of reflection does not happen as fast as it does in the visual process. The experience of balance is being reflected in us throughout our lives.

As children, we experience our sense of balance in a very strong way when we change from crawling to standing and walking. This change is reflected later in mathematics and mechanics. Often, we consider mathematics to be something that we have created. That is not the case. Mathematics is based on the perception of our own organism. Why do we have thoughts that we can relate to the universe, so that out of them we can build a whole universe in our thoughts? This is only the result of the way the human being is positioned in the universe.

And if we compare now the animal's position of balance [with regard to the universe] to that of humans, we can see that animals are bound to the organization of the earth. Humans, on the other hand, by standing in an upright position, lift themselves up, away from the organization of the earth. Our ability to express independent thoughts is a consequence of human beings having achieved an independent position of balance.

As we see, our upright position in the universe is an achievement that is more deliberate than simply following the laws of the organism; and this is not found in animals. In establishing their organism, humans can achieve this only in the [first] years of life. It is a process that affects every single organ. This is how we come to a polarity within the human being.[†] On the one hand, humans stand and walk in an upright position; and everything that started out the same in humans and in animals has to be adjusted to this cosmic position in which humans exist. On the other hand, the soul gives birth to thoughts that transcend the sense perception of what we see or perceive with the five senses; thoughts that, in fact, liberate us from sense perception. Humans detach themselves from the earth through their position in relation to the universe; in the same way, thoughts free themselves from their bond to the sensory world and become, in a sense, emancipated.

Because of my anthroposophic certainty, I would like to pose the following as something more than a postulate. We must see the position of balance, which we have because of the upright position of our spinal axis, as something that separates humans from the animals. At the same time, we should see the special form of imagination, thoughts, as something specifically human. Those of you who can understand these things from an anthroposophic viewpoint (I will touch on this topic later) can also see that through the particular development of their sense of balance and their sense of motion humans achieve a more emancipated system of thinking than one based only on the experience of the eyes or the ears. Having understood this, you would also see that for emancipated thinking the human being must have an inner organization as well. The human being possesses an organization that is simply not to be found in animals—a fact that could surely be proven in material terms. This organization serves the very specific system of thoughts that has emancipated itself from [the bond to the Earth] that animals still have, a form determined by the special human position of balance. Hence, we can say that the human being has established an organ of abstract thinking by coming to an upright posture of the body.

So we see in humans an organization determined by their upright position that at first glance shows nothing more than that the organs, which are the same as those in animals, are in a different position in humans. However, this upright posture affects the organization of the nerves and of the blood. Under the influence of this different position of balance, humans develop something that animals cannot have, and here we find the biological difference between humans and animals. This difference is to be found in the physical organization of the human, and not simply in some theory of metaphysics. This is of fundamental importance. Imagine the transformation of the organization that occurs through the change in the position of balance from the animal to the human. Think for example of the changes in the thigh, the lower leg, the hands, and so forth. [Imagine what it means] to have two hands and not four legs. In fact, humans are supplied with the same forms as animals but the forms are positioned differently, and thus have changed or metamorphosed. This could be proven also in terms of anatomy once the necessary tools and methods of experimentation are developed. We are searching for such tools and methods of experimentation in our institutes in Stuttgart.[†] But to find such methods externally and empirically, we should first form in our imagination an idea about [what the differences must be].† Anthroposophy is not useless regarding the study of the subtle areas of science such as the study of human, animal, and plant forms, since science does not discover these things through imagination Once they are discovered, however, they can be validated [through science].

Looking at the changes caused in organs by the upright position of balance, we can also see that some organs have been transformed into organs of speech; in other words, the organism becomes creative also with regard to speech.

We have now an impression of the special organization of the human being that was established simply because humans are an upright-walking species, a fact that has consequences reaching deep into the physical world. We have also made conclusions regarding the physiological organism of speech—a place where we cannot define any morphological differences between humans and animals, even though we see differences in a biological sense.

These are only a few thoughts that could show how something we search for in an external, profane manner, could be studied in really scientific terms. Today, I could only outline briefly what I wanted to say. However, if you imagine pursuing these thoughts, then science will certainly find a way to explore the differences between human and animal organization in terms of biology.

3.
Anthropoposophy and Philosophy

BERLIN, MARCH 7, 1922

MOST HONORED PARTICIPANTS: it is always difficult when, having a serious scholarly conscience, one tries to translate what we have inherited in the concept of *logos* into one of the modern languages. When we want to translate *logos* we usually say *word*, as the Bible does. However, when we have in mind *logic*, we do not think as much of *word* as of a *thought*, of the way thought functions in the human individual, and of its patterns. For philology, though, "logos" means "consciousness." We develop scholarship that is based on the *word*. I mean that what we understand under *logos* today, according to modern language use, is the basis of all philosophy. And when we speak of philosophy we can sense the reflection of an undefined experience of *logos* in everything that we do not define but rather experience as philosophy.

At the time when philosophy was established, the meaning of the word *logos* was undoubtedly something more than simply its literal meaning. It implied a particular inner experience of the human being. The word *philosophy* implies that the human had a certain interest, *sophia,* in everything that was related to *logos;* this was an interest that, if not personal, was certainly generally human. The understanding of the word *philosophy* was related more to the inner attitude of the human being toward the wisdom-filled content of science than to the possession of scientific knowledge itself.

Our sense of philosophy is not as certain today as it was at the time when the concept of philosophy overlapped with the desire for scientific knowledge (I would not say it overlapped with science itself). The word pointed at the same time to an inner human attitude. As a consequence, our inner feeling when we speak of or deal with philosophy now is extremely unclear. If we try to determine it externally or simply in a dialectical way, it is also very difficult to bring this unclear feeling out of the depth of our consciousness. Our present time requires, rather, that we try to explore the human experience of philosophy in the course of our historical development. Precisely this latter kind of understanding is required.

If as Central Europeans we look back a few decades, we will see that specifically in Central Europe the experience of those who wished to enter into the spirit of philosophy was different from our experience now in the second decade of the twentieth century. Today, we have experienced so much more compared with what people experienced in earlier times through the course of many centuries. We may say that we have more experience, not only in a physical sense, but also in a spiritual sense. And if we look back at the experiences that a student of philosophy could have had as a Central European during the 50s, 60s, or 70s of the nineteenth century, or even later, we will find basically that they were mainly the following.

Scholars looked back at the peak of the development of German philosophy, at the great time of the philosophers Fichte, Schelling, and Hegel.† Then, scholars looked at the world around them, which consisted of educated and knowledgeable people who regarded that era of philosophy as something outdated, and who believed that the rising scientific views should replace the earlier philosophical observations. While they admired the greatness of the sublime thought that could be seen in someone like Schelling, and were fascinated by the energy and power of Fichte's intellectual development, and had perhaps some sense of Hegel's far-reaching creative thinking, people saw this era of classical German philosophy as something science had already surpassed.

At the same time, there was a desire to develop something based on natural science that would become a worldview. We can find this desire everywhere—from the aspirations of the scientists concerning "force and matter"† to those thinkers who were more careful in trying to achieve a philosophical worldview based on natural science, but who also rejected the former idealistic philosophy. Thus, in this area, there were all sorts of nuances in thinking, as well as in research.

There was also a third type of thinker. They were not able to go along with explanations of a worldview based simply on natural science, neither could they go as deeply into the reality of thought as Hegel did. These thinkers were confronted with the big question: how could people relate the objective, outside world to their thinking, which was formed as something that existed only within themselves? So, the specialists in the theory of knowledge unanimously called for "turning back to Kant," though each found a very different way back to Kant. These were intelligent thinkers like Liebmann, Volkelt,[†] and so forth, who remained, however, mainly in the thought frame of theory of knowledge. They did not find an answer to the question of how human thought could bridge over to an external trans-subjective reality using images of their own internal thinking.

The situation that I am describing to you here, the one in which the students of philosophy found themselves in the last third of the nineteenth century, did not bring any resolution. In a sense, it was as if they were in the middle of a drama or in the middle of a piece of art that was developing in time, a piece of art to which no one had found an end yet. The scholarly aspirations were running into the indefinite. They were ending with a large number of questions, but the courage even merely to attempt to resolve those questions was missing everywhere.

The reality now is that the situation in the entire world of philosophy appears to be very different from the situation in the last third of the nineteenth century, which I just described. Now, we face philosophical views that have a completely different foundation, and that force us to characterize the current philosophical situation in a completely different way. If we would like to characterize the situation in philosophy today, with the eyes of our soul we would see clearly something for which our vision was sharpened in the first two decades of the twentieth century, namely, the extremely different philosophical views of Western, of Central, and of Eastern Europe. Today, our inward experience of philosophy is different from the one even of the recent past. It is an experience to which we can associate three names: Herbert Spencer, Hegel, and Vladimir Soloviov.† These three personalities are the representatives of everything that characterizes the situation in philosophy today. Inwardly, this has always been the case, or at least it has been the case for a very long time, but only today we can see this situation so clearly before us.

Let us look at the West. Herbert Spencer. If I want to be precise, I should describe the details of the entire development of this philosophical view: how it led from Bacon and Locke, through Mill, to Spencer.† This tracing of history, however, is not my task today. In Herbert Spencer we see someone who wanted to justify philosophy; but he wanted to justify philosophy using only systems of concepts established in natural science. Spencer unconditionally says "Yes" to natural science, and draws conclusions only on the basis of his own affirmation that philosophical thinking about the world must be founded in natural science. We can see that Spencer is trying to grasp certain concepts of natural science, such as the concept that describes how matter constantly shrinks and expands; and the concepts of differentiation and consolidation. For example, he observes certain processes in the plant that expands in its leaves and shrinks the seed into its germ. He tries to define such concepts in clear scientific terms to establish a worldview in this way. He even tries to think of human society, of the social organism, in a way that would present an analogy to the biological organism.

This, however, immediately creates a problem. The biological organism of the human being is dependent on the combination of everything that helps this organism to relate to the external world, for example through perception, through imagination, and so forth. Each individual organism is dependent on the particular developments influenced by the sensory system. Herbert Spencer does not find a similar sensory system in the social organism. No central coordinating nervous system is to be found there. Nevertheless, built entirely on the foundation of natural science, he produces such a social organism and, in a way, sees it as the crowning element of his philosophical construct.

What does this actually mean in the Western world? It means that in the West, scientific thinking has developed in its fullest, in its legitimate one-sidedness. It means a fine ability of observation and a talent for experimentation have developed from the original dispositions of the different peoples. It means that there is definite interest in observing the external sensory reality down to the smallest detail, without being impatient and wanting to rush to generalizations. It also means that there is a trend toward keeping science in the frame of the external sensory world of facts. It means that there is some fear, as I would call it, of expanding from the sensory world to a larger frame—to an all-embracing world. Since the human being, however, cannot help but live, as well, in a world that is beyond the sensory—where experience is given through more than just the senses—it appears that in the West, knowledge of the entire spiritual world must be completely yielded to the private belief of an individual, and that this belief must develop free of any scientific influence. People do not allow the content of religion to be affected by scientific research. Spencer, in his way, expands the scientific method of thinking to sociology, and then stops there. We see that in the West there is supposed to be a strict distinction between *science*, which is required to be based completely on natural science, and *the human being*, for whom spiritual content now has no connection to science.

Let us now move forward from Herbert Spencer to the points we are confronted with in the case of Hegel. It does not matter that in the second third of the nineteenth century, Hegel, who belonged to the first third, was considered superceded by the philosophers of Central Europe, because Hegel represents in a most significant way the characteristics of Central Europe. Let us look at Hegel: Hegel's emotional disposition speaks of a certain aversion against the Western universalistic scientific manner of dealing with a worldview (as in the case of Spencer). This worldview, however, was prepared by Hegel's predecessors, the naturalists, as well as the philosophers. We can see, for example, that Hegel could not stand Newton; he had no sympathy for the purely mechanical way Newton viewed the universe. Hegel rejected not only Newton's color theory, but also his entire interpretation of the cosmos.[†] Hegel invested a great deal in returning to Kepler's laws of planetary motion.[†] He analyzed these laws and came to the conclusion that Newton did not add anything new to them, but that the entire law of gravity is presented already in Kepler's theory.[†]

Hegel adopted Kepler's theory because he saw that in Kepler's work it is more or less the spiritual experience which gives birth to scientific thinking that is comprehensive. Kepler was trying to explain the externally scientific on the basis of the spiritual. To Hegel, Kepler was simply the person who was able to penetrate the spirit with thinking, and to build a bridge between what was scientifically recognized and what, according to the Western world, could only be believed. Hegel saw Kepler as a person who was capable of elevating science to the level that, in the view of the West, was reserved only for faith. This is the reason why Hegel, like Goethe, rejected Newton's color theory. We see in Hegel's disposition a certain antipathy against everything that seems completely natural from the perspective of Newton's disposition.

At the same time, Hegel had the real capacity to live exclusively within the realm of thought. What Goethe said to Schiller was absolutely self-evident to Hegel: that he "sees his ideas with his eyes."[†] This statement may seem to show some naiveté, but sometimes, if we see it correctly, this kind of naiveté turns out to be the most profound philosophical wisdom. Because Hegel's life was entirely within the realm of thought, he would have simply not understood how people can insist that the *idea* of a triangle cannot be comprehended. To him, a higher world of revelation, a world of higher spirituality, exists for us only because it is reflected in the shadows of a plane filled with thoughts. From above, the spiritual world throws its shadow-images upon the plane of the human soul, where human thoughts develop.

To Hegel, the concept of higher spirituality is based on the fact that the higher spiritual world is reflected in the human soul in the form of thoughts. Hegel tended to experience those thoughts as something spiritual. Therefore, he did not experience natural phenomena in their elementary presence either, but saw them in the thought-images reflected on the plane of the human soul. In this way, it becomes impossible to separate knowledge from faith in Hegel's philosophy in the external manner described above, a manner that is absolutely natural for the Western world.

It became Hegel's lifelong task to unite the sensory-physical world with the spiritual world (which the West, because of its dispositions, wants to simply relegate to the area of faith). He wanted to combine the two worlds into one world that we can know about. In Hegel's case, knowledge was not opposed to faith. Here, however, the human soul is confronted with an important problem. How do we find the bridge between faith and knowledge, between nature and the spiritual, in our inner life? Hegel's tragedy was that he saw the problem (which he was able to set forth in such a grand manner), only in relation to the plane of thought. Although he was able to experience the inner power, the inner life of *thinking*, he did not perceive anything that was alive in its *content*. Let us look at the Hegelian logic: he wanted to go back to the old concept of *logos*! He felt that if we want to have any real concept of *logos* at all, then *logos* must be something that is not simply thought, but that actively penetrates the world and fills it with life.† To him, *logos* is not simply an abstract logical content. To him, it becomes a real content of the world. However, if we consider Hegel's treatise "Logic," one of the three parts of his philosophy, we will see that it contains only abstract concepts.†

Hence, those who are really enthusiastic about Hegel's philosophy are strongly affected by the profoundly correct sense that one can comprehend the principle of creation in the world through the understanding of *logos*. *Logos* must be "God before the creation of the world"—to put it in Hegel's own words.† This is on the one hand. On the other hand, the question is how Hegel developed this concept of *logos*. He began with *being*, then came to *nothingness*, to *becoming*, and to *existence*.† He came to causality, to the purpose, to teleology. We look at the concepts in Hegel's logic and we ask if this could have been the content of the divine before the beginning of creation? It is abstract logic, furthering creativity; *logos* as a postulate, but a postulate of purely human thought. One can almost feel the tragedy in this! One can also feel the tragedy in the fact that Hegel's philosophy counts as being overcome. However, it contains elements that can give birth to something new. It contains seeds. Hegel saw in this philosophy his salvation: *being, nothingness, becoming, existence.*

But today when people learn about Hegel, they say, this is outdated; we do not have to deal with it. However, if we decide to experience this concept in a more internal way, through a process of the soul, in the way Hegel wanted to experience it, then all concepts of empiricism and rationalism disappear; and the thought can be experienced, and the experience can be directly thought. Then the thought becomes experience and the experience pure thought. Those who are willing to do this feel the desire to free thinking from abstraction. They see Hegel's logic as the key to a transformation of thought that could turn into something very different if it could express itself more directly.

Hegel's thought appears to me as the seed of a plant that does not show what it will become, although it contains a multitude of possibilities. It seems to me that when this seed grows, when the human being grows it with care and plants it in spiritual soil using anthroposophic research, then the seed will show precisely that thought not only exists in thinking but also can be experienced as reality. Here we see that Hegel was a Central European.

Moving to the East, we see in Vladimir Soloviov a man whose vocation, unlike any other philosopher's, is to become more and more part of our philosophical search; we see someone who becomes gradually more important as we let his unique ideas influence us. At the same time, we see in Soloviov a representative of an Eastern European way of thinking, which, however, is not the Asian or the Oriental way. Soloviov has adopted everything that is European, but has developed it further in a particularly Eastern variant. What do we see in his philosophy with regard to the human desire for scientific knowledge? We see that Soloviov disdains the kind of thinking that the West appreciates most, particularly in the case of Herbert Spencer. To Soloviov, this kind of thinking merely points to the truth and the knowledge he is looking for. In contrast, Soloviov offers a real experience in the realm of the spiritual. In his philosophy, this experience is not accompanied by full consciousness, but appears, rather, in the unconscious as atavism, albeit in the spiritual realm. It is more or less the attempt to experience knowingly (but almost as if in a dream) what the West shifts (also consciously) to the realm of faith. Thus, in the East we are confronted with things that could be experienced in an undefined way; something that appears as another form of experiencing Hegel's idea of building a bridge between natural existence and the realm of the spiritual.

At first, those with a Central European spiritual background feel uncomfortable exploring Soloviov's philosophy on a deeper level. He recommends something that reminds them of a foggy mysticism; of an excessive life of the human soul; of something that cannot be formulated in terms of the external world but can be experienced only internally. Those people feel the completely undefined character of the mystical experience; they also find that Soloviov uses the same concepts and expressions as Hegel, Hume, Mill—even some that recall Spencer—but he uses them only as illustrations.[†] Therefore, we can say that Soloviov certainly does not get stuck in the foggy mysticism. Rather, the way he treats religion as science, looks for it everywhere and develops it as philosophy, allows us to compare and analyze his teachings in terms of Western concepts.

Currently, we are confronted with the following situation. In the West, we see the effort to develop a worldview based on natural science, that is, the effort to place natural science on one side and the spiritual on the other. We struggle with the problem of finding a bridge between the two sides with the help of Hegel's unclear phrases such as "Nature is Spirit in its otherness";[†] or "Spirit is the concept when it has returned to itself."[†] In these confusing phrases, we see Hegel's tragedy of being able to experience everything he was searching for, but only by entertaining abstract thoughts. In the East, however, we see how Soloviov has preserved the way in which the Church Fathers must have discussed philosophy before the Council of Nicaea.[†] He completely transports us back to the first three centuries after Christ in the Western world. Thus, in the East we can see an experience of the spiritual world that is not yet capable of elevating itself to its own conceptual definitions. It needs Western concepts to express itself, even though in its system these concepts remain unclear, imposed, and alien.

We can see how the philosophical understanding of the world has developed in three different ways. Looking at this threefold way in which the philosophical understanding of the world has developed out of the very character and predispositions of the West, the East, and Central Europe, we realize that now—when science is extending its influence uniformly in every area of human society—it is our task to find something else that goes beyond these three philosophical streams. The three streams are based generally on elements that formerly made philosophy a personal human affair. Today we see that the West, Middle Europe, and the East follow their love of wisdom in different ways. We understand that in ancient times philosophy could have been still an inner condition of the soul. In our times, however, when people are so individualized, the love of wisdom is manifested in many different ways. Perhaps this is precisely the reason for us to realize what our own task is, and particularly what the task is of those who are in the middle, between East and West, where the problem appears in its most tragic and most intense form, even if today it does not yet concern all philosophical souls equally.

If I had to present this issue visually, I would say the following. From a philosophical point of view, the voice of Soloviov is like that of the old priest who lives in the higher worlds and has to develop certain abilities in order to live in those higher worlds. In Soloviov's work we hear everywhere the language of the priest transformed into philosophy. In the West, the voice of Herbert Spencer is like that of a man of the world who wants to adjust to the practicalities of life; he wants to give science a structure that can produce a practical foundation of life—as Darwin does with his theory.† In the middle, we have neither the secular man nor the priest. Fichte, Schelling, and Hegel are not priests like Soloviov. In the middle, we have the teacher, the pedagogue of the people. He is there even where German philosophy is based on religious contemplation. There, the minister has become a teacher. Even Hegel's philosophy has the character of teaching. In modern days, for example in Oswald Külpe,† we see how we have lost philosophy, which now is nothing but a summary of the ideas presented in the individual sciences.

When it comes to non-organic science, we ask ourselves what sort of concepts it brings forth. When it comes to organic science, we ask ourselves the same question: what sort of concepts does it bring forth? The same applies to history, religion, and so forth. We collect those concepts and construct with them, completely superficially, an abstract unity. What I am trying to say is that the subject of the theory in the different sciences should be one common theory. Considering the sensitivity of the people, this is generally the point that science in Central Europe should reach. If, however, we reflect, we see that because we are influenced by thinking like that of Herbert Spencer, we are obligated to stick to unconditional belief in natural science; to the belief in our ability to experience through observation, experiment, and our reflecting reason; even belief in reason that can elevate itself above observation and experiment.

However, we deceive ourselves if we think that there is no problem in transferring the concepts we have gained in such a manner to the higher level of the social organism. In trying to comprehend the social organism with the help of the same concepts we have derived from natural existence, we overlook the fact that the social organism does not have the most important characteristic of the natural organism—the *sensorium*. We see that the strong leaning toward natural science forces people such as Newton to hold on to only the mechanical, and to try to satisfy their spiritual needs outside the realm of science. As we know, Newton tried to explain the Apocalypse, but from the perspective of mysticism.[†] Hence, along with his scientifically established worldview, he was searching for something mystical as well.

Let us look at natural science as it appeared in the nineteenth century and as it was gradually adopted by Central Europe. Here, science was established according to the model of Western scientific thinking. Without our noticing, the entire worldview developed on the basis of the Western model. People went mad when someone once tried to defend Goethe's ideas of physics as contrasted with those of Newton! What about the development of biology? Goethe established a kind of organic science that required the experience of concepts by means of mathematical thinking. Our time urgently presses for us to develop a science of biology that suits modern thought better than the one we have inherited from previous times. In its further progress during the nineteenth century, however, Central Europe did not accept Goethe's biology but that of Darwin, a science full of concepts that relate to those of Goethe as the concepts of the sixteenth century to those of the eighteenth. Concepts kept developing only in Central Europe. The West was satisfied with concepts that were sufficient only for the understanding of nature. This is why certain concepts simply do not exist in the West, and why they disappeared when Central Europe adopted Western thought. For example, Central Europe lacks the idea of the living thought, as we see it in Hegel: the concept of comprehending reality separately from the empirical. This idea was lost because the way of thinking in Central Europe was flooded with Western thought.

Therefore, here, in Central Europe, we have the task to observe exactly what a naturalistic way of thinking really is. People dislike the anthroposophist who is attracted to this naturalistic way of thinking, as much as they dislike the naturalist. I would never say anything against the way of thinking in natural science. Anybody who believes I would is mistaken. However, I must see the kind of thought in natural science in its pure form; and then I must try to characterize it in its pure form. If we confront natural science without prejudice and if we accept the conclusions of Western studies without imposing any philosophical interpretations, what science or Western scholars describe (such as what is described so ingeniously by Haeckel†), would appear everywhere not as solutions, not as answers, but only as questions. To the unbiased thinker, all of natural science becomes gradually a great universal question, rather than an answer to our questions. In everything, one can feel how the best scholarship on natural science—including the atomic theory, which I do not reject, but want only to place correctly—†turns into one big question, which speaks to us with the voice of the West. What are the origins of this question?

We will not discover the complete reality if we look only at the external world and focus simply on the perception of the empirical. We are born into the world as human beings and cannot change the way we are designed. We take into our inner Self a part of reality to build our views based on it. Then, we turn to the external world, to the sensory-empirical, and we fail to integrate into our views that part of reality that lives in ourselves. Only through human struggling can we connect the inner half of reality to the part that looks back at us from the outside world. In the West, we see one half of reality, studied with particular dedication. That half, however, produces only questions, because it is not complete. On one side we see ourselves confronted with one half of reality, the empirical, and if we look carefully it leads us to a question. Central Europe realized the character of questioning in Western thought, and tried to get through to thought itself. This is what the philosophy of Hegel did.

The East grasped what is beyond thought and what affects thought; but it was not able to fully awaken it and to give its body skeletal structure. In his philosophy, Soloviov was able to develop flesh, muscles, and even blood, but it lacked a skeleton. Therefore, he adopted concepts from Hegel, Hume, and others, and gave a foreign skeleton to what he himself had created. What we experience in our spirit can be transformed only when we no longer need a foreign support system. Soloviov's spiritual experience, however, exists like a shadow, because it cannot produce its own skeletal structure, and thus cannot become apparent. If we are not satisfied with only an external skeletal system, but want to live in spirituality and to develop through hard spiritual work, then we should build a skeletal structure for our spiritual experience and develop the concepts for it. The exercises I mention in my study "Knowledge of Higher Worlds—Initiation," published in *An Outline of Esoteric Science*, and others, would be appropriate for that purpose.[†] They can help you develop an inner organism of conceptions. This would be the other side of reality, the side that germinates in the Eastern philosophy of Soloviov.

Central Europe has always had the challenge of building a bridge between nature and spirit. We have to deal with another important historical problem as well: how to build a bridge between the West and the East. This is the task we have in contemporary philosophy, and it leads inevitably to anthroposophy. If anthroposophy is able to give substance to its own experience of thought, then it can also allow for experiencing natural reality in a fully materialistic way, as it is experienced in the West. In that case, the bridge between pure faith and knowledge, between cognition and subjective certainty, would be built with fully engaged scientific effort, and not with abstract concepts. Then, philosophy will develop into real anthroposophy, and science would be able to stimulate philosophy at any time. Hegel's philosophy could be brought back to life only if it is rejuvenated by the blood stream of spirituality introduced through anthroposophy. Then its logic will not be too abstract to be "the Spirit beyond nature," as Hegel wanted it to be. Rather, it will replace the abstract with the living spirit of philosophy.

All this gave anthroposophy the primary task to explore the following. How can we build a bridge between what we now call truth (which must include the full reality) and what we call science (which also must include the full reality), in accordance with our modern standpoint now, many years after the time of Hegel? Briefly, this problem had to be articulated, and it is the most important philosophical problem of anthroposophy: "What is the relationship between truth and reality?

In my introduction later today, I would like to place this problem at the top of my list, with the observations that will follow next.

4.
Anthroposophy and Education

BERLIN, MARCH 8, 1922

Most honored participants: Many repeatedly object to the anthroposophic worldview, stating that it requires people first to study and to develop particular abilities as a basis for accepting its ideas; and that, consequently, from the very beginning, the results of anthroposophic research cannot be tested by everyone. In spite of this, it is claimed, anthroposophy still proclaims its views to all those who are unprepared.

No matter how plausible this objection may sound, it belongs to the most unjustified objections that could ever be made against the anthroposophic movement. The goal of anthroposophy is not to turn everyone immediately into a scholar in the area of the suprasensory. Its goal is to present the results of its study in a way that could be tested by all, simply by using common sense and healthy logic. This does not eliminate the need to put some effort into taking at least some initial steps toward suprasensory studies, for which there are instructions in various publications I have already mentioned here. Simply because of the circumstances in our contemporary civilization, everyone could become an anthroposophic scholar to a certain degree. But that is not necessary in order to prove the results of anthroposophic studies; they could be proven simply by using common sense. One of the areas where such a test could be made practically is the area of pedagogy.

For a very long time, the anthroposophic worldview existed only in the sense that it presented ideas when people asked about the suprasensory. This was before contemporary cultural circumstances made it possible for anthroposophy to intervene in practical life. Anthroposophy is very well suited to helping in practical ways. But even this only became possible in a very limited area and to a very small degree when Emil Molt[†] opened the Waldorf School in Stuttgart, whose administration I am in charge of. The short article "The Education of the Child from the Perspective of Spiritual Science"[†] shows that already in 1907, before the founding of the school, there was an impulse to shape a school according to educational principles based on anthroposophic understanding. However, only after founding the Waldorf School did it become possible to turn these principles into practice, and to apply the pedagogical and didactic aspects of anthroposophy. I will not be able to mention more than a few ideas in the context of these introductory remarks, but I think that these ideas can be developed further in the rest of the lectures today. When using our common sense, we verify for ourselves the things we perceive through anthroposophic ideas. We see that these are not simply theoretical views or abstract ideas, which we hold to satisfy some need for theoretical knowledge. What is expressed in ideas that have an anthroposophic source is real human power, something that concerns the entire human being, something that makes love stronger and that could be transformed into a driving force for the human being. Although the usual scientific ideas and thoughts—related exclusively to the sensory world—are expressed in the fact that they serve theoretical and practical interests related exclusively to the sensory world (to repeat myself), ideas based on anthroposophic studies affect the whole human being. This includes the way we grow stronger, our capability to live, and our understanding of life. Such an understanding of life enables us to react to all possible situations by using our will. If we enrich any given aspect of life through the ideas of anthroposophy and we let these ideas guide us, we will see that our actions gain more strength and become more effective. This power and effectiveness gain validity particularly in the area of pedagogy and didactics.

When the Waldorf School was established, we had no opportunity to choose the external conditions for the education and the process of teaching those children who were entrusted to us. Today, people usually make the point that if we want to have satisfactory work in the classroom and a satisfactory education, we must have an appropriate place for the school or the educational institution. Certainly, there are many arguments supporting these assertions and, to a certain extent, they are also confirmed in practice. Having an ideal space, however, was not possible for us. In the beginning, we had to start the experiment with the children from the Waldorf-Astoria cigarette factory, accepting the existing circumstances. This means that we had to work with a very particular kind of children, and we had to begin our teaching in a building that, of course, was not at all appropriate, since it used to be a tavern. In other words, we were not able to rely on anything but on the pedagogical and didactic aspects that could be established on a purely spiritual basis alone.

We should always emphasize that anthroposophy does not aim merely at an abstract knowledge of the head, but for an understanding of the world and its secrets. Such an understanding involves the entire human being, and it can lead to a kind of knowledge and understanding of the human being that cannot be achieved in any theoretical field. Ultimately, education and teaching are based on an understanding of the human being as this is demonstrated in the relationship between the teacher, who is the educator, and the one who changes, who is the growing human being, the child. Therefore, our Waldorf pedagogical system is established on the immediate basis of anthropogenesis, the child. I will mention only one detail that can demonstrate how real understanding of the whole human being can prove itself in practice.

Today we have a kind of psychology more or less accepted by the acknowledged sciences. However, this psychology theorizes around certain questions that remain always without satisfactory answers. For example, psychology asks what the relationship is between the psychic-spiritual and the bodily-physical in the human; and psychology comes up with all sorts of theories. We have three types of theories. The first type tries to begin with the psychic-spiritual, and aims primarily at defining it somehow. Then theorists create some abstract concept of the psychic-spiritual, and begin to study to what extent the psychic-spiritual affects the bodily-physical. Another, more materialisticallycolored theory assumes that the bodily-physical is the foundation, and that this bodily-physical creates the psychic-spiritual only as a secondary function. A third theory represents the psychic-physical parallelism. Its purpose is to give validity to both the psychic-spiritual and the bodily-physical, and also simply to observe how the functions of the one occur parallel to the functions of the other, without elaborating on any inner connection between the two. All these are psychological speculations. They gain some substance only in living practice, where, through psychology, through the knowledge of the psyche, we find the driving forces of pedagogy and didactics.

In this area, the attitude toward the psychic-spiritual in the human is simply not yet as advanced as the attitude toward the principles in natural science, which we are used to seeing as self-evident. In science, we can observe how somewhere there is heat even though it was not produced in the usual way. We can imagine how this heat was first in a different condition—in the so-called condition of latent heat—and how out of this latent condition the heat became obvious. These principles, which are so common in science, should also be accepted, metamorphosed in an appropriate way, of course, in the observation of the complete human being, which includes the psychic-spiritual.

Even if some of us do not yet understand this at the moment, we will still come to such an attitude, which will be completely validated by science, if we look at the first major metamorphosis that occurs in the human organization—the change of teeth around the seventh year of the child's life. Such changes are usually observed only superficially in the human being. But the change of teeth is something that deeply affects an entire life. If we train our ability to view things in this way, we will learn to recognize that with the change of teeth the entire psychic life of the child becomes different. We will also realize that before the change of teeth, children actually do not live "in themselves"—and I have in mind the real meaning of this phrase. Instead, children are completely dissolved in their surroundings. We will recognize the fact that the most important thing about the forces in the child's organism before the change of teeth is imitation. Children learn how to move through imitation.

Unbiased observation will show exactly how the movements and gestures of the father and mother, and of other people surrounding children, are transferred into their very organism. We can observe that under normal circumstances, children also learn how to speak under the influence of imitation. We can see how their psyche *dissolves* in its surroundings, in the real meaning of this word. This, however, will not be the case during the process of the change of teeth. At that time we will see how the forces that develop in children bring their capacity to produce independent mental images. This ability to produce independent images, which to a certain extent frees children internally from their surroundings, does not exist before the seventh year. Along with the change of teeth, the child develops some inwardness and becomes more capable of abstract thinking.

At the same time, the nature of childhood determines the fact that children perceive everything from the inner life of the people who surround them. Thus, we have to assume that in the second phase of life, which begins with the change of the first teeth and continues until sexual maturity, the child develops internally by adjusting to the adult environment. What is impressed on the child at this stage, is not what the people do, or anything that the child imitates. Rather, it is what *lives* in other people, and what is expressed through words; the way people think, and their inclinations. All this is impressed on the child, no longer through imitation, but through the inner force of authority, to which the child has the same predisposition as to growth or to nourishment. I hope that you will not misunderstand what I mean here by "the force of authority." As the one who wrote *The Philosophy of Freedom*,[†] I would like merely to point out here that the principle of authority plays a role in a particular phase of human life. Therefore, it is not necessary to form the entire process of education around what we currently call the principle of authority. If we pay enough attention to such an observation, things begin to differentiate themselves more and more clearly, and we become more and more capable of observing the metamorphosis in the developing child, not only from year to year but also by the month. So, what is it, then, that happens with a child between the change of the first teeth and sexual maturity?

Those who have an eye for the facts realize that between the ages of seven and fourteen (and these are only the approximate ages), forces that earlier were hidden begin to find their expression in the child's psyche. In the first few years, these forces are hidden below, in the physical body, and they affect the formation of the human organism, including that of the brain. In fact, they affect the entire development of the physical. Thus, we can say that the spiritual human, the soul, which in the first seven years is latent in the physical organism but is expressed in each single movement, in each process of the body, is freed only later—in the same way in which warmth could be hidden in a body and be freed only under particular circumstances. After the seventh year, the physical is left more or less to itself. Consequently, the spiritual in us, the soul, does not grow completely out of the physical, but it does so to a very high degree. The change of teeth is then some kind of an ending point in the first stage of development in which the spiritual in the human being, the soul, was in a way overlapping with the bodily-physical.

You can see that looking at things from such a perspective enables us to recognize the real connection between spiritual or soul matters and the bodily-physical. At this point, one ceases to theorize about the question of how exactly these two aspects influence each other. Rather, at the first stage of life we simply see the spiritual or the soul entirely within the body, as the development of children shows clearly; and then later, when the soul becomes free, we see it in its own form. Thus, we do not start with comparison between pre-formulated abstract concepts. Instead, we observe the work of the spiritual or the soul within the body at the different stages in life.

This approach, however, puts an emphasis on the fact that the same phenomena usually studied in natural science (as if they are accessible only for the external senses) could be studied from a spiritual perspective as well. Anthroposophy as spiritual science is simply a productive continuation of natural science. At least that is the case when the natural-scientific way of thinking is rightfully established. If we do not want to get stuck in superficial definitions, and if we want to analyze in detail the question of what exactly anthroposophy wants, then this becomes clear. If we gain deep human knowledge of the world of concepts and ideas through spiritual science, then any accusation that the world of ideas is alien to life is obviously refuted.

In the area of pedagogy, anthroposophy does not wish to oppose in any way the pedagogical principles defined by the great educational theorists, especially during the nineteenth century. Anthroposophy recognizes that there are major and meaningful pedagogical principles, and it appreciates great educators as much as everyone else. Nevertheless, I should say that even though we have all those great pedagogical principles, currently people do not feel satisfied with educational practice, a fact demonstrated by the existence of diverse educational methods. Why is that so?

Often, this is simply a consequence of the intellectualism characteristic of our time. This intellectualism causes more animosity toward life than we could possibly imagine, particularly toward the social areas of existence. In the world of ideas, intellectualism creates only abstractions. The abstract, however, has no life force. Abstractions are the corpse of the spiritual, to a degree, and are experienced as such. We may have the best principles that inspire us passionately, but as long as they remain abstract, they cannot have a really productive influence on life. Only when these principles are penetrated by a real and living spirituality that is connected to the essence of the human being can these principles become practical. Thus, anthroposophy does not wish to establish new abstract principles of education. It wishes only to provide guidance in pedagogical and didactic skills, in the implementation of the art of education and teaching. It wishes to offer what even the best educational principles have not yet offered: a spiritual foundation for practical implementation, for the inner abilities of the teacher to work in school and in education.

For the very same reason, contrary to what is often believed, the Waldorf School is not organized in a way that enables us to stuff children's minds with our views of the world, as we present them to adults. I must emphasize that even religious education is left to the Catholic priests for Catholic children, and to the Protestant ministers for Protestant children. We have simply added another class, a non-denominational religion class, for the children of non-religious parents. Without this class, these children would not have had any religious education. In this way we can achieve some awakening of religious feelings, because exactly those parents who would not have sent their children to any class on religion, are sending them now. We put forth a lot of effort not to preach anthroposophy in this class, but to build up what is appropriate to be fostered in children of that age. In other words, it is not about forcing anthroposophy into children's minds, but about helping teachers to adjust, through anthroposophy, their methods in a way that corresponds to a true education of developing human beings.

We see, therefore, that through practical methods it is possible to establish education and a way of teaching that focus not only on the child, but also on the whole development of the human being. After all, it would be silly to think that the feet or the hands a child has now, in childhood, are already completely developed. It would be silly to try to force the hands and feet, as they grow, to remain the same as they were in childhood. Obviously, we consider the physical organism of a child to be something that is in a state of becoming, and that later in life will become something different. However, we do not always treat the spiritual development or the soul in the same way. On the contrary! Often, we see that children are being taught stern concepts; and we think that in their psyche, certain things gain sharp contours at a very early age. This is wrong!

Everything that we want a child's organism to become eventually, we need to approach now, but only in a way that will allow it to grow, to keep changing. Later, say when the students are thirty, they will not only remember what they learned when they were young; but as physical growth has transformed their limbs, they will also have the capacity to transform everything they learned. Along with everything spiritual that we offer a child, we must offer something that has the power to grow and to transform itself. This means that we have to make teaching more and more alive.

All this can certainly be expressed as an abstract principle, but it can be achieved practically only in the presence of a really intimate knowledge of the human being. Such knowledge enables us to figure out from the nature of the child everything that we usually call the lesson plan or educational goals. Therefore, the Waldorf school has teaching plans and goals that are based on a real knowledge of the human being. These plans can be redesigned from month to month, in accordance with the nature of the children themselves. We are trying to design education in a living spirit.

I should mention one thing further. We can see great improvement, now, even in public education. Nevertheless, we all know that in the course of an academic year a child suffers, more than we realize, under the system that evaluates the child's progress. On the one hand, we have the achievements of the child; and on the other hand, the evaluations of these achievements by the teacher. Evaluations are expressed in the following way: "satisfactory," "almost satisfactory," "almost non-satisfactory," "less than satisfactory,"and so forth. I have to admit that I was never able to see the difference between "almost satisfactory" and "almost non-satisfactory," and other formulations like this.

To us who teach in the Waldorf School it is important that at the end of the school year children receive certificates recording their individual characteristics and the experience of the teacher with each particular child. The child sees a kind of mirror image of herself or himself. Experience has demonstrated that this mirror image, which does not specify "satisfactory," "less than satisfactory," and so forth, for each subject, is accepted with a certain satisfaction and joy, even when there is criticism in it. This means that children receive potent evaluations, based specifically on their own nature, from which come the ability to learn and which can serve as guidance throughout the following year. If one has the necessary love to go deeply into the living nature of teaching, one can design living methods even under the most unfavorable circumstances.

In this way, we can overcome precisely those abstract pedagogical principles that must be overcome in our times. One can find hardly any indications in external historical sources of the way the human soul has changed during the succeeding epochs of humanity's development. Those who are sufficiently unbiased, however, can understand that the spiritual expression of the soul in the tenth, eleventh, or twelfth centuries must have had a character very different from that of the state of the soul in the civilized world since the mid-fifteenth century. Intellectualism has been developing in our civilization until it reached a culminating point in the twentieth century. However, like the principle of imitation, or the principle of authority, intellectualism has the peculiar quality that it is transformed from a latent into a free form at a later age. We can see that people are able to progress from their basic nature to the intellectual nature only after they are beyond the age of sexual maturity, or even later. Before that, use of the intellect paralyzes and almost kills the work of the psyche.

Thus, we can realize that we live in times that support only the adult; times that have as a cultural impulse a quality that can be manifested only in the adult human being. As a consequence, we no longer understand the world of childhood and youth because we are steeped in everything that gives the tone for the culture of our adult world.

This is the most important thing to consider in our civilization. We should be very clear about the fact that the same forces that have allowed our science and technology to flourish and triumph, also deprive us of the possibility of understanding our children and of analyzing in depth the full nature of childhood. Now we need to find the way to rebuild the bridge to the young person and to the child. No matter how we see the different forms of youth movements today, they are profoundly justified.[†] They are the cry of the youth: "You adults have created a civilization that we simply do not understand when we live in our primal nature!" The bridge between adults and children must be rebuilt, and anthroposophy wants to offer its contribution.

If we move from a general cultural viewpoint down to the details, we will see that an educational plan based on the essence of childhood itself reveals to us exactly how the plan should unfold at the different stages of the child's development. Writing and reading used to be something different from what they are now. Look at our modern letters; they are abstract, out of touch with real life. Let us look back at earlier times. In pictographic writing, we find something that is directly based on life. Today, we do not even think about how intimately connected to life this kind of writing was, and how alien to our modern life writing and reading are today. Yes, we are in the midst of a civilization where it is natural to put things alien to life in the service of civilization. If you look without prejudice at a stenographer or an elderly person sitting behind a typewriter, you would see that such an occupation brings life-estrangement into civilization. Simply articulating this fact does not make us enemies of culture or reactionaries. We are not denying the advantages of such means for modern times; there are advantages. At the same time, we should develop counterforces that could help us heal the things that can only bring culture to a decline, to decadence, if we simply let them affect us without paying attention to the consequences. Real healing can come only from education—from teaching and learning in the classroom—a process that must be constantly redesigned in light of the complexity of upbringing.†

When a child enrolls in the primary school,† the intellect is still in a latent state. The capacity for abstract thinking, which must first be awakened, develops later. This is why we cannot approach a child immediately with abstract forms of writing and reading. Since there is a creative spiritual principle at work in children in a greater and more perfect way than there is in any art form, we can work only with things that allow us to approach the child in a dynamic way. This creative principle works subconsciously. Thus, we have to support the subconscious and try to find special forms, appropriate for the age of the children, that will introduce them to writing through art, and thus will allow them to employ their full human capacity. Then they can take the next step toward reading. If children who are eight or nine years old are not yet able to read and write, teachers should have the courage to say, "Thank God that they cannot yet read and write." The point is not that children should be able to do certain things [at an early age], but that they learn in an appropriate way and at the appropriate age.

This is why teaching in the Waldorf School is designed with art as the basis for every subject. This artistic pedagogical approach is the beginning, followed by a gradual intellectual development. We also take into account that music should be integrated into the classwork as early as possible, since it is directly related to establishing the will. To the classes of traditional gymnastics, also for will development, we have added eurythmy, an art of movement that combines the physical and the spiritual. We develop our methods as we go along, to improve the pedagogical approach. However, we can see that this art of movement, which captures both the human spirit and soul, conveys something meaningful. We see that in these required classes, children adapt to the art of movement in the same way in which they adapt to language at a very young age—naturally, and with joy.

Educational development based on art allows children to experience colors, as well, from very early on. Even though painting with watercolors can sometimes be inconvenient (for instance if we have to spend more time than usual cleaning up), we still see that such a method gives children a much deeper sense of life. We are doing more than simply helping them to "get by"; this approach requires them to interact with the external world. They develop a sensitivity toward the beautiful; toward everything that makes sense in nature and in human life. This is much more important than teaching children specific details from a subject matter.

In addition to what I can describe here, which are only general guidelines, I must mention the anthroposophic basis of the teacher's outlook. When teachers enter the classroom, close the door, and step in front of the children, they bring along pedagogical "imponderables," formed by their way of looking at the world and the human being. Teachers who use their living senses when they observe how children adapt to the surrounding world by imitation, rather than abstract ideas, will know how the soul or the spiritual aspect works inside the child. They get to know the children, and their knowledge forms judgments different from the usual. When we look at life in such a way, we learn certain things. I would like to give you an example.

Once, the parents of a child came to me and told me that, to their surprise, their young son, who had been a very good boy so far, stole something.

I asked: "How old is the child?"

The parent said: "Five."

"Then, we should try to figure out what the child really did. It is possible that he did not steal at all." What did the child do? The boy took some money from a drawer—the same drawer the mother took money from every morning when she was going to shop. With the money he took out of the drawer, the boy bought some sweets, which he did not even eat himself but offered to other children. In this case, we have to say this is not stealing, whatsoever. The child had seen what his mother was doing every morning, and felt entitled to do the same. He simply imitated his mother. Only after the change of teeth can we observe a change in the child's attitude toward the norms of adults that are expressed as *good* and *bad*. Therefore, we have to establish a completely different idea of judgment; and we have to learn that everything we do in the presence of a child has to be done in a way that the child may imitate. Children should be able to imitate everything they see, including the imponderables of our thoughts. This is how the reality of thoughts is expressed. Not only what we do is important, but also the way we think. In the presence of a child, we should not simply yield to the first thought that comes to mind, because thoughts affect the child. We have to consider our thoughts carefully, even if they are only in the form of imponderables.

If we observe how a child deals with the surrounding world before the age of seven, we can see the reflection of how the child must have been before coming down to the physical or sensory world as a human being. Until then, as anthroposophic research shows, human beings are completely surrounded by the spiritual world, which is connected to them in the universe as the body is connected to the physical world. This is why, in a child younger than seven, we can see the continuation of life before birth, or even before conception. This understanding must be transformed into a pedagogical sense, so that, when standing in front of the child, the teacher can think: the spiritual world has entrusted me with a being that I have to understand, and it is my task to pave the way for this being's life path.

In a way, teaching and educating a child become a selfless service to the entire world. Through teaching and education, we sculpt something out of a particular system of views that have power, and without which there is no real teaching and no real education. The most important things in the pedagogical and didactic activities are precisely these views, which are based on an anthroposophic understanding of the world. While this understanding is not externally accepted as the norm, it is, nevertheless, rooted in deep internal work. Such an attitude causes us to look at the secrets of the child's body cautiously, in religious awe; we see how something created in the eternal primordial depth of the world reveals itself step by step in the movements and the gestures of the child. We realize that we must solve a riddle of life in a practical manner. Only in this way are we going to give the right direction to our entire attitude toward education and teaching.

Anthroposophy wants most of all to see that this atmosphere, which radiates from all school activities, is present in the process of teaching, and that it dominates every detail in this process. However, in order for this atmosphere to be predominant, it is first necessary that, through a deep inner conviction, we come to see how the spirit works its way down to the finest detail of each sign of life the child shows. In order to take up and approach a class with the attitude and the skills that are based on internalizing the anthroposophic worldview, a teacher must come to particular understandings and develop the resulting abilities, and these should become instinct.

I have been able to make only a few suggestions, which I will expand in the following lectures. The suggestions I made were intended to show that anthroposophy does not want to be radically against the major achievements in the area of pedagogy. Anthroposophy wants to offer some assistance, which would help bring these otherwise abstract theories into real life, into our daily practice; so that the art of education becomes a living impulse, an effective factor in our social life.

5.
Anthroposophy and Social Science

BERLIN, MARCH 9, 1922

MOST HONORED PARTICIPANTS: in my introductory words today, even more than at the other meetings, I will have to restrict myself to making only a few suggestions. There will be a detailed discussion of our economy in the upcoming lectures, and the main substance of what needs to be said about the social sciences will have to wait until then.

We cannot speak of social science if we take only one theory as a starting point. Today—and I mean our immediate present, the present moment—we can speak of social science only if we see it against the background of the desperate situation concerning the economy of the civilized world. I tried to describe part of this desperate situation in my book *Core Points of the Social Question* [*Towards Social Renewal*] after the end of the catastrophic World War.[†] This work was based on an observation about developments in social science that, considering current conditions, should have been apparent to all. Our present economy is deeply intertwined with something very basic for the entire scope of social conditions—what we could call "the social question." In our times, most people do not think it possible to separate the discussion of social conditions from the question of our economy. Yet, my book aimed at the clarification of this issue. The book aspired to demonstrate that within the social organism, the economy must have its own independent position, a position determined exclusively by economic principles, economic views and impulses. Seen from such a perspective, my book might seem to display an inner contradiction. I am saying this here in a very straightforward way because a lot depends on understanding this. The book was not supposed to be a theoretical work on social science, however. It was intended to inspire most of all the *practitioners*—those who work in a practical and direct way in business, production, distribution, and all areas of economic life. The book was written out of an understanding that came from observing the economy of Europe for decades. Since the book was intended to be thoroughly realistic, and to prompt practical activity, it also had to contain a contradiction. This is nothing but the same contradiction characteristic of our entire society. I am talking about the fact that the chaotic, messy elements of our social life could actually be productive, but only if each element develops naturally under its own conditions and in its own particular section of society.

In my book I discussed the threefold formation of the social organism, a formation that would lead to a completely independent organization of the economy, almost completely separate from the government, the law, and the spiritual life. The economy would be determined by those who are part of it, and by the way they deal with their own impulses. However, we live at a time when this is not yet the case; the economy is still interwoven, too enmeshed with these other elements, in the structure of the social organism. We live at a time when the contradiction is reality. This is why my study—which was written on the basis of reality and was intended to make suggestions for this same reality—implied some contradiction. Nevertheless, the study had to be aimed first of all at achieving some clarity, at the clarification of the circumstances.

And so, making this introduction today, I am in a peculiar position because people in the widest possible circles generally misunderstood the conclusions I made. My conclusions were based on anthroposophic methods of thinking, as well as on decades of realistic observation of the conditions in the European economy. I can only say that I see very well why my original intentions were misunderstood. Misunderstandings themselves are a phenomenon of our time. Nevertheless, I am convinced that overcoming these misunderstandings is what we should aim to achieve in the field of sociology, and in society. I would like to make some suggestions precisely in this respect because they could give us some direction.

My book was first published just after the Treaty of Versailles, immediately following the terrible war catastrophe.[†] Those were times when the currency relationships between Central and Eastern Europe were still very different. The impulses expressed in my book back then did not come "out of nowhere." They were based on the situation in the world at the time, which led me to believe that perhaps there were other people who saw the same things I saw, and were seeking change. If so, then it would have been possible, starting with Central Europe, to spread an economic impulse that could have brought certain progress in the midst of the clearly deteriorating economy, and social life in general, which still has not recovered. Considering the complicated situation in the world, one would have thought that there would be no arguments against acceptance of the ideas in the book. These ideas were founded in the reality of the time. Nevertheless, they could be attacked. Perhaps they could have been formulated in a different way when they were first written down. But the point was not to create impractical, utopian ideas or to paint a picture of a future social organism. Rather, the point was to find people who understood that we were confronted with real, immediate problems in our daily lives; that we had to deal with those problems as best our professional knowledge allowed us, and while dealing concretely with the problems, try to find increasingly better understanding.

Generally, however, what happened was something very different. On one hand, there were economic theorists who endlessly discussed what was written in my book, and who attached all sorts of "demands" to the things I had said.[†] There were also theorists who misunderstood what I had said in a very idealistic way, and who kept asking how this or that could happen. There are no instant answers to such questions; only the passage of time reveals the answers.

In addition, there was also something that really surprised me. The "practitioners" of economics, that is, the "hands on" business people, the entrepreneurs—those who had direct experience in specific areas of economic activity, and who knew what works in their area of business and what does not—precisely those people paid no attention to their own knowledge and experience. They allowed themselves to be influenced by theorists who had no direct experience with their particular branch of the economy. When the practitioners discussed the core points of the social questions, their conclusions showed that they themselves had become the most abstract theoreticians. It became obvious that they could be conventional businesspeople in the old sense easily enough, but they did not understand the new circumstances. These practitioners were absolutely unable to discuss the economic problems that I am talking about, from any other perspective than the one of abstract theory. It could cause real despair to stand in front of business people, trying to have a discussion with them. Some were absolutely not able to look at anything concretely, but instead, kept repeating only the most trivial and general points of economic theory.

Along with the repetition of theory, originally, those who were very thorough practitioners refused to talk about the possibility of looking at the economic problems in the new way that I suggested in the book. I encountered yet another problem with socialists. Despite the vague interest that my book aroused among them, they did not want to look at their goals from this perspective. They made judgments about everything on the basis of whether or not it fit the old socialist party clichés. This is how we came to the terrible currency disaster that prompted me to make those remarks.† It should now be understood and evaluated in a way different from the way we now understand it.

When I first published my "Appeal to the German People and Culture" and then *Towards Social Renewal*,† there were people who had very serious intentions regarding the process of healing the Central European economy. They said, "Yes, such suggestions" (they called my theories "suggestions") "are very good, but we have to figure out first of all how to improve the state of the currency." This was said at a time when the miserable situation of the currency was still a paradise compared to the present circumstances. Such statements demonstrate that all we want is to play around with the external symptoms. There is very little understanding that the currency situation is a superficial symptom, manifesting unhealthy economic conditions, and that such a treatment of symptoms does not even begin to touch the real evil. These statements also show that there is little understanding of the need to go deeper into analysis of the present socio-economic conditions, if we want to discuss the problems mentioned in *Towards Social Renewal* in any realistic way. This is how I came to my appeal, which I expressed at the end of that book and at the end of many lectures:[†] We must come to our senses before it is too late.

To a certain degree, it is already too late, since we are no longer able to approach the issue in the original spirit of *Towards Social Renewal*. Meanwhile, the chaos in our economic life has grown so much more complex that we need many more additional explanations of what, in my view, not only *should* be stated, but also *must* be stated. If we want to discuss what damages our economy, we will not be able to avoid examining a general characteristic of our time.

When I looked at a newspaper yesterday, I noticed an article (here, we can see the most important symptoms in simple sentences formulated by some of our contemporaries). "Postponing of Lloyd George's Resignation until the End of the Conference in Genoa."[†] This title expresses the entire situation of our time. The main characteristic of our time is "to wait." "We want to wait." This is the common principle today, to wait until something happens. We cannot say what will happen, but we want to wait until it happens. This attitude has penetrated our souls, and one can see it in all possible areas.

Now I would like to mention something that is apparently abstract, but only apparently. It is actually realistic, because it points out the forces that are active among us, which gradually, through the centuries, have given credibility to this optimistic principle called "we want to wait." Looking back at the development of past cultures we see that ancient scientific thinking should not be called simply "scientific" (you have heard me talk about this in the lecture I gave recently at the philharmonic hall[†]). If we look at the thinking that was there, we realize that economic circumstances did not grow immediately out of ancient scientific thought. Originally, economic life developed almost instinctively because of trade, more or less independently of human thought.[†] What people did in their economy was born naturally from their daily life. People acted intuitively. Some areas of trade were certainly expanded, but everything happened more or less intuitively. We might raise some objections against the economic conditions of the ancient times, on the basis of modern views of freedom, dignity, and so forth. Nevertheless, it could be helpful to see some remarkable signs of humanity's development, which could teach us a lot, even today.

To give only one example, I will point out the relationships between employer and employee (if I may use these modern terms with regard to ancient times) in ancient Greece, Egypt, and Asia. Considering how we feel today, these relationships may raise harsh criticism, but any such criticism would be unhistorical. We have to admit that the labor relationships in each particular period of time were based on the sensibility of the people who lived at the time. This is the first thing that we should keep in mind.

The other thing that we should keep in mind is the drastic changes in humanity's development that we observe in the fifteenth century, and which affected the entire state of the soul of people in the civilized world. I have emphasized frequently that external history does not tell us much about how the human soul changed its view of life at the time. So, if we ask ourselves how this part of human development relates to the economy, the answer is: The intuitive control of the economy, of the sort I just described, expanded until the fifteenth century, an epoch of drastic changes. Along with those changes, the state of the human soul was affected by intellectualism, by the desire to understand the world through reason and logic alone.

This desire, which became a profound necessity of the human soul, affirmed itself brilliantly in natural science. Technology developed gloriously out of natural science, and celebrated an extraordinary triumph, which cannot be appreciated enough. Yet this intellectualism has proven to be completely unable to aid us in understanding the social context of development in human life, and human beings themselves. Many debates have demonstrated this, including those during this course. Through such intellectual orientation of the soul, we have discovered the laws of the outer nature of the senses. However, intellectualism will not help us comprehend the complex circumstances of social life that penetrate and are entangled with each other, and organize themselves as they become entangled, and materialize as they become organized. The system of intellectual ideas is too loose for the phenomena of social life. From intellectualism, humanity certainly learned how to think scientifically. This kind of thinking covers every subject area, even theology. If we observe it carefully and experiment with it, we will see that intellectualism rules over our entire scientific way of thinking; we consider everything that is not based on intellectualism as simply unscientific. The time of intellectualism overlapped with the transition from a purely instinctive economy to an economy that had to be brought to life by human thought.

Thus, we could say that at the time when people did not think intellectually about the world, economic life was led in an instinctive way. Along with the trend toward a world economy and world trade, people began to think of their economic life in an exclusively intellectual way. One can see two sides or polarities in economic theory as it developed—in mercantilism and in physiocratism, in Adam Smith's ideas of national economy and in the entire development of political economy up to Karl Marx.[†] On the one hand, economic life itself required that economic decisions should no longer be made intuitively, but that they should rather be based on reason instead. On the other hand, since thoughts could be based only on intellectualism, economic decisions become more and more one-sided. As a consequence, there is nothing that came out of economic theory that we could see as applicable in economic practice. On the one hand, we had the theorists of political economy such as Ricardo, Adam Smith, and John Stuart Mill,[†] who produced axioms out of intellectualistic postulates. On the basis of these axioms, they built confusing self-contained systems that were like vicious circles. On the other hand, at the same time, we had economic practice, which might have required a symbiosis with the spiritual but never found access to it. Economic practice continued to develop, however, within the old, almost instinctive life, and thus fell into absolute chaos.

These two movements became more and more commonplace in modern times. On the one hand, there were the political economists who had no influence on economic practice; on the other hand, there were the practitioners who continued the traditional practices, which threw the economies of the civilized world into chaos. We certainly need to articulate things like this in a very radical way, to point out what reality is; what does work; and what should be seen as the real problem.

If we are looking now for some connection, for a synthesis between economic thought (which, however, has been meanwhile completely destroyed by the practice) and the practice itself, we can find this connection in only one area. Most recently, a kind of scientific-economic realism has developed, which acknowledges that we can never come to general economic laws that will always apply. Instead, we should take into consideration economic circumstances as they develop in particular nations, or among specific groups of people. We can find guidelines with regard to trade only if we look at the specifics of external and concrete economic circumstances as they happen. This is the foundation of what appeared as so-called social or economic legislation.

We began to believe that we can analyze the factual economic circumstances in connection with the social conditions that bring them about, and then legislate economic guidelines. In other words, we have tried to bring about through the government some of the things we observe in a rather roundabout way. By doing so, however, we have in fact admitted that real economic laws cannot come out of such observations. Yes, basically this is the situation in which we still find ourselves today. We can see how we are stuck in this situation precisely now, when we are able to have groundbreaking experiences, or shall I say, when we are able to evaluate social phenomena in the right way.

You all know that Woodrow Wilson came up with his so-called "Fourteen Points" exactly at a time when our society fell into such terrible chaos.[†] What were these Fourteen Points really about? Basically they were nothing but the abstract principles of a man who knew little of the real world (a fact demonstrated at Versailles, where he could have actually played an excellent role). A man who was estranged from reality and inspired by intellectualism wanted to show the world how to organize itself. I could only wish that we had been welcomed with such enthusiasm as civilized humanity welcomed those Fourteen Points. However, a large part of the Central European population fell for Wilson's theory, even though only for a little while, and made us the exception.

In 1917, there were people in Central Europe who were interested in these issues, and who asked to speak to me.[†] (I did not pursue these people; they either came to me or were brought to me). I tried to show that the latest social developments were abstract and estranged from reality. I tried to show that everything negative, which we consider to be based on bad educational principles, but that we nevertheless see predominating everywhere, could be summarized in the person of this teacher of the world, Woodrow Wilson. I also showed how people welcomed with enthusiasm the abstract principles of this (in the pejorative sense) "world teacher." In addition, I tried to show that a recovery from the current circumstances could be achieved only if, in contrast to all these abstract views, we stand firmly on the ground; on a ground that does not exclude thought but that nurtures the kind of thought grown out of reality. In this case, we would not create any utopia—and I would like to say that Woodrow Wilson's principles were pure utopia—utopia multiplied by three. In contrast, we should understand clearly that actual impulses are to be found only in the real circumstances of contemporary humanity.

Thus, in all my arguments, I was avoiding any utopian theory. I avoided even mentioning how capital and labor are formed. I gave only a few examples of how we could possibly imagine their developing from the current circumstances into the near future. I said all this, however, only to illustrate what capital and labor should be. In fact, capital capacities could change either in the way I mentioned in my book *Towards Social Renewal* or in some other modified way. I did not mean to paint some abstract picture of the future. My goal was to explain what the basis for a real solution of the so-called social question could be, not to propose an abstract theoretical solution. I did not intend to "define a solution" in general for the social question because I have enough experience to know that it is impossible to do that.

In the 1880s, in cozy Vienna, I used to spend at least an hour nearly every afternoon with all sorts of bright people. Within this hour, every afternoon, the social question was solved several times.[†]

Those who see the present without bias can realize that the current solutions published frequently on the pages of thick volumes are not much better than the solutions negotiated with a few strokes of the pen and the many fanatical words spoken over café tables back then in Vienna. Defining a solution was certainly not my goal, and to accuse me of such an intention was a most terrible misunderstanding.

All I wanted to show was that the solution to the social question could come about only in a natural way; that it could not be the result of discussions, but only of action. However, the conditions for such action must first be prepared. In my *Towards Social Renewal* and in other debates I was referring to precisely these conditions. I was trying to demonstrate that in our social organism we need institutions that would allow the natural development of spiritual life, a development affected only by the conditions and requirements of spiritual life itself. I argued further that we will need a second entity, where only the judicial impulses of the governments would be at work; and then a third entity, dealing with the economic impulses based on the production and consumption of goods.

If this economic entity were to develop out of an associative economic system, it would culminate, in my view, in a healthy pricing policy. By developing an associative economic system, we would not revive the old class system.[†] This is not about dividing people into teacher-class, soldier-class, and worker-class. The human being of modern times has progressed to the status of an individual and cannot be placed into any particular class in a theoretical way. However, simply because of the forces of historical development, the existing institutions tend not to treat the spiritual life, the judicial life of the state, and the economy separately from each other, each on the basis of their own conditions. Only after we create the conditions that would allow the economist, for example, to make changes in the current market or capital relationships, on the basis of purely economic impulses; only then, when such possibilities are created, would we be able to develop what we could call a real "solution" of the social question. This solution, however, would be in a constant state of "becoming."

So, my goal is not to solve social problems, because such a solution, in my view, can never be final at any given moment. Once the social problem has appeared, it remains in constant flux. The social organism is like someone who is young, and will age. The social organism must be constantly instilled with new impulses, and we will never be able to define it in a fixed form. The government can have a real democratic foundation only if it has a healthy organism in which people consider the individual conditions of each specific area of life in its own right. This will not be accomplished by those who sit in parliaments mixing all possible interests—where those interested in the economy make decisions about spiritual issues, or those representing the state make decisions about the economy, and so forth. What needs to be said in a healthy organism, will not be said by only one person in such a mixed parliament. Rather, it will result from constant and continuous negotiations between the different parts of the social organism.

In that sense my book was a warning that we need to stop the futile discussion of "the social question"; instead, we have to stand firm on the ground and deal with social problems on a daily basis. My book was an appeal to those who understand that need—to turn abstract theory into thoughtful and real action. Economic associations should be responsible for these actions in the economic area. Such associations are profoundly different from the processes of nationalization that occurred in recent times, and they could be established at any moment on the basis of existing economic conditions. Such associations should consist of the practitioners, the people who are really connected by the processes of production, circulation, and consumption of goods—things that actually connect all people. These are the people who should organize themselves in associations to establish a healthy pricing policy. In the present situation we are a long way from benefiting from the practical and professional experience that the people organized in these associations would bring to a healthy pricing policy. Such a policy would not be the result of legislation and discussion, but of experience.

Nevertheless, people felt the need to discuss the main ideas that I presented in my book, and which I presented in my introductory words to you today. The world was so well trained in abstract thinking that it saw my suggestions only from the perspective of abstract thought. As a consequence, things are discussed for hours that I mentioned only as examples, and the point is missed to tackle the formation of the social organism on a daily basis in the way proposed in *Towards Social Renewal.*

The point is not to search for theoretical solutions to the social question, but to determine under what conditions people will be living in society. Social life will exist when the social organism is working in the interest of all its three parts, in the same way that the natural organism works precisely toward unity though it is also divided into three parts, relatively speaking.[†] Nowadays, we have to explain what we mean when we say such things, you see. Even when we have expressed them, there is still an expectation that the words we must use will be taken according to the theoretical meaning attached to them. People immediately translate into intellectualism, ideas that obviously are not the product of intellectualism. For example, in my book I speak about capital and about the basic principles of the production process, and about labor, in such a way that the ideas can be related to life. If we begin abstract discussions, we spend a lot of time on definitions. One would say rightfully that capital is crystallized or accumulated labor, while another one would say—also rightfully—that capital is saved labor. We could do this with any concept of political economy if we want to remain within the mind frame of intellectualism. These, however, are not concepts that we can deal with in theory only. On the contrary, we should try to understand how concepts are being formed, and how they live. The practitioners who cling to traditional practice while talking abstract theories, could instead do something new. I would like to clarify this through a comparison.

Ernst Müller[†] is short, and has clearly youthful features and child-like qualities. I see this man twenty years later and I say, "This is not Ernst Müller." Although he is still short and has child-like qualities, the face is completely different! If twenty years ago I have created an image of Ernst Müller and I want it to be identical with the real person I am facing now, I will be making a terrible mistake. No matter how much people are opposed to believing it, this is exactly what they are doing when they think about the economy. They think about capital and labor, and they create their respective fixed concepts in the belief that these concepts will always be valid. In this case, however, we do not need to wait for twenty years. We could simply go from one employer to another, from one country to another, to discover that the concept we have created in one place has no validity in the other unless it has been transformed of its own accord like the person Ernst Müller. We will never be able to recognize what we are looking at unless we have flexible concepts that are fully rooted in life itself.

In our time of scarcity, anthroposophic principles make it possible for economic institutions to find their own expression because anthroposophy, by its nature, deals with the ever-changing spirit, using ever-changing ideas. We can learn from anthroposophy how to infuse our ideas with the force of growth, with an inner flexibility, and how to use such ideas regardless of the disbelief of today's practitioners. We can use flexible thinking in the reality of the social life between individuals, between countries, and throughout the entire world economy, which has now become necessary, although it has been destroyed in such an artificial way.

Thus we could say that the attempt to come, not to social "ideas" but to social "impulses" by means of anthroposophy was not based on anything external. I remember the times when these terms were much discussed. I always had to repeat: "social *impulse*"! This made people terribly angry; according to them, I should have used the phrase "social ideas," or "social thought," because people had in mind only "thoughts." It was terribly upsetting to speak of *impulses*. They did not realize that I needed the word *impulse* because I was working with the reality and not with abstractions.

Consequently, today we have to establish new conceptions of the so-called social problem. Circumstances are now very different from those in 1919. Things are changing very fast, especially in the area of economics. It is necessary to keep seeing movement, even in those ideas that were already considered to be flexible in 1919—and also to preserve the perspective of common sense. Those who are able to see the reality of economic conditions, know that these conditions have changed significantly since I wrote *Towards Social Renewal*, and that we cannot simply deduce the same conclusions we did back then. Nevertheless, they will find in that book at least an attempt to search for methods of social thinking in a realistic way. That attempt was founded on the constant search for reality, to prevent us from falling into the trap of illusions and mysticism. That attempt was nourished by the quest for exact truthfulness, which is characteristic of the anthroposophic view of the world.

6.
Anthropsophy and Theology

BERLIN, MARCH 10, 1922

MOST HONORED PARTICIPANTS: I am compelled to refer to a note in a journal that was handed to me just now, a note in *Die Christliche Welt* (*The Christian World*).† I did not expect to be referring to this in my introductory words today, since I did not know of it. The note in the journal reads as follows:

"Between the 5th and the 12th of March there is an anthroposophic college course ... Friday, the 10th, is the day of the theologians.† The lecture on Friday is an obvious challenge to theologians by Steiner and his followers..." and so forth.

Well, most honored participants, the lecture today may be anything but a challenge. If that is the general belief, it is a profound misunderstanding; this lecture is certainly not a challenge to theologians. I did not initiate these lectures, and I have never been involved in them in any other way, except that I was asked whether I wanted to participate in this college course by giving lectures and making some introductory remarks. I am least involved with today's lecture in the sense that it was not my decision to include this particular topic in the college course; and it never crossed my mind that what we will be discussing here today could be interpreted as "an obvious challenge to contemporary theologians." Therefore, dear participants, in order to avoid any further misunderstandings, repeated or new, of the few introductory words that I will say, today I will limit myself to the topic "the relationship between anthroposophy and theology." So that there are no further misunderstandings, I will give up some of the points I was going to make, because I do not wish to see my intentions misinterpreted again.

Distinguished participants, I apologize if because of this challenge, which was aimed at me, I am forced to include some brief personal remarks in my introduction today. I have never desired, and it was never my intention, to challenge theology in any way. Since the very beginning of our work on anthroposophy, insofar as this is about the field I am involved with, we have never tried to argue with modern theology as such. Nevertheless, this argument has happened, even though I have tried to prevent it. It has happened simply because anthroposophy has been frequently attacked by the theologians; and because some people, not so much I myself but others, have tried to defend it. I would like to say that as a field of study, anthroposophy is intended to remain completely neutral toward theology. Its purpose is to work in the spirit of contemporary science.

Toward the end of the last century science took a particular direction; it used particular scientific methods, which led to particular scientific views. For the same reasons I already mentioned, as well as because of lack of time, I cannot go into detail about these views and these methods. Growing out of the entire historical development of modern times, they have been applied most particularly to the study of natural science, where they led to the greatest possible triumphs in human progress and welfare. I do not mean this in a trivial, but in a very profound, sense. At that time, I would say philosophy was somewhat at a loss with respect to the study of natural science. Philosophy was confronted with methods which were applied primarily in natural science and which were virtually inapplicable in philosophy, a field dealing with completely different subject matter. In terms of theory and in terms of theory of knowledge, we were not sure in what sense we were supposed to use scientific methods in the area of philosophy. As a consequence, experimental psychology was trapped in an area where things were more or less apparent, or more or less right, but where uncertainty remained present.[†]

By contrast, on the basis of different developments, anthroposophy established its own methods. On one hand, it takes account of things achieved precisely through the newest way of thinking and the newest scientific research methods; and on the other hand, it takes account of the human desire for a spiritual world and its understanding. We were confronted with the fact that we must fully accept scientific methods. Regarding our attitude toward the area of science, I am still as much a follower of Haeckel as I was in the 1890s, as I already have mentioned.[†] I do not mean that scientific methods should not develop further, or that what Haeckel wrote should not be criticized precisely from the point of view of science; but this is a completely different issue. With regard to my attitude toward the purely natural world, I am as much a follower of Haeckel today as I was back then.

The question is what we actually experience through the scientific methods of observation and through the fact that we are trained in scientific precision and attitudes. In other words, what ideas and concepts can we form when we simply need to work with natural science? There is one thing that remains true for all methods of observation; because of insufficient time I cannot prove this here, but if the statement that "nothing is in the mind that is not first in the senses"[†] is true for external observation through the senses, then Leibnitz's addition to that statement—"nothing... except the mind itself" is also true.[†]

There is something much more than experiencing only the sensory in experiencing the mind, in other words, in the movements of the soul throughout the categories of the mind, in experiencing ideas that help us study an object and the facts in nature and that allow us to formulate natural laws, in experiencing the world of ideas. Thus, when scientists are facing natural science and they are really unbiased, they must admit that the senses must be the source of everything that is in the mind, but the senses cannot be the source of the mind itself. Once we have fully comprehended this, nothing will prevent us from observing what we see internally, and from further developing the categories of the mind through an inner psychic and spiritual process through a process that represents internally something similar to the external processes of growth in a plant or an animal.

We will be truthful to the natural process of becoming, if we try looking at the human mind itself as if it were an embryo that could grow internally. From this effort, we can learn the truth that the sensory world is not the source of the mind. If we really try this, then the rest will be an immediate consequence of the growing intellect that develops into imagination, inspiration, and intuition; a process I was describing here during these few days and also in other places. This is simply a matter of the further progress in the inner development of the human being. This attitude amounts to a real view of the world.

Anthroposophy is trying, as much as possible, to put this view into words. I admit that sometimes we are certainly forced to use unsatisfactory words for what we observe, simply because in the past few centuries our language, like all modern languages, has adapted to the external materialistic understanding of the world. And we have adjusted our feelings related to the words more or less to that same understanding. This is why we always struggle with words when we try to express in language things we observe through imagination, inspiration, or intuition. This is especially the case when we try to express these observations in words in order to prove them, using our healthy human common sense—which is another goal of anthroposophic study.

In that sense, anthroposophy has always been a field of study—and this is exactly the way in which I understand it. To those who had a desire to hear what we could learn about the suprasensory world through such methods (and in the beginning there was a very small circle of such people), we will show what we can discover in this way. People are not forced to join this movement by any means; they join only by their own free will. The rumors that some hypnotic means were used are slander; in some cases a conscious, and in other cases an unconscious, slandering of the real intentions of the anthroposophic movement. It seems that those who, because of their healthy common sense, contemplate things studied through imagination, inspiration, and intuition, are freer than most people in our times. For example, people of our times run after the movements of their political parties, and allow others to influence them in all possible ways. Anthroposophy must free the human being from precisely these inner psychological dependencies. Those who enter into the spirit of anthroposophy are not simply liberated from the most common, passive way of thinking, they also make their thinking internally flexible and more powerful. Thus they become free individuals through this internally empowered thinking.

For reasons that I do not wish to discuss today, originally very few scientists joined anthroposophy, even though the movement counted precisely on them. Today, we are beginning to have more scientists in our circles. To those more or less naïve souls with strong psychological needs, who joined the anthroposophic movement in the beginning, we have always talked about the discoveries made in a conscientious way within the framework of anthroposophic studies. I have been glad to hear some of the things that people tell me (such as one of the highly respected persons present here today[†]). "It is amazing that you get such a large number of listeners, since you avoid speaking in what people call a popular or commonly comprehensible way. In fact, you speak in a way that always requires that people do some inner work while they are listening, and this is something people usually do not want to do. Thus, I must wonder how you get such a large number of listeners." These approximately were the words I heard long ago from a person who is present here today, and who, back then, visited a series of my lectures. While I always wanted to promote anthroposophy in the world, I have never looked for popularity.

It is remarkable that people from all walks of life and from all denominations came to us. While through its work anthroposophy did establish some kind of relationship to the contemporary religious movements, originally there was never a conflict with the religious needs of the people who joined us, people from all walks of life, as I mentioned. Catholics who are in our circles have often asked me if it is possible to participate in the anthroposophic movement but to remain Catholic with regard to religious practice. I said to them, of course it is possible to participate as a good Catholic in the things that anthroposophy offers, because anthroposophy is not supposed to limit itself to one single confession but simply to speak on the basis of the study of the suprasensory world. It would suit me best to tell people what we have found in the suprasensory world, and not to participate in any polemic.

Those who tell honestly what they have seen know well how it comes to polemics, and how unproductive it actually is. My original desire was simply to tell what could be discovered through anthroposophy and to pay no attention to polemics. These things, however, do not always work out as we wish. Nevertheless, within the anthroposophic movement there were people from all religions, including Catholics, and I said that Catholics can participate in the anthroposophic movement like anyone else. They might be in conflict with their religious practice regarding only one issue—the Confession. Not because this is about confession. Confession itself could be considered simply a matter of conscience. I have seen many Protestant clergymen who long for some kind of a confession in order to establish a more intimate relationship to their congregations. There could be different opinions about that. The issue is that the Catholic Church denies Communion to those who have not first made a confession. Because of this prohibition against participating in the most important sacrament of the Catholic Church, it is very difficult for Catholics to combine the beliefs they have established through their experiences in the suprasensory world with a behavior that does not allow them to feel free, but that the constitution of the Roman Catholic Church forces them to follow. The way confession is treated tears Catholics apart from the free observation of the suprasensory world, not because of anthroposophy, but because of the constitution of the Roman Catholic Church. Catholics could avoid this if they could avoid the Confession. However, they cannot avoid the Confession, because if they did, they would not be able to partake in the Communion. This is the difficulty Catholics are confronted with. Despite that, there are many Catholics who are trying to satisfy their spiritual needs in the anthroposophic movement.

It was only natural that people from all denominations joined the anthroposophic movement; it was only natural that our very time brought the need to discuss questions of Christianity in the Anthroposophic Association. I would like to say the following in that regard. As far as the subject of Christology includes questions concerning both the sensory and the suprasensory in this world, anthroposophy treats the essence of Christology in the same way as any other subject. It tries to explore and to give answers about the essence of Christology through the methods of its suprasensory studies. It is difficult to summarize in a few words the character of the relationship of anthroposophy to Christology.

However, I would like to note the following. We see human beings primarily here in their earthly life, between birth and death; and we realize that their existence, including their psychic and spiritual life, has the form of a physical body. We also realize that they are bound to this physical body when it comes to their views, to processing the phenomena in their environment, to their work or the exercise of their will, and generally to the way they function in the physical-sensory world. Thinking back on what we see in our surroundings when we wake up in the morning, we realize that we first perceive these surroundings through the senses of the body, and through the mind, which combines the experiences of the senses with our perceptions of everything that surrounds us in the physical world.

Provided that sometimes we are able to look away from the environment and reflect sufficiently on ourselves, we cannot deny the fact that the mind or the intellect, which bears in itself the primordial, the intrinsically spiritual, is able to put things together on its own. This process of putting things together culminates in an idea that has now a spiritual content; a content that represents the divine or the Father-idea, if I may phrase it this way. At this point we could involve anthroposophic methods of study. I can describe this only very briefly. Anthroposophy gradually makes the entire process of obtaining human knowledge transparent; this is something that is evident from the content of these lectures, too. Its purpose is to point to the processes that occur within the human being when we try to look away from the external world in order to see what we ourselves have done, and to ask ourselves: What have we actually done? What gives us the right, the capacity, to put together the external world into ideas? As we analyze the complexities of this process sufficiently, we come to the divine Father-experience, if I may use this phrase again.[†] Those who understand the process of arriving at the Father-experience in anthroposophic terms make a very particular judgment. Please, do not misinterpret this judgment, which is a fact that I must express in a radical way.

We make the judgment that only a completely healthy individual, someone whose physical body is completely healthy, can have this Father-experience. This means that those who cannot have that experience must be carrying the traces of some degenerative problems, even if in a hidden way. In other words, anthroposophic study brings us to the conclusion that if we are not able to come to the Father-experience, we must have some illness. This sounds radical, because the illness in question certainly cannot be discovered using the usual physical means. The illness is in the finest elements of the human organization, if I may put it this way. However, for those who can use anthroposophic methods of study, it is clear: atheism is disease.

What I said yesterday about forming a judgment that may be right or wrong, healthy or sick, applies here particularly well.[†] If we pursue only this path, we will come first only to the divine Father-experience. If, however, we continue on that path, and having come only to the Father-experience we realize the deficiencies of our soul, or if we become aware of the fact that basically by limiting ourselves to intellectualism we, as modern people, in a way limit ourselves to this divine Father-experience, then we will understand that we have to go beyond it. External observations could support us in this.

It is remarkable that religion should be preserved in the Western world precisely where scientific views have reached the maximum of their intensity and where these views are not allowed to influence the area of the suprasensory. Precisely in the religious movements in the West, the Spirit represented by the Old Testament intervenes, and is particularly successful in our modern times. We can also see that even though the West accepts and preaches Christianity, it does so completely in the spirit of the Old Testament; we see that it molds Christ into the image of the Father, and that it is not fully aware of the difference between the two.

In the East, where the human soul does not make such a clear distinction between religion and science, where this bridge is treated more or less as a very basic internal experience of the soul, as we can see in the discourses of Vladimir Soloviov—there we see the Christ-experience as an independent experience, even though it is immediately next to that of the Father.[†]

Thus, we can see that those who are completely healthy cannot be atheists if they put together all the impressions of the external world and summarize them in the crowning experience of the idea of God, to which they must add spiritual content. So, at first they stay with the idea of the Father. With this idea, however, we cannot go beyond summarizing the external phenomena of nature. The idea fails immediately if we want to use it only to comprehend our own human development; then we feel abandoned in a way. But if we analyze our own human development on a deeper level, from the level we reach when we internalize the outer world in our souls, and if we analyze the internal development without prejudice, then we will come to the Christ-experience. At first this appears to be only an undefined inner experience. This experience clearly follows the principles of anthroposophy. We can understand the mystery of the historical event of Golgotha on our own, simply through honest observation of the development of humanity on earth. Through the internal forming of spiritual organs [the human being is led] to imagination, inspiration, and intuition. If we analyze human development from antiquity to the event of Golgotha, we will realize that there were traces of preparation for the coming of the Christ-spirit living in earlier religious ideas, not only in those of the Old Testament, but in all religious ideas.

Then, simply through contemplation, we can learn to recognize the fact that at the time of the event of Golgotha, the Christ-spirit was not united with the earth. If we look at everything that people searched for in the mysteries† at the time of the well known pre-Christian religions, we will see how the ideas those people had of God eventually melded together into the Christ-idea. We see how the human soul is elevated to the supra-terrestrial, when people turn to their gods. We also see that in the beginning of human development, simply through the organization of the human being, people were given a great deal more than what their senses and their minds were able to perceive from the environment in their earthly existence. In antiquity (but less and less so as time went by), the human soul possessed the ability for what I would like to call instinctive seeing, a dream-like seeing, the ability to contemplate the spiritual, non-terrestrial world, to which the human felt attached. The human being experiences inner resurrection in the moment when, through the mysteries or through popular religions, the soul is elevated to things it can see as supra-terrestrial and with which, in its deepest essence, it feels united.

If we analyze human development up to the Mystery of Golgotha, we will realize that these inner abilities of the human were gradually diminished, and no longer existed by the time the Mystery of Golgotha happened on earth. Since development is not realized in sudden, drastic changes, some traces of these abilities certainly remained. Some people retained, if not a precise seeing, perhaps at least an instinctive consciousness, of what once was seen. We can find traces of this ability even in art. Then the Mystery of Golgotha happened on earth. Anthroposophy sees in it how the Spirit (which before could have been searched for only in the supra-terrestrial) now flows into a human body, how Christ flows into the human body of Jesus. How exactly this occurred is a discussion we can have in detail only with those who are willing to study this subject scientifically.

Anthroposophy shows that from the moment of the Mystery of Golgotha on, a new era began, an era that all old religions [mention]. Christ, who went through the Mystery of Golgotha, Christ whom Paul saw on the road to Damascus, this Christ remained on earth among human beings. This is the meaning of the words: "I am always with you until the end of time."[†] He lives among us; he can be found again. With some preparation, Paul's experience could be repeated again and again. However, if we take this road to Christ, who has been present on earth since the event of Golgotha, we will experience him through contemplation, by looking at our own inner development. We will find Christ through an inner experience, as we find the Father-God through experiencing the outer world, unless we are sick with atheism.

I can mention only briefly in an outline how, through real study, anthroposophy arrives at the Christ-phenomenon as an objective fact. Anthroposophy tries to present the Christ-phenomenon in all its details, as the most important fact in the earthly life of the human being, as something that has objectively occurred. Thus the entire spirit in which the Christ-phenomenon is presented in anthroposophy supports its understanding as fact. Consequently, within the anthroposophic movement we have seen Jews who in the most genuine, truthful, and honest sense have accepted the Mystery of Golgotha. Perhaps this way, my most honored participants, the anthroposophic movement anticipates something that should occur in the future development of humanity: that by pointing out what we can see in the Mystery of Golgotha, we actually rediscover the path to Christianity.

We have to ask ourselves whether the point Friedrich Nietzsche's friend Overbeck makes in his book (that modern theology is no longer Christian), may not have a very deep meaning after all.[†] Should this question be justified, even only to a degree, we would have the right to say that anthroposophy is capable of bringing people to the Christ-experience in a very living way. At the time when the Christ-phenomenon occurred, many people had retained their ability to see instinctively; thus, they could see the foundation, or shall I say the spiritual substance, of the Mystery of Golgotha; a substance that was recognized later, in the first centuries of Christianity.

After that, however, this phenomenon gradually diminishes. We see it diminishing; we see it was completely extinguished by the time of someone like Scotus Eriugena.[†] We see that more and more medieval theology took root and tried to oppose the intended development of modern humanity's intellect, which, if left to itself and without inner development, could never reach the suprasensory worlds. In a way, theology separated the human soul from its natural development impulse, and divided it between the world of the things humans can gain knowledge of through intellect, and the world of the unknown, which cannot be reached except through revelation.

We could understand the entirety of medieval theology on the basis of this background, especially the Thomistic theology that Catholicism considers the only authoritative one.[†] Today this could be discussed. The goal of anthroposophy was and still is nothing else but to express, in a simple way, what the various possibilities for a spiritual worldview are. And in the same way in which anthroposophy comes to the statement that atheism is actually a hidden disease, it also comes to a second statement: not to find Christ, not to find any connection to Christ is fatal. It is a fatal misfortune, because he can be found in an inner experience. He presents himself as the being who has gone through the Mystery of Golgotha. One can come to the Christ-experience on one's own. No one needs anthroposophic study to become a religious person in the sense of Christianity. However, if you come to Christ, you become part of the spiritual world. In that case we can speak of a rebirth of the human being into the spiritual world, of an extension of the essence of the soul through the experience of the spiritual world. We could also say that one who cannot find Christ is relatively limited in his view of the world. Atheism is a disease; not to be able to come to Christ is a fatal misfortune; not to come to the Spirit is a limitation of the soul.

For all those reasons, anthroposophy deals only with religion, [not with theology]. And with religion we deal only with respect to the fact that people who have religious needs and cannot find satisfaction in the contemporary denominations, turn to anthroposophy. Anthroposophy wants to deal only with what is needed in our times, and what others do not deal with. As I have repeated many times, you can deduce what our fundamental attitude is from the following. Many years ago I gave a discourse on "Wisdom and the Bible" in a southern German city (back then it was a German city; today it is not).[†] Two Catholic priests were present in the audience. After I gave my talk they came to me and said,

"We didn't find anything in your discourse that could be contradicted from a Catholic point of view."

I said, "If I could only be so lucky all the time!"

They replied, "Yes, but there was one thing we noticed. It is not *what* you say but the way you present it, *how* you put it; and here we should say that we speak to people who are in a way prepared. You speak to a community who have a particular kind of education, and we speak to all people."

I told them, "Reverend Fathers, this is not about making decisions according to our subjective feelings, but about moving along with the time in our work. It is important not to imagine that we talk to all people, but to answer the question, 'What is the objective living development of humanity?' I could be wrong imagining that I speak to all people, and so could you. It is very good to imagine this in order to have some enthusiasm, but my question is, 'Does everyone who needs to hear something about Christ today come to you in the Church?'" The two could not say "yes" since they knew well that plenty of people who search for a path to Christ do not go to church. Then I said, "You see, I speak to those who do not come to you in the church, but search for a path to Christ, nevertheless. This means to set myself a task according to current developments, and not to imagine that I speak to all people. It also means to ask myself if there are people whose spiritual development makes them more open to particular ideas."

This is the only approach anthroposophy has ever had toward religious denominations. Even when we came to the point to be able to establish anthroposophy as the basis of our teaching practice in the Waldorf School, we still refrained from turning this school into a place where children's heads will be stuffed with anthroposophy.[†] With regard to the study of religion we have a Catholic priest who teaches the Catholic children, and a Lutheran pastor who teaches Lutherans.

We have also organized some sort of a class in free religion, only for those children who come from dissident families, but that class is taught entirely in the spirit of Christianity, as well. Nevertheless, in this class we do not present some kind of abstract anthroposophy, nor a concrete anthroposophy as it is presented to adults. We put a lot of effort into presenting children with what is appropriate for their stage of development. Of course, first we have to search for the appropriate content and methods, and to find them. Through the introduction of a class on free religion we have brought back to Christianity those children who otherwise would not have had any religious education whatsoever; and they come to this kind of class on Christian religion in large numbers. We never used any kind of religious propaganda within the anthroposophic movement, and anthroposophy was not in the least established to oppose the different theological systems.

The only thing incumbent on anthroposophy is to make the various theological systems understandable in their distinctions, and not to fight them. This is how I have always seen my task when I have spoken to people who have come to anthroposophy: making clear why Catholicism has become Catholicism; Protestantism, Protestantism; Judaism, Judaism; and Buddhism, Buddhism; and how in all of them there is a certain kind of person who, through life, is able to experience in the soul the real Christ—an idea that I believe to be Christian.

Consequently, if there had never been attacks that came from the other side, no argument between anthroposophy and theology would ever have been necessary. Even today, I am saying all this only because it was the wish of those who organized this day of lectures on theology. The only task remaining for anthroposophy is the proclamation of the results of anthroposophic study of the suprasensory world. This is why I have always been reluctant to react to attacks, especially when they came from the theologians. Anthroposophy does not want to act as a fighter. It wants only to satisfy rightful human needs for spirituality, as dictated by the times. Everyone who would like to cooperate with anthroposophy in this sense, to work toward the satisfaction of these rightful spiritual needs that surface from the depths of the human soul—everyone who wants to cooperate with it in this sense—is welcome to anthroposophy.

7.
Anthroposophy and Theory of Language

BERLIN, MARCH 11, 1922

MOST HONORED PARTICIPANTS: the organizers of this course requested that every morning I introduce the observations of a particular day, with some comments. Today, I shall open our work with a somewhat aphoristic discussion. I realize that, precisely today, this is not going to be easy. In a brief course addressing the same issues we will be discussing today, which I held once in Stuttgart in front of a smaller audience,[†] it became very clear to me that one needs a great deal of time to talk about the controversial things that we will be talking about today. Thus, I would like to say in advance a few words about the spirit of contemplation required by anthroposophy with regard to the view of human language.

When we speak of language and are planning to discuss language from a scientific point of view, we should realize that it is more difficult to look at language as an object of scientific study than to discuss nature outside the human being, or even the physical nature of the human. In those cases we have at least one object that is clearly defined for our perception. Of course, we could still argue to what extent perception is the basis of the object; or to what extent the object is grasped through the cognitive human capacity simply as the effect of an unknown cause. These, however, are discussions that occur only on the intellectual level. The object of scientific observation is a given and completed thing.

This is not at all the case with language. When it comes to language, part of what develops while we speak, exists already in the unconscious life of the human psyche. Certain things surface from these unconscious areas and are then combined with conscious elements, which move as waves over an unconscious or subconscious stream. The momentary content present in our consciousness while we are speaking is only part of the real object with which we are generally concerned regarding language. Even if we cannot change contemporary speaking habits, we can still find a way to bring language as an object into our consciousness during the process of speaking.

I would like to give you a humble example to illustrate this. Around Christmas, I gave a series of lectures on pedagogical and didactic topics in the Goetheanum in Dornach.† The occasion was the visit of a number of teachers from England who wanted to come, particularly to hear this series of lectures. When the word was spread that this series of lectures would be held, people from other Western and Central European countries, for example Switzerland, decided to come to the lectures, too. Since I could not give the lectures in the big hall of the Goetheanum, which has more than 900 seats, but only in a small room, I had to give each lecture twice, one after the other. Already before the lectures started I thought that I should separate the English speakers from the rest of the audience, certainly not, however, for any political reasons. I thought I should emphasize that the course was held in German even for the English speakers, because I always speak in German when people want to hear something about anthroposophy, no matter where they are. I believe that this is a way to prove one's German-ness, and that this is in service to the German spirit and the German language. In one of those lectures, I talked about ethics and moral education, and I tried to describe how children can be brought to a level of inner experience that allows them to form ethical and moral attitudes.†

If I were speaking today in front of people who listen in the same way as some people were listening yesterday, then the things that I am saying out of having experienced them immediately would be called artificially constructed, as it happened yesterday when I was speaking about the Trinity. Dr. Rittelmeyer, however, gave a very apt response to that, using the comparison of a head and a book—a response I did not want to give for obvious reasons.†

In the lecture on education in ethics, I wanted to show how we should guide children by awakening their feelings of gratitude, interest in the world, love for the world, and love for their own actions. I also wanted to show how the feelings that we perceive as "duty" develop out of this love for our own actions. Since we are talking about language today, I will mention that, in relation to our immediate life, it was necessary to define a trinity with three words: gratitude, love, and duty. From the first two steps—gratitude and love—I came to the third: duty. I had to give this lecture twice, once from 10 to 11 o'clock for the English speakers, and again from 11 to 12 o'clock for the listeners from other nations, whose state of mind was essentially Central European.

The second lecture could have been simply a repetition of the first. But in fact, because I tried to put myself into the shoes of the listeners, I had to speak to the English in a very different way from the way I spoke to the Germans. Something similar happened on the other days, but it was particularly necessary on this day that I have mentioned.

Why was this the case? While in the hour between 11 and 12 I was speaking about duty to people whose sensibility as listeners was built on the basis of the German language, in the first hour, between 10 and 11, I was speaking to people who perceived what I was telling them about the duty-impulse against the background of their concept of "duty." There is a big difference between the feeling one has when one says the word *Pflicht*[†] and when one says the word "duty." In the hour between 11 and 12, I had to let the nuance of our experience that results from the use of the word *Pflicht* flow into my lecture. In German, when we say the word *Pflicht* we awaken an impulse that arises in our psyche and leads the experience immediately to something else, which I could express by the verb *pflegen*,[†] or to the outpouring of a feeling directed from the action itself to its object. This is the essence of the impulse defined by the word *Pflicht*.

The psyche has a very different experience when we define this impulse using the word "duty." Although the word *Pflicht* refers to the psyche, the word "duty" refers to the intellect, to the spirit—to a principle that guides us internally, as our thoughts guide us when we move to action. We could say that *Pflicht* is something we do out of inner love and devotion. In contrast, we fulfill our *duty* because if we have human dignity we want to be able to follow a law that penetrates us; we must be devoted to a law that we understand with the intellect.

This of course is only an approximate description. My purpose is simply to emphasize that the complex inner experience is different, depending on the use of different words, even though the dictionary tells us that the English word "duty" stands for the German word *Pflicht*. This fact applies to the entire national spirit, to the soul of the nation; and you can see that language reflects the nuances of the soul of a people. You will see in that sense that the soul of the Central Europeans is very different from the soul of the people from other nations; and that psychic life is expressed in language by the Central Europeans in a way very different from that of the English.

Those who have no sense for the fact that the unconscious elements integrated in language are rooted on a much deeper level than the level of conscious experience will find no clear object for the [scientific investigation of] language. We have to be aware that when we observe nature the objects of observation are external, or we create them neatly by some external actions. In this process, the objects remain still outside ourselves; thus, we can definitely observe them. When we observe language, first we have to go through a conscious process of figuring out what is the real object of study that we observe. Consequently, when it is about language, we should observe more than what is in our consciousness. When we observe language we should keep in mind the whole living being that expresses itself in the process of speaking and in language.

We are rarely prepared for this scientific observation of language. For example, if we study the history of language or comparative linguistics, to prepare ourselves properly for the observation of a particular language, we would need to contemplate first its object. That is, the "object" of each language is its inner unconscious content; the unconscious substance of what is only partly expressed in the conscious process of speech.

In addition, at the different stages of human development, the degree of consciousness related to language was different. For example, it was one thing at the time when Sanskrit originated, another when Ancient Greek was formed; and again it is something different here in Germany, or in England, although the nuances here are becoming smaller and smaller, and less visible. To mention only the rough distinctions, there are already major differences between the inner experience of a Briton and that of an American, both using the English language. Moreover, if one studies dialects; if, for example, one analyzes the different experiences people have when they use different German dialects; then one notices how many complicated psychic impulses flow into language expression and into the entire organism of language.

There was a very good reason for why the Greeks felt essentially the same way when they spoke the word *language* and when they spoke the word *reason*, and why they combined these two concepts into one word. This was because the experience within the word and the experience within the thought, within the idea, were to a certain extent still indistinguishable and overlapping for the Greeks, while in our modern epoch there are distinctions in this respect. When Ancient Greeks spoke, they felt that the thought was transformed into word. To them, the thought was the soul and the word merely flowed into the thought like a body, or, shall we say, like the outer dress of the soul. Today, if we become conscious of this process, we may feel when we pronounce a word, on the one hand, as if the word floats away while we pronounce it; and on the other hand, as if the thought somehow swims on top of the stream of words. However, the thought is again clearly distinguishable from the stream of words.

If we return now to Sanskrit, we will first need to go through some real psychological processes and experience certain soul phenomena to be in a position to internalize the feeling one must have had when saying a word at the time Sanskrit originated. We definitely should not look at Sanskrit with the same feelings toward speech and language with which we look at modern languages today.

Let us take, for example, a very well known word: *manas*. If you open the dictionary, you will find various translations of the word *manas*: spirit, reason, mind, and sometimes even anger or irritability. Generally, such translations do not bring us close to the inner feeling of the word that the people of ancient times once had, and could experience so clearly. At the time when Sanskrit was a language fully alive, the state of the human soul was different from our soul state now; in fact, it was significantly different. It should be clear that as human beings have developed, there has been a deep transformation of the state of the soul. I have repeatedly characterized the major transformation that can be placed in the fifteenth century.† However, as human development advances, there are always borderlines between the succeeding epochs. We can understand what was really happening at a particular time, and what the experience of language was part of, only if we can also analyze the inner psychological life of the human being at the time.

At the time when the word *manas* was still perceived internally as something living, there was a phenomenon that I would like to call "experience of the meaning of sounds." The inner experience was felt in an incredibly intense way through the sounds, which today we label as an "m," an "a," an "n," and an "s." When people pronounced vowels and consonants, the life of their soul was moving to a very high degree along with the processes within the organism, even if this was happening as if in a dream, because they were aware of that dream.

If we are equipped with this understanding and if we analyze how language lives within us, we will realize that the use of consonants reflects the attempt of human beings, using their own inner but suppressed gestures, to immerse the Self in external processes in the physical world and to imitate the inner life of outer objects. Consonants are suppressed gestures, gestures that do not become visible but that, nevertheless, include things we are able to experience in the rolling of the thunder, the flashing of the lightning, the blowing of the wind, and so forth. By experiencing consonants, we immerse ourselves in the external world. In fact, we want to repeat the life of external nature through gestures. We suppress the gesture, which transforms itself internally and appears in a metamorphosed form as a consonant.

By contrast, we feel a certain amount of sympathy and antipathy when we are confronted with external nature. These sympathies and antipathies, which represent an inner experience, give birth to the entire "vocalism," or system of vowels. Thus, as we live in language, we create a metamorphosed imitation of the external world through the use of consonants, but express our own inner relationship to the external world through the use of vowels. If we look in detail at the concrete language experience, we could certainly grasp and understand this, even with the kind of life the psyche has today.

When I use the word "imagination," I do not mean some kind of fantasy, but the fact that the inner process of language experience could be really *seen* in ancient times. When the Sanskrit language originated, a dream-like imagination was still alive in the human soul. At that time, people did not have images with sharp contours as we do today. They saw life in pictures, in images; however, these were not images like the ones discussed in anthroposophy today: images of which we are fully aware, images that are similar to our concepts with sharp contours. Instead, they were dream-like instinctive images that, nevertheless, had the effect of driving forces. We could say those images lived in the human being as living forces. People felt those forces as they felt hunger or thirst, but in a somewhat quieter way, so to speak.

In their minds, people were painting pictures, in a way; of course, this is not the same way we paint pictures today. This kind of painting, however, was actualized in the use of vowels, applied as if they were paints applied to a canvas. Using vowels, people were immersing themselves in the element of the consonants, as if they were using the colors to highlight borderlines and contours. This was an inner experience that reproduced an experience of the imagination. At the same time, the experience represented an objective reproduction of external nature. It was an experience of the dream-like imagination. People yielded to the images that worked internally in their organisms, and, through the organs of speech, dressed the images in words.

This is the only way we can imagine the inner process of the language experience in the early stages of human development. If we experiment with this observation and take it further, using, for example, the experience of the sound that we call "m" today, we realize that in an earlier time this sound was at the borderline between consonant and vowel. The pronunciation of the word *manas* could be compared to the way we would paint a picture today without applying surface colors that would highlight the outer borderlines of the inner distinctions. On the other hand, when the sound "a" was pronounced, people felt something like the inner world of the human being. And if I want to describe the entire word *manas* in this way, then I would have to say that in those ancient times, language gave life to people's dream-like images, as our consciousness today gives life to language. As for language now, we do not live in dream-like imaginations any longer. Our consciousness goes beyond the use of language.

But for Sanskrit speakers in the past, the old dream-like images kept flowing into language. Those who pronounced the word *manas* felt as if they were in a shell; they felt as if the physical body, consisting of water and other liquids, was some kind of a shell, and as if the other body was carried by a vessel of air. When people of ancient times pronounced the word *manas*, they experienced all this as in a dream. In their souls, they did not feel the same way as we do today. They felt themselves to be vessels of the soul life. The soul was experienced as something given by the supra-terrestrial and supra-human forces of the shell.

If we want to grasp the old content of a word, we should first awaken this experience. We should also know that today when we feel the Self, our inner psychic experience is very different from the experience that people in earlier times had when they said the word *Ego* or from what people in earlier times experienced when they pronounced the Sanskrit word *aham*. Today, we experience the Self as something that has shrunk into a single point, a point that we regard as the center of our inner being and all of our soul forces.

This feeling was not the basis of the concept of the Self revealed to the people of ancient times. In those ancient days, the Self was still felt as something that we carried, not as something that we were inside of. In a way, the Self was perceived as something independent that swims on the waves of the psychic life. However, nothing in the composition of sounds suggested such perception. Thus, the content of the Sanskrit word *aham* is something surrounding the Self, or something that carries the Self.

In our time, we experience the Self as an inner impulse of the will, which seems to penetrate our inner being as the center of a heat source, irradiating heat rays in all possible directions (to use a comparison). In contrast, to the Ancient Greek, and even to the Roman later, the Self was something like a ball of water, and this ball seemed to be completely filled with air. To state the analogy precisely: It is one thing to experience the air expanding in the ball of water, and another to experience the internal radiation of a heat source that spreads warmth in all directions but must be perceived as a ball filled with air.

These, of course, are all symbols. However, the words in any given language are symbols, too; and those who argue that words cannot be defined as symbols would not be able to participate in such observations. Therefore, if we want to discuss language, first we should be able to understand the essence of the object of linguistics. Then we would realize that in ancient times the character of language was very different from the character language has in modern civilizations. We would also realize that in the past, the physical, bodily element played a more major role in the producing of sounds and in the configuring of words. People invested language with their inner life much more than they do now. This is why they had the "m" in the beginning of the word *manas*, because it included the idea of the human and gave it contours.

When we look at Sanskrit expressions, we soon notice that they represent the experience of both consonantal and vocal elements. We notice that there is some inner immersion in the external processes and the physicality of the external world. We realize that the formation of words and the entire process of speech are the result of imitation in the consonants and the feeling of sympathies and antipathies in the vowels. There was a much more physical nuance to the way all this came to be in ancient times. An ancient language was experienced more fully.

We still could have a similar experience today. If you listen to people who speak Sanskrit or any other language of the Eastern civilizations, you can hear how the sounds they produce reflect their entire being, including their physical bodies, and how their speech has the character of music. It comes from the same kind of an inner experience as music. Only at a much later stage of human development was music separated from logic or from the soul that lived in simple images.

We could notice this today, too. If we compare the inner experience of the German language to that of English, we would realize that in English the process of living within the framework of abstract ideas is more advanced. If we want to live in the German language, we have to immerse ourselves in those forms that emerged with New High German.† Dialects allow our psyche to dive into even more intense, more vigorous experience. The real spiritual experience of the German language becomes possible only at the stage of High German. This is why someone like Hegel was formed under such conditions. He was a person formed entirely by the belief that the idea is something independent, in itself; yet, it is experienced exclusively through a particular element of language. For that reason, it is impossible to translate Hegel into another of the Western languages, for in his works we still experience language in an immediate way.

In the West, you will notice everywhere in people's experience that the psyche unfolds when it is devoted to the use of language. The psyche is capable of intense experience, but everywhere language is being thrown out of the immediate experience of the psyche. In English, for example, the stream of speech flows and flows, and out of the flowing water people constantly build something like sheets of ice that swim on top of the waves as firm meanings. When we speak High German, we realize that in the stream of speech there is something liquid and that, in contrast to English, in the stream no ice floes have formed to fall out of the language. This contrast is a phenomenon connected to the human soul and the human spirit.

In the East, you will find the same process at an even earlier stage of development. There, you will not see ice floes being thrown out of the stream of language; neither will you experience the complete overlap between thought and word as in High German. Instead, you will find that the word is experienced in a way that keeps it in the organism, although the thought is something that escapes the word; something that we have to run after or that moves ahead of us.

If we want to understand language, these are the things we need to become aware of. We cannot deal with them if we do not accept, at least to a certain degree, Goethe's phenomenological approach to observation, which he established in relation the living world of plants. When we follow it consistently in our inner experience and in our inner practice, such an approach leads to the development of imaginative abilities mentioned in anthroposophy. Those who want to analyze language should generally approach it in a way that allows them to experience the inner metamorphosis of its organization in a concrete way. Only then can we see the real language process.

As long as we are not able to lift ourselves to the level of such language analysis, we will be looking at language only from an external point of view, and we will not be able to make any progress to the discovery of its real object. This is why, in our present culture, there are so many different theories of language. Thinking about language has become, in many respects, thinking about the origins of language; and there are a number of theories established with regard to this question. Wilhelm Wundt lists them in his *Theory of Language* and takes them apart in his criticism.[†]

We see the same happening in many other areas, and we saw the same thing here yesterday as well.[†] When the supporters of a particular school of thought in modern science begin to contemplate and analyze the facts offered by the science they represent, they begin to speak of a "downfall." This is certainly not what anthroposophy wants to tell you. Yesterday, for example, almost nothing was mentioned about a downfall from the perspective of anthroposophy. Those who discussed theology, however, spoke a good deal about a downfall.

When people philosophize about language, we also hear of the downfall of theories, such as the *theory of invention*. Wundt lists and discusses various theories. According to the theory of invention, language was established, or "invented," as people gave things certain definitions. Today, according to Wundt, this explanation no longer sounds plausible; how would deaf-mute people have determined forms of language, even very primitive forms? As second choice, Wundt mentions the *miracle theory*; according to this theory, at a particular stage of human development, the Creator gave language to the human being as a gift. As Dr. Geyer mentioned yesterday, no scientist the least bit respectable is allowed to believe in miracles today.[†] This is forbidden; thus, the miracle theory is no longer acceptable. Next on this list is the *theory of imitation*, which contains some plausible elements, since it says that the consonant-element of language is based on a process that is much more internal than the one we usually imagine. Next, Wundt mentions the *theory of natural sounds*. This theory implies that what humans attempted to find in language on the basis of their inner experience was the overlap between the sound of the words and the perceptions of external nature, accompanied by sympathies and antipathies. All these theories could be formulated in a different way, too. Currently, simply on the grounds proposed by those who have criticized those theories, it is possible to show that none of them can grasp the real object of language.

As a matter of fact, although people say that they do not need to turn to anthroposophy, it can demonstrate that it offers certain productive thoughts that could help science find the purest, most clear objects of observation, even in an area such as the theory of language. We can certainly discuss many things, including language, even if we do not yet see language as a pure object of contemplation. Anthroposophy, however, has a profoundly scientific character, and it aims first of all at the clarification of the question: What kind of reality can we find in a particular scientific field, to experience within ourselves the connection between the things we perceive as truth or knowledge in a field, and a specific kind of reality. Some people say about our work (which is not any easier than the work in any other branch of science), that anthroposophy "sticks its nose in everything," as was mentioned here yesterday. We will have to give the following response. It certainly turned out that in the process of its development, anthroposophy had to stick its nose in everything. But if we do not want this superficial perception that anthroposophy "sticks its nose in everything" to leave a permanent mark, rather, we should move on and pay attention to and study the questions that arise when anthroposophy investigates things seriously. Then and only then, when we come to this second stage of our relationship to anthroposophy, will we be able to realize how fertile anthroposophy is, and to what extent it is vindicated, when confronted with the kind of judgment just mentioned, which appears to be only a superficial observation.

REPORT

on the Anthroposophy Course at the University in Berlin

Excerpts from the talk given to members
in Dornach, March 18, 1922

My dear Friends! Allow me to say a few words about the way the College Course in Berlin went. The program of the course in Berlin was organized in a very special way. The goal was to present the relationship that different scientific fields and different areas of life have to the anthroposophic view of the world. Each single day was dedicated primarily to a particular scientific field or area of life. The week was organized in such a way that we began on Sunday with a topic dedicated to the branch of natural science dealing with inorganic matter. The following Monday was dedicated to the sciences dealing with organic matter and to medicine, Tuesday to philosophy, Wednesday to education, Thursday to political economy, and Friday to theology. Saturday was supposed to be dedicated to linguistics, and we were supposed to round up the whole course on the second Sunday with a eurythmy presentation in the Deutsches Theater.[†]

The program was designed so that each day began with a short lecture given by myself. Only the first Sunday could not begin in this way, because I was not able to be in Berlin on that day. Thus, in my introductory words on Monday, I offered a summary of the sciences dealing with both organic and inorganic matter. The rest of the day maintained the usual character: After my introductory words in the morning, there were two more lectures, and after that we had a half-hour snack break. But, as you have already heard, there were no snacks offered in the rooms of the Vocal Academy.[†] Then, from 1 to 2 we had a discussion, followed, from 2 to 3, by the last lecture scheduled for the morning. It was an exhausting program. In the evening, there were lectures held partly by myself in the Philharmonic Hall and partly by others in the rooms of the University of Berlin.† There was one lecture every evening, and after each lecture, (with the exception of mine), there was some time left for people to express themselves on the topic. As you see, all these days were extremely busy.

The structure of the program was very interesting, particularly because of the formulations given to the separate daily programs. To a degree, each day had a general title and the formulations of these general titles were particularly interesting because they implied some very significant issues. With the exception of Friday, the day dedicated to theology, there was something very positive in the formulation of the title for each day. This already is something important, not so much because it spoke of the spirit of the time but because it showed the attitude toward anthroposophy of those who created the program. Those who created the other programs felt some pressure to formulate their daily schedules in a positive sounding way. We could see the importance only by looking at these formulations.

Sunday, March 5th: *From a mechanical approach hostile to life to true phenomenology*. In the title of this program we see the expression of the hope that through anthroposophy we will find a kind of phenomenology that will represent the foundation of natural science, including its branches dealing with inorganic matter.

The program for Monday was summarized in an even more positive way: *Ways of achieving anthroposophic knowledge of the human being in biology and medicine*. The same could be said about the Tuesday program for philosophy: *Justification of Anthroposophy on the basis of the contemporary philosophical consciousness*. Similarly positive was the program for Wednesday: *From the modern pedagogical requirements to their realization through anthroposophy*. This title also demonstrates the idea that today there are pedagogical requirements that could be fulfilled through anthroposophy.

The formulation of the general title for Thursday, the day dedicated to social sciences, was even more auspicious, though the lectures held on that day were not so promising. The title, however, was extremely hopeful and sounded very positive: *Prospects for the national economy.*

The title for Sunday, the day dedicated to linguistics, was *From a dead to a living theory of language.*

You can see that all these formulations have as a common basis the intention to show us the ways from our contemporary times into establishing the respective spiritual paths with the help of anthroposophy. We now have some idea of how different disciplines begin with the existing contemporary scientific formulations but move toward other ways of cognition, which could be offered by anthroposophy. In other words, all the sciences have very concrete ideas of alternative approaches. However, on Thursday, as I said, we had a particularly auspicious title—*Prospects for the national economy*—an abstract formulation that, precisely in its abstractness, points out that we should not walk but we should leap, if I may put it this way.

If you look now at the general formulation of the title for Friday, you will read: *The downfall of religion in contemporary theology and its re-definition in anthroposophy.* At first, the formulation here appears to be very negative: The downfall of religion in contemporary theology and its re-definition in anthroposophy. This title points out in a very negative way that there is something like anthroposophy through which theology and religion could be renewed. However, the title does not explain in any concrete way how we are going to get from the mess in which we are today to an anthroposophic attitude. If you compare this to the formulation of the Sunday topic, *From a mechanical approach hostile to life to true phenomenology,* already can be seen in the word *phenomenology* a very concrete definition of what is supposed to come. The phrase *knowledge of the human* in the title on Monday also emphasizes something very concrete. The day about philosophy emphasized the philosophical consciousness of our time—another very concrete point; the day on education focused on the requirements of modern times and the title on the day of linguistics says: *From a dead to a living theory of language,* a formulation that also leads to very concrete ideas.

It is really telling that this College Course, which from both an inner and an outer perspective culminated with the performance on

Friday, and which had basically a theological character (or at least it felt that way)—it is telling that this College Course, which was very well attended anyway, attracted such a number of people on Friday, on the day of theology, that the room was filled with people to the point of overflowing. It is also telling that precisely the formulation of theology as a topic of the day was the only one in this College Course to sound negative. These formulations were certainly based on the existing circumstances, and people tried to formulate the topics in a very honest and direct way, on one hand as a reflection of modern consciousness, and on the other, as a reflection of the idea of a transformation of this consciousness through anthroposophy.

If we look now at the individual days we would certainly see things that we are familiar with to some degree. From a mechanical approach hostile to life to true phenomenology. This is also about making a point that we should overcome all speculations about atomism and about a mechanical conception of inorganic nature. It discusses how we could achieve pure observation of the essence of phenomena, how these phenomena could speak for themselves, and how they could offer their own theories. The idea that we should practice Goetheanism[†] with regard to natural science was clearly expressed in this formulation. In addition, the formulation about the scientific branches dealing with organic nature expresses the fact that we should build our entire scientific conception of organic nature on the basis of our knowledge of the human being. In other words, this title tells us that we must not look at the different kingdoms of nature as if they were broken pieces, as we do today. Rather, we should give priority to the study of the human being, and we should explore the rest of the kingdoms of nature on the basis of that knowledge.

Regarding philosophy, the lectures on Tuesday demonstrated that philosophical thought has come to a dead end, of sorts. It is interesting to consider this formulation in the context of Hegel for example. Already in the beginning of the nineteenth century[†] Hegel said in his philosophy that all contemporary philosophy is at some kind of an end and that generally we only could look back at the course of the historical development of philosophy, but that no further development is possible. On that Tuesday, a suggestion was made that the end of philosophy could be turned into a beginning, a new beginning, if that beginning is formed in the framework of anthroposophy.

The lecture on education emphasized that everyone who is really thinking has some requirements with regard to pedagogy, but that these requirements cannot be fulfilled using the methods that contemporary pedagogy is developing; in other words, the requirements that generally all thinking people have with regard to pedagogy could be fulfilled only with the help of anthroposophy.

The lecture on theory of language demonstrated that language itself should not be perceived as something found in dead documents, as the case is in contemporary linguistics, but that it has to be perceived as a living organism and in relation to the human being.

About social science I can say only that Emil Leinhas[†] made very important points about today's financial problem in a very competent and very positive way. However, as you yourselves must feel sometimes, we cannot say very many positive things about today's financial problem. You can feel this even here in Switzerland, the country with almost the highest currency value, but you can certainly believe that we cannot say many positive things about today's financial problem if we cross the border. In brief, we cannot say many positive things at all. The following two lectures did not mention anything positive, and this day dedicated to the national economy showed that the way we treat the national economy within our anthroposophic movement has failed over and over. Despite the fact that precisely with regard to this area we have repeatedly emphasized the necessity for those who have insight into our economic life to come up with something more certain about the future of political economy, basically we have not been able to offer any ideas that could satisfy the requirements of our present time. In this sense, the title of that day, *Prospects for the national economy*, represented an attempt to dance with a promise. What the day actually brought about, however, was more or less a crippled partner limping after the dancer. Regarding theology, I should say that the titles of the three lectures following my introductory discourse were as interesting as the formulation of the program for this day. The title of the first lecture by Licentiate Bock[†] was "The Fall of Religion into Psychologism," the title of Dr. Rittelmeyer's[†] lecture was "The Fall of Theology into Irrationalism," and the third lecture, given by Dr. Geyer was entitled "The Fall of Theology into Historicism." So, in these few days we heard three different descriptions of the downfall of theology or religion.[†] In a way, the situation today resulted naturally in the fact that it was theologians who, on the basis of their very specific experience in thinking and feeling, described how they have come to a dead end in theology.

If we remember then the positive things we heard on that day, we could summarize the lectures on that day in the following way: The way theology looks at religion, according to Licentiate Bock, leads to seeing only the experience of the soul, defined as religious experience or as an experience of God. We find that among other experiences of the soul, the human being has also some religious experience or some kind of an experience that somehow points at the divine. However, if we are unbiased toward this experience, we could say: yes, this is simply a subjective experience, a purely psychological experience. We cannot find any proof that there is anything in the objective world that corresponds to this experience. In modern theology the subjective experience of God does not lead to the real acceptance of God, and certainly not to a particular view of the nature of the divine in the world. To a certain degree, the religious element in human consciousness is suffocated by the psychological fact that, yes, we need some religious life, but there is nothing that can give us an assurance that this need could be satisfied. The psychological fact that the human being needs religion is given, but our times do not know how to give religion some content. This was approximately the conclusion in the first lecture by Licentiate Bock. After that, Dr. Rittelmeyer explained why theology had enough of rationalism and how it had come to the point when it did not any longer want to be defining the essence of God in the world of thought, when it did not want any longer to say that this or that is the content of the divine that penetrates the entire existence of the world. Thought had to be excluded from theology. Rationality and everything else based on reason had to be taken out. Instead, the irrational, everything that excludes intellectual thought, is supposed to become the content of theology. In other words, theology is supposed to deal exclusively with the most superficial abstractions. We do not dare say that God's being could be grasped through thought. We dare say only that God's being is the unconditional, the absolute.[†] Thus, we construct a completely abstract concept—the irrational, something that cannot be grasped by reason.

Is it not true that in any other area it would seem very strange to characterize things in such negative terms? Imagine, for example, that someone asks who the head of the Goetheanum is, and the answer is: someone who is not head of any other institution. In this case, we will have no information about who really is the head of the Goetheanum. Similarly, we cannot get any idea about the divine when we say that the rationale of the divine being consists of the fact that God is something irrational that cannot be grasped by reason. All of this is only negating.

Rittelmeyer established a connection between these explanations and what contemporary irrationalists have to say; for example, what the inner behavior of people is, who are trying to elevate themselves to this God who could be understood only in an irrational way. What is one's experience of such an attempt? It is a silent experience. However, this is not the silence in a mystical experience, which could be very positive. This is rather the point of not saying anything, of ceasing to speak in thoughts, even to oneself. We heard further how this silence grows roots into the ritual. In fact, the reason to seek refuge in silence is the absolute inability to formulate just about anything.

Later, it was interesting to hear two gentlemen, a professor and a priest,[†] who were defending this irrationalism and were trying to prove particularly that irrationalism is predominant in our time. The professor, for example said: Yes, this is right. It would be silly to say that God could be figured out only in the spirit but not in nature. Nature is not further away from God than the spirit. He also said that with regard to God, the knowledge of the spirit does not offer more than the knowledge of nature, for God is the unconditional that penetrates everything. He was repeating this statement frequently, namely that God is the unconditional that penetrates everything.

"Theology!" Faust would use here the word "alas" not once but three times. Faust's lines: "Philosophy and jurisprudence, medicine and even, alas, [alas, alas] theology"[†] should be rewritten if we get to hear such statements all the time. God is the unconditional that penetrates everything. We imagine what is called *everything,* and then something appears, something surfaces, but this *something* is actually the undefined!

The last lecture was given by Dr. Geyer. He was talking about the downfall of theology into historicism. Geyer was trying to demonstrate how theology has gradually reached the point when it cannot come up with any creative ideas on its own; when it can only observe what has already passed. In other words, in order to discover some content, it emphasizes the constant study of history or of what has already passed. Naturally, this approach leads us, in the best case, to the possibility of saying: In the past, people had religious consciousness, but today they are only able to analyze the different stages of past religious consciousness and to choose something that they still would like to preserve. Unfortunately, when they try to choose, they find that there is nothing left of what the different epochs in the past offered them.

I myself introduced this program with the remark that anthroposophy certainly does not try to found a religion, but wants to achieve the cognition of the suprasensory world instead. Thus, if theology wants to be inspired by it, this will be very welcome. Anthroposophy will say what it has to say about the suprasensory world and, in its own turn, it will wait to see what use it could make of theology. Those who have a sense for the complex situation of our times noticed a deficiency, particularly on that day, which, however, resulted from the circumstances. If we were supposed to exhaust the topic of the day completely, as we tried to do and that we achieved to a certain degree with the rest of the daily topics, with the exception of the topic on social science, then we should have had a Catholic theologian speak as well. All of the lectures that were held on that day were grounded in Protestant consciousness. A Catholic theologian would have been in a completely different position than the three Protestant speakers. A Catholic theologian is well served not only by a theology that is historically inherited, but by a theology that is historically inherited and eternally valid—a theology that is supposed to be as alive today as it was in the third or the second century A.D. The Church councils and the institution of the Pope, which became infallible in the nineteenth century, have added something to that theology. However, this was only about particular dogmas, about additions. The essence of Catholic theology is in fact something that, firstly, does not depend on the developments in different times, and that, secondly, should have a perennial or everlasting character. If a more progressive Catholic had spoken about Catholic theology, he probably would have been in a very interesting opposition to the struggle of a Catholic thinker such as Cardinal Newman.† If a less progressive Catholic theologian had spoken, he would have presented the essence of the everlasting doctrine of salvation or a Catholic theology. Then, people would have had questions of great importance, as for example the question: What does Catholic theology bring to people of today?

There is no doubt that in its present state Catholic theology cannot offer any living ideas to modern consciousness. Its content is rooted exclusively in the experience of old spiritual, if even atavistic, knowledge. The concepts of which Catholic theology consists, such as the creation, or redemption, or the essence of the Trinity—all those concepts have some essence but their essence cannot be comprehended any longer by the modern consciousness. Instead, they are transformed into abstract, incomprehensible dogmatism, unless they are not even transformed but are simply accepted as incomprehensible, dry dogmatism.

Especially in the nineteenth century, Catholic theology developed in a way that made it impossible to recognize what the contents of the different dogmas contained. During the College Course in Berlin we had an interesting experience related to this. In my introductory remarks on Friday I said something that was based on my immediate experience, and which I had already mentioned to you. I said: Unless they are crippled, those who can experience our immediate natural environment and everything related to it will come to the consciousness of God-the-Father. If during the course of their lives some of them find the experience of God-the-Father unsatisfactory and come to some kind of an inner rebirth, they will experience God-the-Son, or the Son of God. In the very same way, if we continue taking further steps, we will come to the experience of the Holy Ghost. To this, a Protestant professor, Licentiate Tillich† made a remark: Aha! here is the Trinity that has to be constructed—and he called the fact a construction. He did not notice at all that at the basis of all this is experience. This was alien to him. The experiences that were at the basis of the Catholic dogmas were also alien to the modern consciousness of the nineteenth century. Originally, the Catholic dogmas were certainly based on spiritual reality, too, but today we do not understand this reality any longer. We deal simply with empty concepts. In the nineteenth century, Catholic theology had to revive its content at least a little bit, even if only superficially. You may well know that the desire to be able to understand again, at least a little bit, appeared particularly strong under the pontificate of Leo XIII.† This is why we had the Catholic ordinance, or shall I say the ordinance of Rome, for all Catholic theologians to go back to the study of the Thomistic philosophy, the philosophy of Thomas Aquinas, since the entire philosophy after him was no longer useful for the understanding of the Catholic dogmas. In order to give natural science its foundations, the philosophy following that of Thomas Aquinas can help us only to understand the existence of nature. It cannot help us understand spiritual facts, which Catholics do not understand well either, but which were formulated in the Catholic dogmas at a time when people still knew something about those facts. The entire later, post-Thomistic philosophy is useless in the attempt to understand these spiritual facts.

When people felt again the desire to understand some of the Catholic dogmas, Rome requested the renewed study of Thomistic philosophy, the real endeavor of Roman Catholicism regarding philosophy until today. There are certainly historical reasons for that. However, if we draw a comparison to the needs we have today, in order to come back to spirituality, we will see that Thomism is not enough to revive the old rigid Roman dogmas. We have to come to a completely different observation.

Please remember my view that Hamlet is a student of Faust regardless of time and space, a view I presented to you in my last few lectures before I left Dornach, and which a contemporary literary historian would find completely perverse.† I said that Hamlet must have been sitting at Faust's feet for ten years—for the same ten years when Faust was leading his students by the nose—and that Hamlet must have been one of those students who was lead by the nose in all possible directions. Such connections are appalling to any contemporary literary historian. But today, we cannot say anything significant about the spiritual that will not be appalling for the official representatives of the sciences. Today, the stigma of the real truth is exactly what appalls the public representatives of the sciences.

So, if you take this interpretation for something profane, you will see that we need to achieve a certain mobility of the spirit, a mobility that could offer a foundation for the understanding of the essence preserved in the dogmas. You will realize that we have to go back to a completely different state of the psyche in order to learn the art of living within such dogmas, and this shows precisely the process of the development of Cardinal Newman.

In Berlin today, it may be very normal to speak in a college course like this only from the perspective of Protestantism, and to ignore the Catholic standpoint. However, we are not going to get the picture of what is really predominant today if we are not capable of discussing the Catholic perspective in some way. Exactly in our time, when we need to look at the entire world as a whole, this is impossible. Today, you see, we have overcome the speaking of church-tower science, of church-tower worldviews alone. You already know the church-tower politics, but there is also such a thing as church-tower worldviews. We are confronted with it in a powerful way, especially when we experience something like Dr. Theberat's† lecture on Friday, for example, when he spoke on the topic "Atomistic and Realistic Approaches to Chemical Processes." Dr. Theberat, who is employed in our Research Institute in Stuttgart, tried to show that atomism has to be abandoned and that phenomenology should be introduced into chemistry. Dr. Kurt Grelling† entered the debate too. At this point I do not wish to talk about Dr. Kurt Grelling, who carried on with approximately the following prescription, "Yes, the anthroposophists talk about just about everything, but none of it seems to me very likely. What is certain, is that 2+2 = 4, and we should stick to what is certain: 2+2 = 4—this is certain." He asserted this opinion already last summer in the course in Stuttgart,† and on one particular evening, he even brought two more university professors to support his assertion that 2+2 = 4. One could not argue with him. By mentioning this, I would like only to suggest symbolically, what he said, namely that 2 + 2 is really 4. I could not argue against it. I could not argue even last Friday when he said, completely out of context, that in Stuttgart I admitted that 2 + 2 = 4. I certainly cannot deny that. I don't mean now literally 2 + 2 = 4. I am talking about things that he discussed back then and which are equally valuable in the broader context. Then he said: Yes, regarding the question raised here, the question of phenomenology, we should say that we cannot make judgments about it from the point of view of natural science, we have to judge it from the point of view of philosophy.

I do not wish to say that this is a typical attitude for Göttingen† but this statement was at least not very sophisticated or scientific. In England, for example, no one would understand a statement that says that we cannot judge something from the point of view of science, but only from the point of view of philosophy, because this is precisely what a church-tower worldview is. Only particular Central European circles would know what this statement means. In any event, when we speak of questions like that today, we need a much wider horizon. For example, we cannot possibly keep talking about East, West, and the Center between them. The formulations in the program for the Congress in Vienna† repeat constantly the words *East*, *West*, and *Central* and I do not object. I think that talking about East, West, and Central is in the spirit of great ideas, but I believe that our concepts should be a bit broader and that they should really cover those regions. We surely cannot embrace the entire world by looking at it from a narrow-minded perspective.

Thus, [in the lectures on religion and theology in Berlin] there was something missing, for example, with regard to the Western development of religious life because Catholicism was completely ignored, even though there is nothing tangible in the Western religious life if we look at it only from the Protestant perspective. We did not even touch upon the question of the development of English Puritanism or the High Church.

I do not mean to criticize all this, since the points that we did discuss were excellent. However, in our close anthroposophic circle, I would like to talk about the issues that should have been mentioned in relation to the discussed processes. In such relation, it should have been demonstrated how our contemporary way of thinking is not capable at all of even approaching the old sources of theological content. In Berlin we did not see any bridge between modern evangelical theology and the ideas that anthroposophy should offer to revive religious consciousness. There were only references to the fact that these ideas should come from anthroposophy, but basically nothing was said about the way all this should materialize.

This will probably give you an idea of the struggle in the arena of anthroposophy that recently found its most beautiful expression in Berlin. The lectures, even the morning lectures, attracted a very large audience, and thus, the participation of various different circles showed that there is some life in the anthroposophic movement—a life that appeals strongly and with great intensity to contemporary human consciousness.

At the same time we did not spare sharp phrases that could characterize the truth. It gives me some inner joy to remember that on Sunday evening Dr. Schubert tried to show, within the framework of the topic "Anthroposophy and Theory of Language," that language plays a role in the political life of peoples and races, and that during the debate he passionately explained what language theory is today and what it should become with the help of anthroposophy. He was very passionate when he said that, yes, he has been in Berlin, that he has studied linguistics with various professors, and then he turned to anthroposophy to give life to the linguistics he had studied. Only then did he have a revelation, and he understood what contemporary linguistics really is: a piece of garbage. And then he slammed the table with his fist. So, he was very generous with the phrases characterizing our time. The opponents were not much better. I cannot avoid saying that they were passionate, so I would rather not say anything.

During the evening panels some people tried to offer some idea of what the content of anthroposophy is. It was very important that both Dr. Stein and Dr. Schwebsch† showed vivid images illustrating the pedagogical effect achieved in the Waldorf School. What I want to say is that we could experience some remarkable moments, just reading between the lines.

The course closed on Sunday. I gave the closing lecture on the last evening, and the morning panels ended with an extremely successful performance of eurythmy in the Deutsches Theater, which was filled to the last seat.

I do not need to say that if you get hold of any newspaper you will read the opposite of what really happened in Berlin. However, there is a gentleman who had written an article in one of the Berlin newspapers, and his article was considered to be pro-anthroposophy (I do not wish to express an opinion about this.). The same person then asked another big newspaper whether he could write an article about the College Course in Berlin. They asked him: "Pro or against?" He answered "pro" because he thought that his article would be pro-anthroposophy. Then the newspaper people said: "No, we take only articles against it." This means that no one cares what people write about Anthroposophy. Rather, they buy only articles against it. Consequently, if you read any outsiders' reports, you will not get any idea of what really happened in Berlin.

It is a pity that, except for the performance in the Deutsches Theater and the short performances on Thursday and Sunday,† there were no more eurythmy performances because, following the example of the Anthroposophic Congress in Stuttgart,† they could have helped the overwhelmed participants to take the burden of those fully occupied days somewhat better. I can imagine that it was very hard. Think, for example, of any one of those days, say an average day when we did not have additional meetings for more people. On such a day, someone who participated in all the panels would have heard five lectures and one discussion. It is too much for people today to listen to five lectures and one discussion. In fact, on a normal day, there were two discussions. This means that we had the opportunity to live continually with such thoughts from 9 to 3, and then again from 8 until half past 10 in the evening. It would have been certainly much better if there had been some short eurythmy performances in between, just for a change, as they did in Stuttgart. Overall, however, the result was significant.

APPENDIX

College Course in Anthroposophy
Berlin, March 5–12, 1922

Administrative Office: Berlin W 35, Potsdamer Street 39-39a

INVITATION

After many other cities have hosted a College Course in Anthroposophy, for the first time there will be one held in Berlin. It will attempt to give an impression of the possible incentives that Anthroposophy could offer to different scientific fields. There is no better way for Anthroposophy to address the increasing number of harsh attacks it is subjected to. Since in the most cases these attacks lack any basic knowledge of the matter, the course will offer an opportunity to those who would like first to test the waters, before they make judgments and pass sentences, for gaining some general idea of the role of Anthroposophy in our contemporary spiritual life.

The lectures will have a scientific character. Each day will offer four consecutive lectures held by different speakers on one particular area of the humanities: inorganic natural science, organic natural science and medicine, philosophy, education, social science, theology, theory of language. The order of the topics was defined with regard to the profile of the speakers. Additional lectures of more general character will be held for a wider audience on each of the evenings. The event will close with an art performance in a very special style. There will be as many opportunities as possible to ask questions and to express concrete criticism/objections, without jeopardizing the main goal of the event, namely, the diverse presentation of the humanities containing an anthroposophic orientation. The chairs of the separate panels will try to satisfy any serious wishes for a more profound understanding and discussion of Anthroposophy.

Those who confront our time without prejudice may be shocked by the negative developments we see in all areas of our spiritual life. There are young people even among the scientists—and sometimes they are some of the best—who are searching more and more seriously for new impulses that could revive us spiritually, give us fresh life energy, and help us found a different culture. In Anthroposophy, you can find a movement that believes itself to be able to inspire new life into our dying contemporary culture through the pure forces of the spirit. Those who feel a responsibility toward their time, culture, and people would want to make their own judgment rather than rely on someone else's.

Anthroposophy is still looking forward to finding its best co-workers and allies. It hopes to look for them among youth who are not burdened by prejudice and not satisfied with the existing spiritual life, and who keep their eyes open and their hearts young and ready for the big things that are yet to come. So far, the anthroposophic college courses organized in the past have demonstrated that an enormous number of people could come together for the sake of serious and difficult questions and tasks in all possible areas of science if the main spiritual forces in charge manage to have a convincing and energizing influence. As practical proof, we should point out that turning academic research into empty specialization, breaking up science into separate disciplines, alienating spiritual work from real life, and the whole fatal divorce of human cognition from action, as seen in our time, are to be overcome. We should be moved, instead, by a new, vivid, and much stronger spirit, based on spiritual cognition that seizes Thought and Research at the same time. Those who are looking for deliverance from the downfall of Western civilization are invited to a test of the possibility that Anthroposophy might offer the spiritual power that could lead to a new ascent.

Organizers of the Anthroposophic College Course in Berlin
Dr. Rittelmeyer

Association for Anthroposophic Work in Academia
Local Group Berlin
Theodor Lauer, stud. jur. et rer. pol. Emil Bock, lic. theol.†

Anthroposophic Society
Section Berlin
Rudolf Meyer. Karl Stahlbusch

Association for a Threefold Social Organism†
Local Group, Berlin
Bernhard Gantenbein. Prof. Dr/ Ludwig Oehninger. Hans Raether

Union for educational reforms on the basis of Anthroposophy
Erich Wetzel

Anthropsophic College Course, Berlin 1922

OUTLINE OF THE PANELS

I. Day-time panels in the Vocal Academy

Sunday, March 5: 9:30 a.m. **Opening**: Dr. Rittelmeyer
Inorganic natural science (Chair E.A. Karl Stockmeyer)
From a mechanical approach hostile to life to true phenomenology

Lecture by Dr. Steiner: *Anthroposophy and Natural Science.* – Monday
10:15-11:15: Dr. von Baravalle: Trends in the development of physics to follow Ernst Mach
11:30-12:30: E.A. Karl Stockmeyer: The philosophical foundation of physical imagination
(12:30-1: Snack break. During the break we offer the opportunity to address the academic chair of the panel with questions or to reserve time for comments.)
1-2: Conversation
2-3: Prof. Dr. Wohlbold: A contribution to theory of color

Monday, March 6: **Organic natural science and medicine** (Chair Dr. med. Kolisko)
Ways of achieving anthroposophic knowledge of the human being in biology and medicine

9-10: Dr. Steiner: *Anthroposophy and Natural Science*
10:15-11:15: Dr. med. Kolisko: Organization of the human and the animal in their biological opposition
11:30-12:30: Dr. med. Husemann: New directions in medical therapy based on anthroposophic spiritual science
(12:30-1: as on Sunday)
1-2: Conversation
2-3: Prof. Dr. Römer: On the alveolar pyorrhea and its relation to the entire human metabolism

Tuesday, March 7: **Philosophy** (Chair Dr. Unger)
The philosophical consciousness of modern times as a source for the foundation of Anthroposophy

9-10: Dr. Steiner: *Anthroposophy and Philosophy*
10:15-11:15: Dr. Unger: Discovering the process of thinking, a psychological study.
11:30-12:30: E.A. Karl Stockmeyer: Establishing new ethics with the help of *The Philosophy of Freedom*
(12:30-1: as on Sunday)
1-2: Conversation
2-3: Dr. Stein: Justifying suprasensory research results before ordinary consciousness

Wednesday, March 8: **Education** (Chair Dr. Caroline von Heydebrand)
From modern requirements in the area of pedagogy to their fulfillment with the help of Anthroposophy

9-10: Dr. Steiner: *Anthroposophy and Education*
10:15-11:15: Dr. von Heydebrand: Antiquated processes in modern pedagogy. Experimental pedagogy as the art of education
11:30-12:30: Dr. Stein: How to base real pedagogy on psychology
(12:30-1: as on Sunday)
1-2: Conversation
2-3: Prof. Dr. Schwebsch: The element of art in the pedagogy of the Free Waldorf School

Thursday, March 9: **Social Science** (Chair President Emil Leinhas)
Prospects of the national economy

9-10: Dr. Steiner: *Anthroposophy and Social Science*
10:15-11:15: Dr. Emil Leinhas: The financial problem of the world
11:30-12:30: Dr. jur. Krüger: Character and changes in private property in relation to law and economy
(12:30-1: as on Sunday)
1-2: Conversation
2-3: Walter Kühne: On the history of the national economy

Friday, March 10: **Theology** (Chair Lic. Dr. Rittelmeyer)
The downfall of religion in contemporary theology and its re-definition in Anthroposophy

9-10: Dr. Steiner: *Anthroposophy and Theology*
10:15-11:15: Lic. Bock: The downfall of the faith of revelation into psychologism.
11:30-12:30: Lic. Dr. Rittelmeyer: The downfall of the faith in God into irrationalism.
(12:30-1: as on Sunday)
1-2: Conversation
2-3: D. Dr. Geyer: The downfall of the faith in Christ into historicism

Saturday, March 11: **Theory of language** (Chair: Prof. Dr. Beckh)
From a dead to a living theory of language

9-10: Dr. Steiner: *Anthroposophy and the Theory of Language*
10:15-11:15: Prof. Dr. Beckh: Poetic and musical elements in language
11:30-12:30: Lic. Dr. Rittelmeyer: The downfall of the faith in God into irrationalism
(12:30-1: as on Sunday)
1-2: Conversation
2-3: Hahn: The pedagogical element in language

II. Evening Events

Sunday, 8:00 pm in the Philharmonic Hall (Oberlicht room): Dr. Steiner: Harmonizing Science, Art, and Religion through Anthroposophy.

Monday, 8:00 pm at the university, auditorium 122: Dr. Unger: Anthroposophy and Psychology

Tuesday, 8:00 pm in the Philharmonic Hall (Oberlicht room): Anthroposophy in Its Scientific Character

Wednesday, 8:00 pm in the university, auditorium 122: Dr. Schwebsch: Methods of Spiritual Science as the Basis for the New Views of Music

Thursday, 8:00 pm in the Philharmonic Hall (Oberlicht room): Dr. Steiner: Anthroposophy as Content of Life

Friday, 8:00 pm at the university, auditorium 122: Dr. Theberat: Atomistic and Realistic Observation of Chemical Processes

Saturday, 8:00 pm at the university, auditorium 122: D. Dr. Geyer: Anthroposophy and Christianity

Sunday, 8:00 pm in the Philharmonic Hall, (Oberlicht Room): Dr. Steiner: The Requirements of Our Time and Anthroposophy

The panels at the university are organized by the Association for anthroposophic work in academia, Local group Berlin

III. Art Performances

Eurythmy Presentation

In Deutsches Theater, Sunday, March 1, 11 o'clock in the morning, introductory remarks: Dr. Rudolf Steiner – Recitation: Mrs. Marie Steiner

Further art presentations will be announced

Commercial Information

While the course is held, in the rooms of the Vocal Academy, from 9 o'clock in the morning until 3 o'clock in the afternoon, there will be:

Book sales of publications by the Philosophical-Anthroposophical publishing house, Berlin, and the publishing house The Coming Day Ltd., Stuttgart; information booths, particularly about the Association for Anthroposophic Work in Academia, the Free Waldorf School in Stuttgart; representatives of the company The Coming Day in Stuttgart and the enterprises related to them, such as the Institute for Clinical Therapy "The Coming Day" in Stuttgart; a Lost and Found office; and a Mail desk.

Mail sent to the participants in the course should be addressed as follows: Vocal Academy Berlin C 2, Unter den Linden. Anthroposophic College Course.

Admission Fees:

Full Subscription for all events organized in the Vocal Academy: 100 Marks

Day tickets for the panels organized in the Vocal Academy on one single day: 20 Marks per day

Evening tickets for lectures in auditorium: 122 at the university, 5 Mark per night

Evening tickets for the lectures in the Oberlicht Room in the Philharmonic Hall: 30 Marks for the first evening, 20 Marks for the second, and 10 Marks for the third. Ticket prices and sales locations for the art performances will be announced separately during the course.

Student Discount:

Students may have either partially or completely free entrance, according to their own judgment. Requests for such discounts should be addressed to the local group of the Association for Anthroposophic Work in Academia. Where no such office exists, the discount should be requested from the Local Group of the Association for Anthroposophic Work in Academia, Berlin, West 35, Potsdamer Street 39a.

Registration:

Advanced booking of full subscriptions, day-tickets, and evening tickets in writing is preferable. We ask also the members in Berlin for advanced registration in writing. The requests should be addressed to the commercial office of the Anthroposophic College Course, Berlin, 1922, at Berlin W 35, Potsdamer Street 39a Gartenhaus. Please send your registration request at the latest by February 25. The deadline for students registration with the local groups of the Association for Anthroposophic Work in Academia is February 20. In the case of very strong interest, we will not be able to guarantee seats for those who have registered later. Payments must be made to the local group of the Association for Anthroposophic work at the Friedrich-Wilhelm University Berlin, account number 119294 by the postal check office,* Berlin NW 7, marked "College Course" on the back of the slip, or perhaps to Mr. Bernhard Gantenbein, Berlin SW 19, Krausen Street 30.

The tickets will be mailed upon receipt of payment.

Full subscription, day and the evening cards will be sold between March 1 and 4 in the Vocal Academy Berlin, Unter den Linden, every morning between 9 and 11.

Depending on availability, tickets will be sold also during the course in the Vocal Academy beginning Sunday, March 5, at 9:30 a.m.

If there are any tickets available for the evening events, a special evening box office will be opened.

Room and board:

Guests from out of town will be asked to book accommodation on their own. We will try to guarantee free or discounted accommodation for students. Applications should be sent in connection with the requests for partially or fully reduced entrance.

There is no cafeteria in the Vocal Academy.

---

*The first attempts to establish easy ways for money transfers and check transactions in Europe dated from 1876, but a common regulation for check transactions was introduced in Austria-Hungary only in 1884. Originally only postal check offices (*Postscheckkontostellen*) were dealing with check transactions before they became postal giro offices and later postal banks.

Two letters by the Chair of the Berlin Section and Organizer of the College Course Rudolf Meyer and Rudolf Steiner:

Berlin S. O.* 36, Cottbuser Ufer 25
August 26th, 1921

Dear Dr. Steiner,

May I ask you, in the name of the Berlin movement, to give one or two open lectures that we would organize at the time following the lecture of the concert director Wolff? I think that one or two big open lectures given by you would better prepare the ground for the anthroposophic College Course we are planning for next spring. Mr. Raether** who has donated 25 000 Marks for a grand performance of eurythmy in Berlin, as I mentioned to you this spring in Dornach, has made the realization of the college course possible through his renewed support. Like myself and all other friends who are passionate about this movement, he would like to see this college course as an event on a generous scale. We believe that two or more big open lectures given by you now in September would attract the interest of the society in Berlin to a degree that would assure a strong participation in the college course next March that corresponds with our plans.

With cordial regards to you and your esteemed wife Mrs. …

Unchangeably obedient,

Rudolf Meyer[

---

*Berlin Süd Ost (South East). Part of the Postal Code.

**Hans Raether, no biographical data is available. At the time, a member of the administration of the Rudolf Steiner-Branch in Berlin.

Berlin, Sunday, November 6th, 1921

Dear Dr. Steiner,

For a while we had such difficulties reserving appropriate rooms for the college course next spring that sometimes it was as though the circumstances were going to force us to postpone the course. At this point, there is a possibility to book rooms in the Vocal Academy in Berlin from March 1 till the 15. The main events of the college course would be well organized here, if we do not book rooms for the evenings too, but only for the time from 9 till 3. We will find other appropriate rooms for the evening panels. It seems to us that even if the panels are going to be in two different places it is better to schedule the course for March 1922 than for 1923 in *one*.

Since from the very beginning you were supposed to give the Berlin college course its real weight and assure its desired effect, the possibility to schedule the course for the time between March 1st and 15th depends mainly on the question of whether you would be able to be in Berlin at that particular time.

May I ask you to let me know briefly if it would be possible for you to give some lectures in Berlin between 1 and 15 of March, so that we could rent immediately the rooms in the Vocal Academy and in another place. Hereby, I am sending an addressed envelope.

Warm regards from our friends, and me to you and Mrs. Dr. St.

Your
Unchangeably obedient,

Rudolf Meyer

VOICES FROM THE PRESS

Excerpt from the report "The Anthroposophic College Course in Berlin" by Ernst Uehli, published in the journal *The Threefold Formation of the Social Organism*, Stuttgart, 3rd year, No. 38-40, March 23, 30, and April 6, 1922.

The entire event was marked by a lively oscillating spirituality, felt by everybody and expressed in the full attendance at each lecture. The course found a remarkable resonance, and even the skeptics could not very long fail to notice this. The fact this resonance was so explicit considering Berlin's cold milieu of a big city, should serve as proof of the life forces springing out of anthroposophy as a spiritual science. Serious observers realized that this event achieved the effect of uniting people not only on a spiritual but also on a social level.

The lectures in the Vocal Academy started at 9 o'clock in the morning and continued almost uninterruptedly until 3 o'clock, with the exception of a very short break. They were scheduled in a way so that each day was dedicated to one particular branch of science. Dr. Steiner gave an introductory lecture to each of the discussed branches of science. An hour for discussion was included before the last lecture of the day. Unfortunately, one definite disadvantage of this schedule was the fact that the discussion could not be really productive, since most speakers did not have enough time to reply to questions and objections in the necessary detail.

There might have been some concern about the attendance of the last lecture because of the way the panels were scheduled. However, this concern turned out to be unnecessary because the number of attendees seemed to remain generally the same throughout the daily six-hour panels. This fact, in my view, seems to be of great importance for the evaluation of the course [...]

Each day Dr. Steiner opened the session dedicated to a particular branch of science with an introductory lecture in the respective field. In a one-hour lecture one could hardly say much about the respective field. Thus, what Dr. Steiner said in his seven introductory lectures on seven scientific fields, had more the character of a fresco. These were amazing sketches—sketches with an illuminating clarity and a sure brush stroke. Through this particular kind of a presentation, Dr. Steiner painted a picture of each respective scientific field exactly as it was supposed to be in the future, seen from the anthroposophic perspective. With regard to the future tasks, which will have to be defined in each individual area of science if science is not to become gradually a giant expanse of atomistic ruins, these introductory lectures were like scientific sketches of an artist, in which the whole painting could be revealed to the viewer. [...]

In contradiction to the profound effect Rudolf Steiner achieved with his lectures on anthroposophy, and particularly on science, among the educated or, more specifically, among the academic circles, that was obviously the case in Berlin, the press insisted that it was all hypnosis. To those who have some idea of the human and spiritual context, it is obvious that these opinions were simply meant to bury the whole idea of anthroposophy. Seen from such a perspective, such a report could also be qualified as personal and subjective. In fact, my goal is exactly to share my personal experience, and to juxtapose it to the big-city-dirt that journalists of a particular kind have uploaded in the columns of their newspapers, calling it personal experience of anthroposophic events. I would define the most profound experience I was able to gain out of Rudolf Steiner's lectures as *objective love*, objective love in the sense that its entire content reveals itself in a cognitive form valid for all humanity. This, in my view, is the core of Dr. Steiner's success.

The specialized lectures of the other speakers, following Dr. Steiner's introductory lectures, created an overall fine and relatively complete image of the ways anthroposophy could contribute to science today. The scientists who represent anthroposophy know better than anyone else that we are only in the beginning of this process. What is important is that a respectable and growing number of scientists from all fields have found the courage to confront the consequences of the way science is treated today, and to make a new beginning. This fact, along with the content of the lectures themselves, obviously made a great impression on many of the best among the audience in Berlin. [...]

These lectures were driven by enthusiasm, a fact emphasized by one of the neutral discussion speakers. One could feel the common ground—the anthroposophic spiritual science—whose life energy was to be perceived in a particularly intimate way on the day dedicated to pedagogy, which, in my view, represented a high point in this academic week. The pedagogical methods of the Waldorf school presented here summarized the significance of the Free Waldorf School in the life of our contemporary civilization in a beautiful overall impression. This includes the last lecture on the day of the theory of language, which should be considered as well since it ended with the Waldorf school pedagogy and the sensitive criticism of experimental pedagogy. [...]

A number [...] of teachers in the Waldorf School spoke. In his lecture, Dr. Stein offered an idea of the character of educational psychology. In fact, he offered more than simply an idea. He vividly described an ideal of education that was already tested in the Waldorf School, and that presented the teacher as a servant of the child's soul. Dr. von Heydebrand spoke against experimental psychology, and at the same time she made us feel that she was a person who had the finest understanding for pedagogical errors, too. She mastered her subject not only as a specialist, through her knowledge, but also through her superior sense of humor and her lovely way of being relaxed. Her criticism was at the same time reconciliatory on a very human level. One felt confronted with a developed soul in the best sense of the word. Dr. Schwebsch's sparkling lecture on the use of art in pedagogy gave us a view of what pedagogy could actually be if it is not based on prescribed methods but uses creativity at every individual moment instead, and, precisely by doing this, offers the child effective moral values. Dr. Hahn's lecture, which discussed various issues of language teaching in the Waldorf School, was profoundly thorough and had a fine personal touch. This person conveyed the spiritual and social elements of language. Dr. Schubert spoke about the word and showed the cultural and the historical perspectives of the morally characterized use of the word. He wrought and formed sentences containing complete views, and was often extremely original. He was trying to transform cognitive material into art. [...]

The day of theology enjoyed a particularly strong formal interest. The program, including the topic of the downfall of religion in contemporary theology and its re-definition in anthroposophy, was perceived by the theologians as a challenge on the side of anthroposophy rather than as a scholarly confrontation with the contemporary state of theology. Thus, Dr. Steiner felt the need to explain that he himself does not see any other task set for himself except the one to describe the relationship of anthroposophy to theology. However, the following three key lectures defined the difficult crisis of religious life in an objective manner, from three different perspectives. The conclusion made in this three lectures had to be accepted as correct during the discussion. One could think that we were partaking in the funeral procession of theology (and the black gowns of the many priests who participated in this panel only intensified this impression.) The discussion took a very unproductive course. Even the opposition got involved in embarrassingly emotional polemics. While the theologians' opposition was stressing its existing piety, at the same time one of them managed to accuse Dr. Steiner of consciously misleading the public with his lectures. Nevertheless, this accusation turned to the better, too. If the lectures had offered an academic, theoretical description of the crisis in theology, the debate supplied an immediate concrete example. We did not simply listen about the crisis, we experienced it.

The decisive, key appearance of Dr. Rittelmeyer left an important impression in the course of this modern council-like argument. His lecture was also a decision that represented a redemptive balance to the heavy negation the subject brings with itself [...]

One of the four evening lectures given as part of this course at the university was the one on anthroposophy and Christianity by Dr. Geyer from Nürnberg. The clever way he grilled theology as well as his own views brought him the excited applause of the large audience. Regarding anthroposophy, he has the positive attitude of a fighter. He wants to see the anthroposophic movement in good terms, and he called upon his contemporaries to do the same. In an inspiring and stirring way, Dr. Schwebsch spoke about "new ways of looking at music using spiritual science as a basis," and Dr. Theberat offered in his talk a fine view of "atomistic and realistic approaches to chemical processes."

On Sunday, March 12, in the Deutsches Theater there was a matinée dedicated to the art of eurythmy and directed by Mrs. Marie Steiner. [...] In Berlin this exquisite program [...] was transferred to an environment completely different from the one in Stuttgart. The mood was somewhat cold, yet there was interest. Some people became angry. I consider this a good sign. There are always people who become angry when they see originality. Berlin was no exception. Some newspapers were obviously upset and were swearing in quite a wild tone of voice.

This is an even better sign. It is the objective confirmation that what was presented as a new kind of art is really new. Indeed, the scenes from Rudolf Steiner's mystery plays were particularly gripping in the atmosphere of a big city. The gnomes and sylphs made people feel very clearly the endless melancholy of the big city milieu, with its stone-cold character. In a strange way, the yellow bony figure of Ahriman, whose weak movements seemed to be dramatizing the fixed fate of the big city, was an especially strongly expressed touch that left a remarkable impression.

The Deutsche Theater was full to the last seat. Since there were not enough places to satisfy the demand, two additional performances, which were also sold out, had to be scheduled in a different, smaller hall. Considering the artistic qualities of this performance as well as the demand, it seems that the last two performances in the Deutsches Theater should have been planned, and that they should have been integrated into the main events in accordance with their significance.

The College Course in Berlin was a clear success. Those from the large audience who have experienced this success personally will appreciate the work of the people who contributed to it publicly or behind the scenes. We should thank among others the deserving leader of the anthroposophic work in Berlin, Rudolf Meyer, who had the initiative and started the first preparations for this course, and who, unfortunately, because of illness could not participate as planned as a speaker. We should also consider the fact that Dr. Rittelmeyer was of great service for taking over the coordinating work during the course in place of Rudolf Meyer. [...]

The College Course in Berlin was the renewed realization of a small part of a free spiritual life. The people who represent this life are profoundly convinced that Central Europe, particularly, should be seeking it for the sake of its future. [...]

The unending applause at the end of the last [evening] lecture in the Philharmonic Hall, which was also the end of the entire College Course, [...] was the expression of something more than a momentary excitement. It was the expression of many people's deep gratitude for the prospect of a new image of humanity, which appeared as an ideal that could be a driving force leading us beyond the endless spiritual misery of our time.

* * *

Report: "On the Anthroposophic College Course in Berlin" by Dr. Eberhard Kurras, published in *The Goetheanum*, Dornach, 1st year, No. 33, March 26, 1922.

Now Berlin has also experienced an anthroposophic event of great style. A number of presentations, each with a different theme, have attracted more than one thousand participants, among whom were many young academics, and kept them engaged for eight days. The morning panels in the Vocal Academy offered specialized discussions of different scientific fields: inorganic and organic science and medicine, philosophy, education, social science, theology, and theory of language were treated each on a different morning. The audience followed these presentations with untiring interest: a real achievement, since, beginning at nine every morning there were four lectures with only very short breaks. Dr. Steiner guided the audience into the different scientific fields with introductory speeches suggesting a new orientation. When the second speaker scheduled for Monday did not appear because he was ill, Dr. Steiner jumped in and talked about the announced topic, showing his sovereign mastery of the subject. In order to give listeners the word as well, there was a special time for conversation scheduled at noon. After the discussion, the fourth lecture rounded out the day.

On Sunday, Father Licentiate Dr. Rittelmeyer, who was in charge of the course administration, opened the meeting with a strong and inspiring address. Anthroposophy, he asserted, is aware of the fact that it is still in a far from a perfect state. Nevertheless, it is determined to continue developing the spiritual movement of German idealism further and to carry it out in an independent and original way, regardless of the Western and Eastern spiritual traditions. The most significant opponents and the most decisive battles, according to him, are yet to come. However, those who are unbiased and would like to test the waters before they make their own judgments and pass sentences, are invited to this course. The two days dedicated to natural science showed the way from a mechanical outlook on nature, alien to life, to a true phenomenological view and a profound knowledge of the human being. This is the kind of scientific research practiced by

Goethe, who had the ability to think in mathematical terms and to grasp things inwardly, even though he was not a gifted mathematician.

The day of theology was anticipated with intense excitement, for theology appeared for the first time at an anthroposophic forum. The topic of the day, "the downfall of religion in contemporary theology and its re-definition in anthroposophy," was by no means meant as a challenge, as it was perceived in the theological press, which gradually started paying attention. Rather, it was supposed to be an attention-calling approach to the scholarly work on theology. In his introductory lecture, "Anthroposophy and Theology," Dr. Steiner developed his idea that a person with a healthy body and spirit, who truthfully experiences the spiritual and divine reality, will arrive at the differentiated knowledge of the Father-God, Christ, and the Spirit. At the same time, atheism is a real illness; the impossibility to find Christ—destiny; and the impossibility to discover God—narrow-mindedness. The fundamental details in the methodological exposition of the following paper on the "downfall of faith in revelation into psychologism" by Licentiate Bock demonstrated that the psychological method destroys all faith in God's revelation and all consciousness of the existence of a spiritual world because it falls back to the subjectively-psychological and gradually loses the objectively-divine. Then, Dr. Rittelmeyer spoke of the "downfall of faith in God into irrationalism." This was an intellectual investigation of the attempts to define the divine as irrational by Rudolf Otto, Christoph Schrempf, and Paul Göhre. The *irrational*, according to him, is an empty definition of the divine, which should not be sustained by a theology and a piety that are supposed to be full of life. Anthroposophy, on the other hand, is able to explain faith in a new and better way: not through logical proof and psychological explanations but through a spiritual education that leads to the immediate experience and knowledge of the individual. Lastly, Dr. Geyer spoke about the "downfall of faith in Christ into historicism." He led us through the different phases in the history of faith in Christ, demonstrating an extensive knowledge of the subject, and determined the contemporary state of this faith: On one hand, because of the purely historical research of the person Jesus, Christ who lives in spirit was lost; on the other hand the historical Jesus was lost for the sake of the abstract principle of Christ. These theological discourses finished successfully with Dr. Geyer's second lecture on Saturday night. The elderly theologian spoke with a truly youthful enthusiasm about "Anthroposophy and Christianity." In an extremely fascinating and humorous way, he explained that originally anthroposophy and Christianity had nothing to do with each other, since the former is a science and the latter is religion. Yet, they both have much to do with each other for piety and worldview, according to Neumann's statement, belonging together as the vine and the wall that supports it. At the end, he recommended that we look at anthroposophy with a "good look," but also that most of all we test it in practice through exercises of the soul. The discussions following the lectures on theology showed that the opposition has not yet achieved a profound understanding.

The participants in the course gathered on the other evenings as well. A whole series of lectures, organized by the local group of the Association for Anthroposophic Work in Academia, was given in the university. There, in a lecture entitled "Anthroposophy and Psychology," Dr. Unger energetically rejected the unscientific treatment of anthroposophy by the professor from the University of Berlin, Dr. Max Dessoir. Dr. Steiner spoke on the last four evenings in the Philharmonic Hall. Here he revealed the great prospect of harmonizing science, art, and religion through anthroposophy. The different areas of the spiritual, he asserted, are only different forms of the same original phenomenon, and as they were united in the mysteries ages long ago, they will come back together, this time in a higher form of unity. This form of unity will be achieved by ascending to the higher forms of cognition through imagination, inspiration, and intuition. The content of life, which anthroposophy is able to offer, does not consist in something finished, in something given that should simply be accepted. Rather, it is expressed in the possibility to reap the fruit of our inner labor; fruit that does not mean simply the result of thinking, but the ability to live, understood in the sense of Goethe's statement that "only those deserve freedom and life who have to conquer them every day." On the last evening Steiner spoke with contagious passion about the needs of our time.

Through its ideas full of life and energy and through its constructive impulses, anthroposophy, according to him, will manage to find treatment even for the terrible social ills. It is not "a tortuous path to the right and necessary goals" as one of the opponents has said. It is the true way to redemption from the great cultural crisis. Strong and lasting applause showed how touched emotionally the audience was. The course ended on an artistic note with several performances of eurythmy. The performances, organized under extremely difficult circumstances, deserved the gratitude and the applause of the unbiased audience.

We could say that the course in Berlin was a complete success. One could hear from different sources what the overall impression was: that a large number of people have invested us with a great deal of culturally creative energy through the unusual spiritual content and the uncommon inner and explicit liveliness of their performance. This impression could be even increased through Dr. Steiner, whose speeches were truly powerful spiritual deeds. Thus, the course in Berlin was a historical cultural event, an event that one could hardly find anywhere else today. The participants in the College Course in Berlin were left with the strong impression and the hopeful conviction that our contemporary science, which has an intellectual, materialistic character, could be complemented and developed further by the initiation-like science grown out of anthroposophy.

* * *

Excerpt from Heinrich Frick's article "Who has challenged whom?" in *Die Christliche Welt* (The Christian World), Nr. 13, March 30, 1922, p. 226:

There was a huge crowed of visitors. Particularly the evening lectures, but also some during the morning hours, especially on the days of pedagogy and theology, enjoyed a massive audience of hundreds of people. The morning meetings were in the Vocal Academy. One had the opportunity to see and to buy anthroposophic literature at many tables placed at the entrance. These books, along with the medications produced by the pharmaceutical company The Coming Day, the photographs of the Goetheanum, and the flyers, created a first impression of the suggestions that one could expect anthroposophy to make in different areas.

Excerpt from Heinrich Frick's article "Anthroposophy and evangelical theology," in *Die Christliche Welt*, No. 17, April 27, 1922, p. 303:

The Berlin Course caused me to see in anthroposophy an educational and cultural phenomenon and not a religious movement. Since the discussion over the course of these eight days included almost all areas of knowledge and all current questions and concerns of modern humans, from the state of the currency to the question of God, a big part of the attraction for the audience was the encyclopedic character of the event. For those hungry for knowledge, this compendium-like, abbreviated universal knowledge is generally the main motivation that brings them to Steiner. The program, however, makes us feel as if we have revived here the epoch of Goethe: from broken-up, narrow specialization to the whole, from formless pieces of knowledge to organic unity, and all of this arranged logically around one center—anthroposophy.

EDITORIAL AND REFERENCE NOTES

About the publication of Rudolf Steiner's lectures:

The Collected Works of Rudolf Steiner are divided into three major parts: Treatises, Lectures, and Literary Works.

Originally Rudolf Steiner did not wish for his many lectures to the members of the Theosophical Society (and later the Anthroposophical Society), or the more spontaneous public talks, to be written down. He intended them to be "verbal messages, not designed for print." After more and more notes by listeners (which often were incomplete and full of mistakes), were copied and distributed, he considered it necessary to direct the taking down of notes. He gave this task to Marie Steiner-von Sivers. She was in charge of selecting the stenographer, supervising the transcriptions, and the proofreading of the text in preparation for publication. Because of insufficient time, Rudolf Steiner was rarely able to correct the notes himself; therefore, one should keep in mind that he had reservations in respect to all published lectures: "It should be assumed that in these documents, which I have not been able to check myself, there will be errors."

After the death of Marie Steiner in 1948, the work on Rudolf Steiner's Complete Works continued in accordance with her guidelines.

Comments by the German editors:

The College Course in Berlin was organized by the Association for Anthroposophic Work in Academia and the Berlin Section of the Anthroposophical Society. The goal of the organizers was to try to "give an impression of the possible incentives that anthroposophy could offer to various scientific fields" through a series of lectures given by a number of speakers on organic and inorganic natural science, medicine, philosophy and theology, education, social science and theory of language. To each topic of the day Rudolf Steiner gave an introductory lecture. Additionally, on the second day of the course, he spoke on the topic "The Organization of the Human and the Animal," in place of the original speaker Eugen Kolisko. The pastor Friedrich Rittelmeyer chaired this panel in place of the chair of the Berlin Section, Rudolf Meyer, who was absent because of sickness. (The two letters by Rudolf Meyer and Rudolf Steiner included in the Appendix give some idea of the preparations for the College Course.) Since Rittelmeyer was a well-known personality in Berlin because of his position as a main pastor of the New Church, the connection between his name and a public anthroposophic event attracted particular attention among the Protestant theological circles. At this point Rittelmeyer was still a pastor in his parish in Berlin, but at the same time, he was already actively involved in the movement for religious renewal that was the basis for the foundation of The Christian Community* in the autumn of

---

**Christengeimeinschaft,* a Christian denomination founded with Steiner's help in Dornach in 1922 by a group of theologians and pastors lead by Friedrich Rittelmeyer.

1922. Many of the prominent participants in the religious renewal movement had come to Berlin for the occasion of the College Course. They were meeting at Rittelmeyer's in the free afternoons. Twice, Rudolf Steiner was also present at these conversations. Even though these meetings had nothing to do with the College Course, and even though the College Course did not discuss the movement for religious renewal, the day dedicated to theology got special attention due to the presence of this group. No notes were taken on that day during the hours designated for discussions of the individual daily topics. Only the report by Eberhard Kurras, later a priest in The Christian Community, which is included in the Appendix, gives us some impression of the discussion on the "theologians' day."

Along with the course panel in the Berlin Vocal Academy, there were also a number of open lectures given by prominent people in the building of the Philharmonic Orchestra. Rudolf Steiner held four evening lectures on the following topics: "Harmonizing Science, Art, and Religion through Anthroposophy," "Anthroposophy in Its Scientific Character," "Anthroposophy as Content of Life," and "The Needs of Our Time and Anthroposophy." These lectures are not yet published in the Complete Works (Gesamtausgabe).

Text documents:

Rudolf Steiner's lectures were simultaneously written down in shorthand by the stenographer Walter Vegelahn. They were printed following his transcription. The original stenographic notes are not preserved. Missing words and mistakes were considered in the printed version of the text. Words completed or added by the [German] publisher are given in square brackets. There are also changes in the syntax of some sentences, which were made because without the intonation of the living speech the word order alone did not make the meaning clear enough. No notes of lectures given by the other speakers or of the discussions are available.

Publications in journals:

The lectures were published first in the journal *Blätter für Anthroposophie* (Paper for Anthroposophy), 14th year, 1962, No. 2, 3, 4, 5, 6, 7/8, 9.

The Dornach Member Speech from March 18, 1922, was published in the newsletter of the journal *Das Goetheanum* (The Goetheanum), 22nd year, 1945, No. 46-50.

* * *

Works by Rudolf Steiner are referenced by Gesamtausgabe number (GA) when they are only available in German; the English edition Collected Works (CW) number is referenced where available. See also the overview of Rudolf Steiner's Collected Works (CW) starting on p.157ff.

Page 2, "if I may repeat the phrase of du Bois-Reymond"
Emil du Bois Reymond (1818-1896), German physician and physiologist. "On the limits of the cognition of nature. Lecture given second public session of the 45th Meeting of German natural scientists and medical doctors in Leipzig on August 14, 1872." Leipzig, 1872.

Ibid. p. 2: "Cognition of nature, or better scientific cognition, or cognition of the physical world, achieved with the help and in the sense of theoretical natural science, is reducing the changes in the physical world to the motions of atoms caused by their core forces, independently of time; in other words, it is the reduction of natural phenomena to the mechanics of the atoms. It is a matter of a psychological experience, that whenever we manage to reduce the meaning of things in this way, our need to find causality is satisfied for the time being." (translation by J. W-A.).

Page 3, "the great natural scientist Virchow"
Rudolf Virchow (1821-1902), medical doctor and anthropologist, professor in pedagogical anatomy and temporarily president of the Frederick William University [University of Berlin], Berlin. "The founding of the University of Berlin and the transition from the era of philosophy to the era of natural science," speech given on August 3, 1893. Berlin, 1893.

Page 3, "Ernst Mach"
Ernst Mach (1838-1916), Austrian physicist and philosopher of materialism. He was one of the founders of empirio-criticism, and revived Berkeley's and Hume's views of the theory of knowledge.

Page 3, "We can find Goethe's explanation in his statement that ..."
See J. W. Goethe: *Naturwissenschaftliche Schriften* [Treatise on natural science] with introduction, footnotes, and explanatory notes to the text by Rudolf Steiner: Photo-mechanical reprint of the first edition in *Kürschners Deutsche National-Literatur* [Kürschner's German national-literature] (1884-1897), 5 volumes, GA 1 a-e; Vol. 5, GA 1e, "Verses in Prose"; Part 1 "Das Erkennen" [Cognition], p. 376: "It will be best to understand that each fact represents already a theory. The blue color of the sky reveals the basic principle of chromatism. We shall search for nothing beyond the phenomena: they are the teachings themselves" (translation by J. W-A.). See in English, CW 1, *Nature's Open Secret.*

Page 3, "This is how Goethe came to the realization ... "
Ibid. Vol. 3, GA 2c, Part 2: "Physical colors," X. "Dioptric colors. First class," p. 135 Par. 150f and p. 141f. Par. 174-177. In a note to par. 175-177, Rudolf Steiner added the following (p. 141): "Goethe expresses here his view of the real task of natural science. Our immediate perception of nature is apperception of phenomena that depend on different conditions. If we change one or more of these conditions, the phenomenon will change too. So, the questions is when is a change secondary, when minor, and when radical. All phenomena that were caused to change only insignificantly because of the changes

in the conditions point at a basic or original phenomenon that is the core of each one of them, in which we can see the expression of one of nature's laws. Thus, the task of the natural scientist would be to put together a number of such phenomena that are only modifications of one single original phenomenon caused by a change in the conditions. This original phenomenon is the objective law of nature. No explanation as such could go beyond the natural phenomena. It is a great illusion to believe that we could prove or explain further the existence of natural phenomena. Even if it becomes possible to find proof for the existence of the atom anywhere in the world, we will still be able to express the effect one atom has on another through nothing else but an original phenomenon. Therefore, Goethe's profound understanding of nature should not be qualified as dilettantism any longer. Rather, we should realize that it distinguishes itself from modern natural science precisely through its strongly philosophical conceptualization and method. Not even philosophy can go beyond the original phenomena. Its task is only to set apart from each other the original phenomena discovered by science and to treat them separately in their ideal sequential order. While the scientist puts phenomena together in order to find in them the expression of the original phenomenon, the philosopher puts together the original phenomena in order to find in them the expression of the ideas of nature. See also Rudolf Steiner, Vol. 2 , GA 1b, Chapter "The relation of Goethe's way of thinking to the views of others," p. LXI; Vol. 3, GA 1c Chapter "Introduction," 2. "The original phenomenon," p. Xff.; Vol. 4, GA 1d Chapter "Introduction," 3, p. VIff. (This citation corresponds to pp. 226ff., 266ff., and 311ff. in "Introduction to Goethe's treatise on natural science and fundamental principles of spiritual science (Anthroposophy)," GA 1. See in English, CW 2, *Goethe's Theory of Knowledge* and CW 1, *Nature's Open Secret.*

Page 4, "I said before the end of the last century"
In my introduction .... *which I wrote in the 1880s*: In "J. W. Goethe: Treatise on Nature." (See the third note to p. 3) Vol. 1, GA 1a, p. LXXIII; resp. in "Introductions to Goethe's treatise on natural science," GA 1, p. 107. See in English, CW 1, *Nature's Open Secret.*

Nicolaus Copernicus (1473-1543), astronomer, mathematician, medical doctor, jurist, humanist, and domicellarius. Founder of the heliocentric view of the world.

Johannes Kepler. See note to p. 32.

Page 4, "Kant's statement"
See "Metaphysical Foundations of Natural Science," 1786, in *Immanuel Kants sämtliche Werke* [Immanuel Kant's collected works], Leipzig 1897, Vol. 4, Preface, p. 360; this is literally: "I assert, however, that in each particular branch of natural science we could find only as much real science as we can find *mathematics.*"

Page 4-5, "Finally, he concluded . . . the concept of a mathematical function"
"*It is sufficient to characterize the law of causality by saying that it presupposes an interdependence between the phenomena.* This understanding eliminates some pointless questions, such as whether the cause precedes the effect or they are simultaneous. Let us call the complexity of phenomena upon which a single phenomenon *x* is considered to be dependent, the cause for *x*. If the complexity does exist, then *x* is determined, unequivocally determined. Thus, we could formulate the law of causality also in the following way: 'The effect is determined by the cause.'" "History and origins of the axiom of receiving work," (lecture given on November 15, 1871, 2nd edition, Leipzig, 1909, p. 35 and 37).

Page 5, "Goethe . . . he defined himself as such"
See J. W. Goethe: "Treatise on natural science" (see note 3 to p. 3), Bd. 3, GA 1c *On the Theory of Color*, Part 5 "Neighborly Relations," "relations to Mathematics" p. 27, Par. 723: "The author cannot pride himself with any culture regarding this side (mathematics), and thus remains only in the areas independent from the art of measuring, which in modern times are spreading everywhere." Compare: Rudolf Steiner's essays "Goethe and Mathematics" from 1887 in GA 1, p. 237, and from 1923 in GA 36, *Goetheanumgedanke* [The thought of the Goetheanum], p. 150, (the latter is a review of the book *Goethe* by Benedetto Croce, in German, 1920). See in English, CW 1, *Nature's Open Secret.*

Page 6, "the famous conversation. . . that Goethe and Schiller once had"
See J. W. Goethe: "Treatise on Natural Science" (see note 3 to p. 3), Vol. 1, GA 1a, "Progress," "Happy Event," p. 108ff. See in English, CW 1, *Nature's Open Secret.*

Page 6, "the natural scientist Batsch"
August Johann Karl Batsch (1761-1802), botanist, professor of natural history in Jena.

Page 6, "Jena Society of Natural Science"
Jenaer Naturforschende Gesellschaft (1650-1820).

Page 6, "roots and stem, leaves, blossoms, and fruit"
In the argument that follows, we can see the influence of Plato's concept of ideas or forms on Goethe's and Steiner's views, especially how Plato presents the concept of ideas in the speech of Diotima in the *Symposium*.

Page 6, "In my introduction . . . I tried to repeat the drawing"
Rudolf Steiner: *Nature's Open Secret: Introductions to Goethe's Scientific Writings*, CW 1, see also Chapter "The Origin of Goethe's Concept of Metamorphosis." Between 1883-97, Rudolf Steiner edited in four volumes Goethe's works concerning natural science in Joseph Kürschner's (1853-1902) 220-volume collection of the greatest works of German literature entitled *Deutsche National-Literatur.*

Page 6, Goethe … ended the conversation summarizing"
Ibid., p. 112. Literally: "I like the fact that I could have ideas without realizing it, and that I could even see them with my eyes."

Page 7, "he wrote from Italy … developing the idea of the original plant"
See Goethe: *Italian Journey*, Sicily, Letter from April 17, 1787 (Palermo) and from May 17, 1787 (Naples). Compare further the letters from September 27, 1786; March 25, 1787; and September 6, 1787.

Page 7, "In this context he said"
See note above. In his letter from May 17, 1787, Goethe writes to Herder:

> Undoubtedly and clearly, I have found the main point, where the germ is; I can see everything else in the whole [plant]. There are very few points that still have to be determined better. The original plant will be the most wonderful creation of this world, a creation that even nature will be envious of. Then, with the help of this model and the key to it, we will be able to create an endless number of further plants that will have to be consequent. This means, that even if they do not exist, they nevertheless could exist, and that they are not some picturesque lustrous shadows but that they have their inner truth and necessity. We would also be able to apply the same law to everything else that is alive.
>
> … In fact I realized that the true Proteus,* who can hide or reveal himself in all possible forms, is actually in the organ of the plant, which we usually call a leaf. In the front and in the back, a plant is always a leaf, so inseparably united with the future germ that we should not imagine the one without the other. (*Goethe-Works*, Hamburg Edition (Deutescher Taschenbuch Verlag, India paper), Munich 1982, Vol. 11, p. 323f.

Page 7, "It is completely wrong to insist, as Schleiden later did"
Steiner refers here to Schleiden's article "Goethe als Naturforscher" [Goethe as natural scientist] published in *Westermann's Jahrbuch der Illustrierten Deutschen Monatshefte* [Westerman's almanac of the monthly German journals], Vol. 23, Braunschweig: George Westermann, 1868. pp. 614-625.

Matthias Jakob Schleiden (1804-1881). German botanist who specialized particularly in plant embryology. Cofounder of the cell theory.

The Plant and its Life, 6th edition, Leipzig, 1864, lecture 4: "The morphology of plants," p. 86. "The suggestion that there is such law, and that it applies to the formation of plants, was expressed first by Goethe in his idea of the original

---

*Proteus is a Greek deity whose name is related to the concept of the "first" (from Greek *protos*, "first") or the "primordial." He is the son of Poseidon in the Olympian theogony (*Odyssey* iv. 432), or of Nereus and Doris, or of Oceanus and a Naiad. He can change his shape and he answers only to someone who is capable of capturing him. From this feature of Proteus comes the adjective protean, with the general meaning of "versatile," "mutable," "capable of assuming many forms."

plant, by which he meant an ideal plant whose materialization is a task nature, and which has achieved more or less its complete form in the individual plant."

Page 10, "In his speech du Bois Reymond..."
Steiner quotes here du Bois-Reymond's famous 1872 speech, "Über die Grenzen des Naturerkennens."

Page 10, "Laplace's worldview"
Pierre Simon Laplace (1749-1827), French mathematician and astronomer. He developed further the theory of the celestial mechanics established by Newton.—*Exposition du système du monde*, 1796; *Traite de Mecanique cèleste*, 5 volumes, Paris, 1799-1825.

Page 10, "'the astronomic conception' of the entire existence of nature"
See note to p. 2: "I use the term astronomical knowledge of a physical system for such knowledge of all its parts, of their positions in relation to each other, and of their motions, that allows us to calculate their positions and their motions at any time in the past or in the future with the same certainty with which we calculate the positions and the motions of the celestial bodies, given the presupposed necessary sharpness of observation and completeness of the theory.... Considering our inability to comprehend matter and force the astronomical knowledge of a physical system is the most complete knowledge of them that we could achieve. It is the knowledge that usually satisfies our drive to understand causality. Even the demon that Laplace thought of* will know that under the condition that Laplace's universal formula of the system is appropriately applied."

Page 13, "This is why Goethe remarked naively"
See last note to p. 6.

Page 13, "anthroposophy is really capable of accounting to anyone"
J. W. Goethe: *Naturwissenschaftliche Schriften* [Treatise on natural science]. (See note 3 to p. 3), Vol. 2, GA 1b, Chapter "Der Versuch als Vermittler von Objekt und Subjekt" (The experiment as a mediator between subject and object), p. 19, literally: We should learn this careful way of thinking, to put together only things that are close to each other, or even more, to deduce from each other only

---

*In *A Philosophical Essay on Probabilities* (translated from the 6th French edition by Frederick Wilson Truscott and Frederick Lincoln Emory, Dover Publications (New York, 1951) Laplace, who believed in causal determinism, says that "An intellect which at a certain moment would know all the forces that set nature in motion, and all positions of all items of which nature is composed, if this intellect were also vast enough to submit these data to analysis, it would embrace in a single formula the movements of the greatest bodies of the universe and those of the tiniest atom; for such an intellect nothing would be uncertain, and the future just like the past would be present before its eyes." (p. 4) This intellect is frequently referred to as Laplace's Superman or Demon.

things that are in immediate closeness. Even in the cases when we cannot make any calculations, we still have to approach the issue in such a way as if we were obliged to give an account to the strongest geometrician. See in English, CW 1, *Nature's Open Secret.*

Page 14, "Goethe's goal when he formulated his idea of the original plant"
Goethe's comments on the original plant are spread throughout his entire work. See especially "Metamorphosis of the plant" in J. W. Goethe: *Naturwissenschaftliche Schriften* [Treatise on natural science], (see note 3 to p. 3), Vol. 1, GA 1a, p. 17. On the topic of the original animal, Goethe wrote a poem, which was published only in 1820 in the first number of the *Morphologische Hefte* [Studies on morphology], included later in the *Gedichtensammlung* [collection of poems] under the title "Metamorphosis of the animal," (ibid., p. 344ff., see also p. 12ff., 239ff, and 331ff.) See in English, CW 1, *Nature's Open Secret.* Compare further among others his two essays "Goethes Naturanschauung gemäß den neuesten Veröffentlichungen des Goethe-Archives" [Goethe's view of nature according to the most recent publications of the Goethe-Archive], (1894), and "On what our views have gained through the publications of Goethe's works on natural science by the Goethe-Archive," (1891, in *Methodische Grundlagen der Anthroposophie* [Basic methods of anthroposophy...], GA 30, p. 69ff and 265ff.

Page 14, "I demonstrated already in the 1880s"
See Rudolf Steiner: *Nature's Open Secret,* CW 1, Chapter 4: "The Nature and Significance of Goethe's Writings on Organic Morphology," and Chapter 5: "Concluding Remarks on Goethe's Morphology," as well as *Goethe's Theory of Knowledge* (CW 2), Chapter E: "Knowing Nature."

Page 16, "Eugen Kolisko"
(1893-1939), 1920-1934 school doctor and teacher in the first Waldorf school, Stuttgart. Kolisko, who had agreed to give a lecture on the topic "the organization of the human and the animal in their biological opposition" on that day, was not able to come to the College Course in Berlin because of illness. Dr. Steiner gave this lecture in place of Dr. Kolisko.

Page 16, "one of Goethe's first achievements in the area of science"
In 1784 Goethe succeeded in finding proof that humans also have an intermaxillary bone. He published his study *Dem Menschen wie den Tieren ist ein Zwischenkieferknochen in der obern Kinnlade zuzuschreiben* [Humans as well as animals have an intermaxillary bone in their upper jaw], Jena, 1786. See J. W. Goethe: *Naturwissenschaftliche Schriften* [Treatise on natural science], (See note 3 to p. 3), Vol. 1, GA 1a, p. 277. See also Rudolf Steiner's "Die Entstehung von Goethe's Gedanken über die Bildung der Tiere" [The origin of Goethe's thinking on animal morphology], ibid. p. XXXIV; resp. in *Einleitungen zu Goethe's naturwissenschaftlichen Schriften* [Introductions to Goethe's scientific writings], GA 1, p. 40. See in English, CW 1, *Nature's Open Secret.*

Page 17, "Goethe did assume a transformation"
In addition, see Rudolf Steiner: "Die Entstehung von Goethes Gedanken über die Bildung der Tiere" [The origin of Goethe's thinking on animal morphology]. See note above.

Page 18, "As I have been telling some of you for years"
See Rudolf Steiner's remarks on the theory of senses in the following volumes:

Riddles of the Soul: The Case for Anthroposophy. "Anthropology and Anthroposophy, Max Dessoir on Anthroposophy, Franz Brentano (Obituary). Expansions as an Outline," (1917), (CW 21)

Anthroposophy. A Fragment, 1910, (CW 45)

A Psychology of Body, Soul, & Spirit: Anthroposophy – Psychosophy – Pneumatosophy, 1909-1911, (CW 115)

Toward Imagination, 1916, (CW 169)

The Riddle of the Human Being, 1916, (CW 170)

Die Wissenschaft vom Werden des Menschen [The science of the development of the human being], 1918, (GA 183)

What Is Necessary in These Urgent Times, 1920, (CW 196)

Spiritual Science as a Foundation for Social Forms, 1920, (CW 199)

Menschenwerden, Weltenseele und Weltengeist – Zweiter Teil. Der Mensch als geistiges Wesen im historischen Werdegang. [Human development, world-soul and world-spirit – Part II. The human as a spiritual being in historical development], 1921, (GA 206)

The Foundations of Human Experience (also translated as *The Study of Man*), 1919, (CW 293)

See further, No. 14 of the *Nachrichten der Rudolf Steiner-Nachlassverwaltung* [News of the Rudolf Steiner Heritage Administration]. Dornach, Micheli 1965 (H. Knobel), and No. 34 of the *Beiträge zur Rudolf Steiners Gesamtausgabe* [Contributions to Rudolf Steiner's complete works]. Dornach, summer 1971. (Rudolf Steiner's notebook entry and essay by H. Knobel).

Page 20, "Ernst Haeckel"
(1834-1919), zoologist. See also his works *Anthropogenie oder Entwicklungsgeschichte des Menschen Keimes* (Anthropogenesis or history of the development of the human embryo), Two parts. Leipzig, 1874, and *Natürliche Schöpfungsgeschichte. Gemeinverständliche wossenschaftliche Vorträge über die Entwicklungslehre* (The history of natural creation. Scientific lectures on evolutionary theory for the common reader). Two parts, Berlin, 1868.

Page 21, "Once, years ago ... at a lecture in Munich"
It is not clear which lecture Steiner refers to here. Compare regarding this topic to, among others, the lectures from November 13, 1907, in *Myths and Legends. Occult Signs and Symbols* (CW 101), and from November 10 and 17 in *Antwort*

der Geisteswissenschaft auf die grosse Frage des Daseins [The response of spiritual science to the great questions of existence] (GA 60).

Page 23, "In the previous lecture I just gave"
See the lecture "Anthroposophy and Natural Science" from the same day.

Page 24, "[external experience]"
The following comments were recorded only sporadically by the short-hand typists. The text added by the German publisher in square brackets, is based mainly on the following lectures given by Rudolf Steiner: March 16, 1921, in GA 324, not translated; September 1 and October 3, 1920, in *The Boundaries of Natural Science* (CW 322).

Page 25, "this is how we come to a polarity within the human being"
In the original there is text added by the transcriber in square brackets—[as opposed to the animal]. This text is unnecessary and only confuses the reader. Steiner explains here the polarity within the human being and not the polarity between humans and animals.

Page 26, "in our institutes in Stuttgart"
To the joint stock company for the promotion of economic and spiritual values belonged also a therapeutic clinic with its laboratories for pharmacological research and production of healing remedies, as well as a scientific research institute for the study of physics, chemistry, technology, and biology.

Page 27, "we should first form in our imagination"
See among others, the two articles "Wie erlangt man Erkenntnisse der höheren Welten?" 1904-05, GA 10 and " Stufen der höheren Erkenntnis," 1905-08, GA 12. See in English, CW 10, *How to Know Higher Worlds* and CW 12, *Stages of Higher Knowledge.*

Page 29, "Fichte, Shelling, and Hegel"
Johann Gottlieb Fichte (1762-1814), philosophy professor in Jena, Erlangen, Königsberg, and Berlin. First president of the University of Berlin.

Friedrich Wilhelm Joseph Schelling (1775-1854), later von Schelling, was a German philosopher. Standard histories of philosophy place him at the midpoint in the development of German idealism, situating him between Fichte, his mentor prior to 1800, and Hegel, his former university roommate and erstwhile friend.

Georg Wilhelm Friedrich Hegel (1770-1831), philosophy professor in Jena, editor-in-chief of the Bamberg Newspaper, later a teacher in Nürnberg, then Heidelberg, and from 1818 in Berlin. Regarding the present lecture see particularly his *Wissenschaft der Logik* [The Science of Logic], 2 Parts, 3 volumes, 1812-1816, *Encyklopädie der philosophischen Wissenschaften im Grundrisse* [Encyclopedia of philosophical sciences in outline], 3 parts, 3 volumes, 1817,

Second edition Berlin 1843-1847 (the second part was published under the title: *Lectures on natural philosophy from the encyclopedia.*)

With regard to Fichte, Schelling, and Hegel, see also Rudolf Steiner's work *The Riddles of the Human Being*, 1916, (CW 20).

Page 29, "concerning 'force and matter' "
Steiner uses the term *force and matter* in reference to the theories of one of the most prominent representatives of German scientific materialism, Ludwig Büchner (1824-1899). See his work *Force and Matter. Empirish naturphilosophische Studien in allgemeinverständliche Darstellung.* [Empirico-philosophical studies intelligently rendered], 2nd edition, Frankfurt 1856. Also physicists such as Hermann von Helmholtz (1821-1894) and Julius Robert Meyer (1814-1878).

Page 30, "Liebmann, Volkelt"
Otto Liebmann (1840-1912), philosopher. Steiner refers here to Liebmann's work *Kant and the Epigones* (1865).

Johannes Volkelt (1848-1930), philosophy professor.

Page 31, "Herbert Spencer, Hegel, and Vladimir Soloviov"
Herbert Spencer (1820-1903), English philosopher and sociologist. Works (selected): *Education, intellectual, moral, physical,* 1861; *Principles of Biology,* 1864; *Sociology,* 1877.

Vladimir Sergeievich Soloviov (1853-1900), Russian philosopher, poet, and religious thinker. Studied natural science and philosophy. Works (selected): *Die geistige Grundlage des Lebens* (The spiritual basis of life), 1882-84, in German 1957; *Die Rechtfertigung des Guten* (Justification of the Good), 1897, in German 1916; *Russland und die universale Kirche* (Russia and the universal church), 1889, in German 1954; and *Der Sinn der Liebe* [The meaning of love], 1896, in German 1930. See in English, *The Meaning of Love*, Hudson, NY: Lindisfarne Books, 1985.

Page 31, "Bacon and Locke, through Mill, to Spencer"
Francis Bacon (Bacon of Verulam; 1561-1626), English statesman, advocate, philosopher, medical doctor, theologian.

John Locke (1632 -1704), widely known as the Father of Classical Liberalism, was an English philosopher and physician regarded as one of the most influential of Enlightenment thinkers. Considered one of the first of the British empiricists, following the tradition of Francis Bacon, he is equally important to social contract theory. His work had a great impact on the development of epistemology and political philosophy. His writings influenced Voltaire and Rousseau, many Scottish Enlightenment thinkers, as well as the American revolutionaries.

John Stuart Mill (1806-1873), English philosopher and national economist.

Herbert Spencer (1820-1903) was a renowned English philosopher and sociologist known for applying evolutionary theory to the study of politics and ethics. He coined the term "survival of the fittest" before it was used by Charles Darwin.

Page 32, "We can see, for example, that Hegel could not stand Newton"
See "Lectures on natural philosophy as encyclopedia of philosophical sciences in outline," 2nd edition, Berlin, 1847, 2nd Part, p. 317ff. (Par. 320) and p. 97ff. (Par. 270) and *Dissertatio Philosophica de Orbitis Planetarum.* [Philosophical deliberations on the planetary orbits], translated and with an introduction and comments by Wolfgang Neuser, Weinheim, 1986.

Isaac Newton (1642-1727). English physicist, astronomer, and mathematician. Regarding his mechanistic view of the cosmos see *Philosophiae naturalis principia mathematica* [Mathematical principles of natural philosophy], 1687; Regarding his theory of color see *Optics*, 1704.

Page 32, "Kepler's laws of planetary motion"
Johannes Kepler (1571-1630), German astronomer, mathematician, and physicist. To calculate his three laws of planetary motion Kepler was able to use the observations of his predecessor at the Court of Prague, Tycho de Brahe. However, generally the point of departure for finding the three laws was the planetary system of Copernicus. Kepler was the first one to try to interpret the dynamics of the planetary orbits, and he located the force of gravity in the sun.

Page 32-33, "He analyzed laws"
Hegel: *Encyclopedia....*, 2nd Part, p. 97ff (Par. 270).

Page 33, "What Goethe said to Schiller"
See last comment to the note for p. 6.

Page 34, "He felt if we want to have any real concept of *logos*..."
See Hegel: *Science of Logic.* 2nd edition Berlin, 1841, 1st Part, 1st Volume, Introduction, p. 33: "Thus, logic is to be understood as the system of pure reason, as the kingdom of pure thought. *This kingdom is the truth, as it appears in itself, without a shell.* Hence, we could say that this content is the presentation of God, *as he is in his eternal being, before the Creation of nature and of his finite Spirit.*"

Page 34, "Hegel's treatise 'Logic', one of the three parts of his philosophy"
The 1st Part of Hegel's *Encyclopedia...* is entitled "Logic."

Page 34, "*Logos* must be 'God before the creation of the world'"
See the comment above.

Page 34, "He began with *being*..."
See Hegel's *Science of Logic* (see the comment above). Compare Rudolf Steiner's lecture in Berlin, November 13, 1908, "Producing concepts and Hegel's

theory of categories" in *Die Beantwortung von Welt und Lebensfragen durch Anthroposophie* [Answering existential questions about the world and life with the help of anthroposophy], (GA 108).

Page 36, "Hume"
David Hume (1711-1776), English philosopher and historian.

Page 36, "Nature is Spirit in its otherness"
See Hegel: *Encyclopedia…* (See comment for *Hegel,* note to p. 29), 2nd Part, par. 247, p. 23: "Nature has presented itself as the idea in the form of *otherness.*"

Page 36, "Spirit is the concept when it has returned to itself."
Ibid., 3rd Part, 3rd volume, par. 381, p.14f.: We should describe the distinct definitiveness of the concept of spirit as *ideality* or the annulment of the otherness of the idea, an annulment resulting from the returning of the idea to itself, from its self-inwardness" and p. 20: "Seen in such terms, the finite spirit should be understood as *totality,* as a real idea—an idea in itself, an idea that, in the very contradiction with itself, returns to itself." *

Page 36, "before the Council of Nicaea"
Steiner means here the First Council in 325 A.D. at which the creed (identity of the substance of the Father and the Son, not a similarity of substance) of Athanasius was accepted as the orthodox faith. About the times between the first centuries of Christianity and this council compare the lecture "Anthroposophy and World Orientation. East-West in history," Vienna 3.6.1922 in *Western and Eastern world oppositions…,* GA 83, especially p. 102f. See in English, CW 83, *The Tension between East and West.*

Page 37, "as Darwin does with his theory"
Charles Darwin (1809-1882), English natural scientist, medical doctor, geologist, and botanist.

Page 37, "Oswald Külpe"
(1862-1915), philosopher and psychologist.

Page 38, "Newton tried to explain the Apocalypse"
See Isaac Newton: *Observations upon the prophecies of Daniel and the Apocalypse of St. John,* 2 parts, London, 1733.

Page 39, "Haeckel"
Ernst Haeckel: See comment to p. 20.

---

* With regard to Hegel, the German word *Geist* is frequently translated into English with two words: mind (spirit). In this context, however, it was clearly understood only in the sense of spirit. Also, the German word *Begriff* is frequently rendered with notion. In this context, however, the issue at stake is clearly the concept.

Page 39, "the atomic theory, which I do not reject"
See in regard to this statement, notebook No. 63 of the *Contributions to Rudolf Steiner's Complete Works*, Dornach, Michaeli, 1978, dedicated entirely to the topic "Rudolf Steiner on atomism."

Page 40, "the exercises I mention in my studies"
Rudolf Steiner: *An Outline of Esoteric Science* (1910) CW 13, and *How to Know Higher Worlds* (1904/05) CW 10.

Page 43, "Emil Molt"
Emil Molt (1876-1936), councilor of commerce, industrialist, director of the Waldorf-Astoria cigarette factory in Stuttgart, and co-founder of The Coming Day, Ltd., Stuttgart. He organized educational courses for workers employed in the factory. His wish to have a school for children based on Rudolf Steiner's ideas was the incentive for the establishment in Stuttgart of the first Waldorf school. See Emil Molt: *An Outline of My Life Story*, "The Waldorf School."

Page 43, "'The Education of the Child in the Light of Spiritual Science'"
This essay by Rudolf Steiner was published for the first time in 1907 in the journal *Lucifer-Gnosis*, and after 1907 as an independent publication in many editions. Printed in the volume "Lucifer-Gnosis. Fundamental essays on anthroposophy and reports from the journals *Lucifer* and *Lucifer-Gnosis*, 1903-1908," GA 34. Included in *The Education of the Child*. Tr. George and Mary Adams. Great Barrington, MA: Anthroposophic Press/SteinerBooks 1996.

Page 46, *"The Philosophy of Freedom"*
Rudolf Steiner: *Der Philosophie der Freiheit* (1894), GA 4. See in English: *Intuitive Thinking as a Spiritual Path*. Tr. Michael Lipson. Great Barrington, MA: SteinerBooks 1995; *The Philosophy of Spiritual Activity: A Philosophy of Freedom*. Tr. Rita Stebbing. London: Rudolf Steiner Press 1992; *The Philosophy of Freedom. The Basis for a Modern World Conception*. Tr. Michael Wilson. London: Rudolf Steiner Press 1964; *The Philosophy of Spiritual Activity*. Tr. William Lindeman. Hudson, NY: Anthroposophic Press 1986, CW 4.

Page 51, "youth movements today"
A protest movement of the German youth around 1900, which turned against traditional bourgeois conceptions in search of its own natural forms of life (*Wandervogel*, etc.).

Page 52, "complexity of the upbringing"
Erziehung in German. This word has no precise equivalent in English. It means both education and upbringing. Steiner emphasizes precisely this double meaning.

Page 52, "primary school"
Volksschule: eighteenth-century system of state-supported primary schools established in Prussia (in 1717) and the Habsburg Empire (in 1840).

Page 56, *"Core Points of the Social Question"*
Rudolf Steiner: *Kernpunkte der sozialen Frage* (1919) [Core points of the social question in the existential necessities of our time and of the future], CW 23. Published in English as *Towards Social Renewal: Rethinking the Basis of Society.*

Page 58, "The Treaty of Versailles"
This peace agreement between the Allies and the Third Reich was signed on June 28, 1919, and came into force on January 10, 1920.

Page 58, "economic theorists who endlessly discussed..."
See e.g., the journal *Tribüne. Halbmonatssachrift für soziale Verständigung.* [Tribune. Fortnightly journal for social understanding], Tübingen, which dedicated its first number (June or July 1919) to the discussions about Rudolf Steiner's idea of the threefold formation of society. The respective essays are printed in the *"Contributions to Rudolf Steiner's Complete Works,"* No. 106, Dornach, Easter 1991.

Page 59, "we came to the terrible currency disaster"
After World War I, the German currency entirely lost its value because of constantly increasing inflation. (By Novemebr 1923 the American dollar was worth 4,210,500,000,000 German marks. Judith Coffin, *Western Civilizations, Their History and Culture.* New York: Norton & Company, 2011).

Page 59, "Appeal to the German People and Culture"
"Aufruf an das Deutsche Volk und die Kulturwelt." Written by Rudolf Steiner and signed by a number of famous personalities of public life, was printed as a leaflet and widely distributed in March 1919. Published in CW 24, *The Renewal of the Social Organism*; and as an appendix in *Towards Social Renewal* (see note to p. 56).

Page 60, "which I expressed at the end of that book and at the end of many lectures"
See the series of lectures *Neugestaltung des sozialen Organismus* [New forms of the social organism], 1919, GA 330.

Page 60, "an article ... Lloyd George's"
Unknown.
David Lloyd George (1863-1942). English Prime Minister (1916-1922).

Page 60, "the lecture I gave recently at the philharmonic hall"
A reference to the public lecture "Anthroposophy in Its Scientific Character," which Rudolf Steiner gave in the wide framework of the College Course on March 7, 1922. (Not yet published.)

Page 60, "Originally, economic life developed"
See here the more detailed explanations in the lectures from August 27, 28, and 29, 1922, in *The Spiritual Ground of Education*, CW 305.

Page 62, "Adam Smith's ideas ... up to Karl Marx"
Karl Marx (1818-1883), founder of scientific socialism and of historical materialism. Main works: *Critique of Political Economy* (1859), *Capital. Critique of political economy.* (1867/94).

Adam Smith (1723-1790), English national economist and philosopher. Main work: *An Inquiry into the Nature and Causes of the Wealth of Nations*, 4 volumes, 1776, German translation by Max Stirner: *Untersuchungen über die Natur und die Ursache des Wohlstandes der Nationen*, 1846/47.

Page 62, "Ricardo ... and John Stuart Mill"
David Ricardo (1772-1823), English national economist, student of Adam Smith, teacher of Karl Marx.

John Stuart Mill: See note to p. 31.

Page 63, "Woodrow Wilson came up with his so-called 'Fourteen Points'"
Woodrow Wilson (1856-1924), American President (1913-1921). In 1918 he presented his world peace program to Congress. The program is known as "The Fourteen Points." It did not become part of the Versailles peace agreement of 1919. See *Woodrow Wilson's Speeches*, English and German, Der Freie Verlag Berlin: Bern, 1919.

Page 64, "In 1917, there were people in Central Europe..."
Already in 1917, after several conversations with Count Otto Lerchenfeld and Count Ludwig Polzer-Hoditz, Rudolf Steiner wrote two memoranda, in which he expressed his opinion about a few fundamental political questions with respect to the current situation.

The two individuals mentioned above brought these memoranda to the attention of influential politicians, including the German Secretary of State Kühlmann and Arthur Polzer-Hoditz, the Head of Kaiser Karl of Austria's cabinet (Kaiser Karl I of Austria, known also as Charles IV of Hungary [1887-1922], reigned 1916-1918).

The two memoranda were published first in Roman Boos' *Rudolf Steiner während des Weltkrieges* [Rudolf Steiner during the World War], Dornach, 1933. See also *Aufsätze über die Dreigliederung des sozialen Organismus*, GA 24. See in English, CW 24, *The Renewal of the Social Organism*. "Essays on the threefold formation of the social organism and the current situation 1915-1921."

Page 64, " ... the social question was solved several times"
Compare his *Autobiography*, CW 28, Chapter VIII.

Page 65, "the old class system"
The formulations *Nährstand* (working-class), *Wehrstand* (soldier-class), and *Lehrstand* (teaching-class) belong to Erasmus Alberus (1500-1553; German humanist, reformer, and poet), and also Luther; they summarize what Plato says

about social classes in the *Politeia:* see the "Phoenician mythos" in which, when they were born, God has mixed gold in the substance of the rulers (the sages), silver in the substance of their helpers (the watchmen), and iron ore in the substance of the craftsmen (*Politaeia* Book III, 414f). See also Vincenz Knauer: *Die Hauptprobleme der Philosophie* [Main problems of philosophy], Vienna and Leipzig, 1892. This book was found in Rudolf Steiner's library. There, in the lectures on Plato (p. 124) it says: "In the same way as the soul is divided between the reasonable, the irascible, and the concupiscible, the state is divided into three classes for which we can use the well-known definitions teacher-class, worker-class, and soldier-class."

Page 67, "the natural organism works precisely toward unity . . ."
Compare Rudolf Steiner: *Riddles of the Soul* (1917), CW 21, Chapter: "Physical and spiritual dependences of the human being." In this chapter, Steiner describes the threefold formation of the soul consisting of thinking, feeling, and willing.

Regarding concepts such as labor and capital, see also Rudolf Steiner's deliberations in the series "Course on national economy. The tasks of a new science of economics," Volume I. Dornach, 1922, CW 340, key words index. See, in English, *Rethinking Economics: Lectures and Seminars on World Economics*, CW 340-341, SteinerBooks 2013.

Page 67, "Ernst Müller"
(1880-1954), German anthroposophist.

Page 70, "a note in a journal"
The following note appeared in the weekly *Die Christliche Welt* [The Christian World], Marburg, year 36, No. 2, March 2, 1922, p. 157f. "[. . .] The event on Friday represents an obvious challenge by Steiner and his followers of modern theologians. By saying this I do not imply an accusation. The science of theology, like any other science, is not sacrosanct, and our readers know well how glad we always are to subject it (and ourselves) to critique. Rittelmeyer knows this best of all [. . .]. Thus, the round with Steiner's group is also welcome. Now, the glove has to be picked up. So far, we had to satisfy ourselves only with a pro or con [. . .] These men are right: we cannot keep neutrality forever, and they want to offer a battle which they will either win or lose. Personally, I could only wish that this session will bring about a definitive result. Even if it were only a conclusion whether we should all study Steiner seriously or not [. . .] We are more interested in this discussion than any other group in contemporary theology because both Geyer and Rittelmeyer belong to our most recognized and appreciated friends [. . .]" (D. Rade)

Heinrich Frick, reporter of the *Christliche Welt* (Christian World), wrote about this event in No. 13 on March 30, 1922, p. 227: "Right away, I have personally explained to Dr. Rittelmeyer and also publicly, in the beginning of my comments (Dr. R. kindly asked me to speak first to offer my explanation) that the phrase 'challenge' used in the C[hristliche] W[elt] was not meant to be directed to a particular person as an accusation, but (since none of us knew who has actually formulated the topic) but that the formulation itself (purely objectively in its wording) must be perceived as a challenge. I reminded everybody of the fact that if we read the program in an unbiased way we cannot fail to notice that this was the only day when a subject of the magnitude of theology was not only put forward but also assessed. This is what the program says about theology: 'The downfall of religion in contemporary theology [...] and then it repeats the key word three times 'downfall – downfall – downfall' in some kind of an ...Ism! It is only human to take this as a challenge, and I asked the listeners to reject the idea that in the CW [Christian World] there exists some animosity against anthroposophy.

To this, Dr. Rittelmeyer explained personally to me, and in public, that he, who has formulated the topic himself, never thought of any challenge. Rather he wanted to pose a serious question and emphasize it energetically in order to imprint it on the conscience of theologians."

Page 70, "the day of the theologians"
Regarding the day of the theologians in the College Course in Berlin see the reports by Ernst Uehli and Eberhard Kurras in the Appendix, pp. 119 and 124.

Page 71, "As a consequence, experimental psychology"
Refers to a particular direction in psychology, represented most of all by scholars such as Wundt, Stumpf, Lange, James, Ziehen, Külpe, Ebbinghaus, G. E. Müller, Stern, and Neumann.

Page 72, "I am still as much a follower of Haeckel"
See note to page 20.

Page 72, "'nothing is in the mind that is not first in the senses'"
This is a reference to Thomas Hobbes' statement of empiricism, "Nothing is in the mind that is not first in the senses"; and Leibniz's paraphrase of John Locke's idea that the mind furnishes itself with ideas.

Nihil est in intellectu, quod non fuerit in sensu. We find this formulation of the statement first in Thomas Aquinas (*Quaestiones de veritate* II, s. Coloniae, 1475), but it was formulated in a similar way already by Cicero (*De finibus* I, 19). However, it corresponds with the explanations in Aristotle's study *De anima.* See particularly Book 3, chapter 8: "Since it seems however, that there is nothing that exists separately, outside the entities perceived by senses, we must assume that forms perceived through the senses contain also what becomes thought; what is said by means of abstraction; the very constitutions and all conditions of the things we sense. Thus, we can neither learn nor understand anything if we do not have sense perception (translated by J.W.A.).

Page 72, "Leibniz's addition to that statement"
Nihil est in intellectu quod non fuerit in sensu, nisi ipse intellectus. See Gottfried Wilhelm Leibniz (1646-1716): *Neue Abhandlungen über den menschlichen Verstand* (New treatise on the human mind), Book II, chapter I (Theophilus): Some might

want to object to me, pointing out the axiom, recognized by the philosophers, that *there is nothing in the soul that does not originate in the senses.* However, we must exclude the soul itself and its affections from this axiom. *Nihil est in intellectu quod non fuerit in sensu, excipe: nisis intellectus ipse.* The soul includes in itself the existence, the substance, the One, the same, the cause, the perception, the wise thinking, and many more concepts, which the senses do not convey (translated by J. W. A.). See on this topic also Rudolf Steiner's lecture from September 17, 1915, published in *Der Wert des Denkens für eine den Menschen befriedigende Erkenntnis. Das Verhältnis der Geisteswissenschaft zu Naturwissenschaft* [The value of thinking for the knowledge that would satisfy the human being. The relationship between spiritual science and natural science], GA 164.

Page 74, "one of the highly respected persons present here today"
Friedrich Rittelmeyer (1872-1938) was a Protestant clergyman. From 1902 to 1916 he became a well-known preacher in Nürnberg, and then in the Neue Kirche (New Church) in Berlin. He was also the author of theological treatises. Since 1911, he had been in contact with Rudolf Steiner (*My existential meeting with Rudolf Steiner*, Stuttgart, 1928); and in 1921 he published a volume of selected works entitled *From Rudolf Steiner's oeuvre.* He chaired the College Course in Berlin and was the first minister (*Erzoberlenker*) of The Christian Community, a movement for religious renewal founded with Steiner's help in Dornach in 1922 by a group of theologians and pastors led by Rittelmeyer. From 1923 he was also a member of the board of the German Section of the Anthroposophical Society. There is a short biography of Friedrich Rittelmeyer in Rudolf Gädeke's publication *Die Gründer der Christengemeinschaft* [Founders of The Christian Community], Dornach, 1992. He expressed himself to the same effect also in his essay "Johannes Müller and Rudolf Steiner" in the journal *Die Christliche Welt*, No. 22/23, 30 from May 1918. There, Rittelmeyer replied to Müller's accusation that "Rudolf Steiner makes a sensation out of the occult world to satisfy the curiosity and lasciviousness of people's superstitious instincts" in the following way (p. 215, footnote): "Neither the topics nor the lectures contained anything even remotely related to speculation. Steiner expects, especially from the public lectures audience, certain spiritual effort, which scares all listeners who are not very serious; but he does not acknowledge people's curiosity and the desire for sensation [...]."

Page 76, "Father-experience"
Compare in this relation for example the lectures from February 20 and March 13, 1917, in CW 175, *Building Stones for an Understanding of the Mystery of Golgotha* and "How do I find Christ?" from October 16, 1918, in CW 182, *Death as Metamorphosis of Life.*

Page 77, "What I said yesterday about forming a judgment"
This is a reference to the evening public lecture "Anthroposophy as a Content of Life," given on March 9, 1922, on the occasion of the College Course.

Page 77, "discourses of Vladimir Soloviov"
See also his *Lectures on Divine Humanity*. Tr. Peter Zouboff. Revised and edited by Boris Jakim. Great Barrington, MA: Lindisfarne Books 1995.

Page 78, "If we look at everything that people searched for in the mysteries"
Steiner refers here to the ancient mystery cults associated usually with Dionysus, Persephone, and Demeter. We have very limited knowledge of the mystery cults. However, the information we have about the Eleusinian mysteries, adopted by the Athenians around 600 B.C.E., shows that in contrast to the other more rational forms of worship, the mysteries aimed at a mystical experience of the gods.

Page 79, "I am always with you until the end of time"
Matthew, 28:20.

Page 80, "the point Friedrich Nietzsche's friend Overbeck"
Friedrich Nietzsche (1844-1900), philosopher.

Franz Overbeck (1837-1905), professor of theology in Basel, friend of Friedrich Nietzsche. *Über die Christlichkeit unserer heutigen Theologie* [The Christian substance of our contemporary theology], 1873.

Page 80, "Scotus Eriugena"
Johannes Scotus Eriugena (c.815-c.877), Irish theologian and Neoplatonist philosopher, predecessor of scholastic philosophy.

Perhaps Steiner refers to the fact that to Eriugena reason was primary to religion, which he saw as a secondary phenomenon, derived from philosophy.

Page 80, "Thomistic theology"
Thomas Aquinas (1225-1274), Christian Church teacher, philosopher, scholastic. Canonized in 1323.

Page 81, "Many years ago I gave a discourse … in a southern German city"
In Colmar, in 1905. There are no notes of this lecture available. Rudolf Steiner spoke in many places on the topic "Wisdom and the Bible." The lectures in Berlin from November 12 and 14, 1908, were published in *Wo und wie findet man den Geist?* [Where and how can we find the spirit?], GA 57, separate edition Dornach, 1993.

Page 82, "our teaching practice in the Waldorf School"
On this topic, see the lecture "Anthroposophy and Education" starting on p. 42 in this volume.

Page 84, "In a brief course"
Rudolf Steiner: *Geisteswissenschaftliche Sprachbetrachtungen. Eine Anregung für Erzieher* (6 lectures, Stuttgart, 1919/1920. See GA 299. See in English, CW 299, *The Genius of Language*.

Page 85, "Around Christmas, I gave a series of lectures"
GA 303, 16 lectures and 3 sessions of answering questions, Dornach, 1921/22. See in English, CW 303, *Soul Economy. Body, Soul, and Spirit in Waldorf Education.*

Page 85, "In one of those lectures"
Ibid., lecture from January 7, 1922: "Religious and Moral Education."

Page 85, "Dr. Rittelmeyer ... gave a very apt response to that"
Regarding Friedrich Rittelmeyer, see the note to p. 74. Perhaps, in this discussion Rittelmeyer quoted the famous aphorism by Georg Christoph Lichtenberg: "When a book and a head hit each other and you hear a hollow sound, do you think that it is always the book that is hollow?"

Page 86, "Pflicht"
The German word for duty, obligation.

Page 86, "pflegen"
To care for, to look after.

Page 89, "the major transformation ... in the fifteenth century"
See among others the Berlin lectures from: January 16, 1911, in *Antworten der Geisteswissenschaft auf die grosse Frage des Dasein* [The answers of spiritual science to the major questions of existence], GA 60; February 15, 1912, in *Menschengeschichte im Lichte der Geistesforschung* [The history of humanity in light of spiritual studies], GA 61; and February 13, 1913, in *Ergebnisse der Gesteswissenschaft*, GA 62. See in English, CW 62, *Spiritual Research: Methods and Results.*

Page 93, "forms that emerged with New High German"
According to Wilchelm Scherer's (1841-1886) traditional division of the different stages in the development of the German language, *Neuhochdeutsch*, known in the English language sources as NHG (New High German) was established in the mid 1600s. The first two stages were *Mittelhochdeutsch* (Middle High-German) and *Frühneuhochdeutsch* (Early New-High-German). The term *high* refers to the higher geographic areas of the Southern uplands and the Alps where the dialects of German (Saxony, Bavaria, Switzerland, and Austria) developed, in contrast to *Niederdeutsch* (Low German), which refers to the dialects of the lowlands and the flat seacoast of modern North Germany.

Page 94, "Wilhelm Wundt"
Wilhelm Wundt (1832-1920), medical doctor, philosopher, psychologist, and professor at Heidelberg, Zurich, and Leipzig. He was one of the founding figures in modern psychology. See his *Social Psychology. A study of the laws of development of language, myth, and custom*, Volume 1: *Language*. Part 1, Leipzig,

1900, chapter 9: " The origin of language": I. "General views" and II. "Critical overview of the main four theories," pp. 584-603.

Page 94, "yesterday as well"
See the lecture "Anthropsophy and Theology" in this volume.

Page 94, "Dr. Geyer"
Christian Geyer (1862-1929), Evangelical theologian, chief minister in the Sebaldus Church in Nürnberg. The topic of Geyer's lecture was "The Downfall of Christianity into Historicism." His comments are not known.

Page 96, "eurythmy presentation in the Deutsches Theater"
On Sunday, March 12, at 11:00 o'clock, there was a eurythmy performance. There are no notes available of Rudolf Steiner's introductory remarks.

The Deutsches Theater (German Theater) in Berlin is one of the most famous German theaters. It was built in 1850 as Friedrich-Wilhelm-Städtisches Theater and transformed into the Deutsches Theater by Adolf L'Aronge in 1883. However, its reputation as one of the most significant theaters in the world was established after the legendary theater director Max Reinhardt took over the directorship in 1904 and founded a theater school in 1905.

Page 96, "Vocal Academy"
The *Sing Akademie zu Berlin* is a music (originally choral) society founded in Berlin in 1791.

Page 97, "in the rooms of the University of Berlin"
Steiner must have been referring here to the Humboldt Universität zu Berlin (Humbolt University of Berlin) founded in 1810 as Berliner University (University of Berlin).

Page 99, "the idea that we should practice Goetheanism"
Steiner's neologism based on the word Goethe.

Page 99, "Already in the beginning of the nineteenth"
It is possible that this is an error of the stenographer due to mishearing or mis-rendering.

Page 100, "Emil Leinhas"
Emil Leinhas (1878-1967), co-founder and later director general of The Coming Day, Ltd, Stuttgart. From February 1923, a member of the board of the Anthroposophical Society in Germany.

Page 101, "Licentiate Bock"
Litentiatus (Latin). Academic degree used in different ways according to the area of study, the country, and the particular university, which allows a person to teach.

Emil Bock (1895-1959), Licentiate theologiae. In the autumn of 1922 co-founder and minister (Oberlenker) of The Christian Community; from 1938 first minister of the same. For his biography, see *The founders of the Christian Community* by Rudolf Gädeke. Dornach, 1922, and Gunhild Kacer-Bock: *Emil Bock. Life and Work*. Stuttgart, 1993.

Page 101, "Dr. Rittelmeyer"
Dr. Friedrich Rittelmeyer: (see footnotes to pp. 74 and 85).

Page 101, "the downfall of theology or religion"
Here Rudolf Steiner renders the titles freely.

Page 102, "God's being is the unconditional, the absolute"
In an essay, "Anthroposophy and evangelical theology," published in the journal *Die Christliche Welt* [The Christian World], No. 7, from April 27, 1922, Heinrich Frick wrote: "The way anthroposophy was presented in most of the lectures during the course makes me feel that it is very intellectualistic. For example, what does 'higher worlds' mean? The comparative form and the word itself are borrowed from the perception of space. Indeed, a large part of our concepts originate in spatial relations. So we must use such concepts when we speak of the non-spatial too. However, there is a great danger in this, namely that we will not distinguish clearly enough between concept and what we mean by it. Concepts give things an additional nuance. If for a very long time we have used spatial concepts to express the non-spatial, we will come to a point when our way of thinking becomes spatial. The anthroposophic idea of the world, and particularly the anthroposophic concept of God, show precisely such a transformation of the way of thinking as if it is all about space. *Levels, path, higher and lower worlds:* those who speak of God in such a way, turn Him eventually into a final point that human motion should be leading to.

This, however, is intellectualism. For no human motion brings us closer to God. *The non-spatial can never be perceived in spatial images.* God can be defined only in paradoxes. The holy is always of such a kind that it objectifies itself in space and at the same time destroys its own successful objectification. We may come *higher* and higher through a thousand worlds, but this will not help us come even one step closer to God. *For he is not in a place to which we can come thanks to our own power*, but He is there, where He wants to reveal Himself. He becomes comprehensible in a revelation. Here, I am only repeating what others have said long ago, and what during the course especially Tillich [Paul Tillich, see below] described appropriately in an image. He was told that he is only in the antechamber, anthroposophy being the all-highest, to which he objected saying that before God, we are all in the antechamber. Because God does not reside in a temple built by human hands; rather, there is a temple where God breaks through reality as a paradox. Let it be called a forecourt, or anything else, it will still become a temple only through such a revelation of God. *God is there or He is not there, but there is no place where we are 'closer' or 'farther' away from Him in our human way.*"

Page 102, "a professor and a priest"

a professor: At the time Paul Tillich (1886-1965) was professor at the Department of Theology in Berlin, from 1924 professor for the science of religion and social philosophy in Leipzig, Dresden, and Frankfurt, among others. In 1933 Tillich emigrated to America where he became a leading Protestant theologian in the US. See here the report " Who has challenged whom?" by Heinrich Frick in the *Christliche Welt*, Year 36, No. 13, from March 1922, p. 225ff.

and a priest: Carl-Gunther Schweitzer (1889-1965). In 1921 Schweitzer founded the apologetic center for argumentation in the name of evangelical theology against different spiritual movements of the time.

Page 103, "'alas ... theology!'"

Goethe, *Faust*, Study lines 354ff. Philosophy and jurisprudence, medicine and even, alas, [alas, alas] theology, from end to end with labor keen..."

This is a citation of the opening words of *Faust* I—"Night."

Page 104, "Cardinal Neuman"

Steiner refers here to the fact that, on the occasion of his elevation to the status of cardinal, John Henry Newman (1801-1890) declared that most of his life was a struggle against the spirit of liberalism in religion.

John Henry Newman (1801-1890). English religious philosopher, originally Anglican clergyman. He converted to Catholicism in 1845 and became a cardinal in 1879. Regarding Newman, compare also Rudolf Steiner's lectures in Stuttgart, from June 15, 1921, in CW 342, *First Steps in Christian Religious Renewal I;* and in London, from April 24, 1922, "The Threefold Sun and the Risen Christ," in CW 211, *The Sun Mystery and the Mystery of Death and Resurrection.*

Page 105, " Licentiate Tillich"

Paul Tillich: See note to p. 102.

Page 105, "pontificate of Leo XIII"

Leo XIII: Pope from 1878-1903. He declared Thomas Aquinas as the first teacher of the Catholic Church

Page 106, "in my last few lectures before I left Dornach"

See the lectures from February 24 and 26, 1922, in CW 210, *Old and New Methods of Initiation.*

Page 106, "Theberat's lecture"

Hans Theberat (1891-1971), Doctor of Chemistry. From 1921-1924 he was working in the Research Institute of The Coming Day, Ltd. Later, following Steiner's advice, he became teacher at the Goethe School in Hamburg.

Page 106, "Dr. Kurt Grelling"
Kurt Grelling: There is no information available about Kurt Grelling, since there were no notes taken of the debates. There is no information about Grelling's appearance in front of the Congress in Stuttgart either.

Page 107, "in the course in Stuttgart"
The first general public congress, "Cultural Views in the Anthroposophic Movement," took place in Stuttgart from August 28 to September 7, 1921. Rudolf Steiner gave a series of lectures entitled "Anthroposophy, the sources of its knowledge and the fruits of its life, with an introduction of agnosticism as a destroyer of true humanity," See in English, CW 78, *Fruits of Anthroposophy.*

Page 107, "Göttingen"
Georg-August University Göttingen, founded in 1737 as a university of the Enlightenment.

Page 107, "the Congress in Vienna"
The Second International Congress of the "Anthroposophic Movement for the understanding of the oppositions between the Western and the Wastern world" took place between June 1-12, 1922, and was entitled *West and East.* See CW 83, *The Tension between East and West.*

Page 109, "Dr. Stein and Dr. Schwebsch"
The speakers mentioned here: Karl Schubert (1889-1949), Walter Johannes Stein (1891-1957), and Erich Schwebsch (1889-1953) were teachers at the first Waldorf school, founded in Stuttgart. See "The circle of teachers surrounding Rudolf Steiner in the first Waldorf School," Stuttgart, 1977. No notes of discourses of these individuals were written down.

Page 109, "short performance on Thursday and Sunday"
There is no information about these "two short eurythmy performances." See note to p. 96 about the performance in the Deutsches Theater.

Page 109, "Anthroposophic Congress in Stuttgart"
See note to p. 107.

Page 112, "Theodor Lauer ... Emil Bock"
The full title used for Theodor Lauer is *Studiosus iuris et rerum politicarum* (Latin), a student of jurisprudence and political science (or political economy). This abbreviation represents an informal descriptions used in academia, and not formal titles. In common usage, the first letter of the Latin word *iuris* [i] is replaced with the first letter of the corresponding German word *Jura* [j], (law or jurisprudence).

The full title used for Emil Bock is Licentiate theologiae (see the note to page 101).

Page 112, "Association for a Threefold Social Organism"

The ideal of a threefold social system was established by Rudolf Steiner between 1910 and 1920. According to Steiner, social life had to be decentralized and not governed or coordinated by a state. Instead, it was to be divided into three autonomous systems—spiritual life, legal life, and economic life—which were to hold each other in check by applying the principles of freedom, equality, and brotherhood, respectively.

RUDOLF STEINER'S COLLECTED WORKS

The German Edition of Rudolf Steiner's Collected Works (the *Gesamtausgabe* [GA] published by Rudolf Steiner Verlag, Dornach, Switzerland) presently runs to 354 titles, organized either by type of work (written or spoken), chronology, audience (public or other), or subject (education, art, etc.). For ease of comparison, the Collected Works in English [CW] follows the German organization. A complete listing of the CWs follows with *literal translations* of the German titles. Other than in the case of the books published in his lifetime, titles were rarely given by Rudolf Steiner himself, and were often provided by the editors of the German editions. The titles in English are not necessarily the same as the German; and, indeed, over the past seventy-five years have frequently been different, with the same book sometimes appearing under different titles.

For ease of identification and to avoid confusion, we suggest that readers looking for a title should do so by CW number. Because the work of creating the Collected Works of Rudolf Steiner is an ongoing process, with new titles being published every year, we have not indicated in this listing which books are presently available. To find out what titles in the Collected Works are currently in print, please check our website at www.steinerbooks.org, or write to: SteinerBooks; 610 Main Street, Great Barrington, MA 01230.

A. Written Works

I. Writings 1884–1925

CW 1	Goethe: Natural-Scientific Writings, Introduction, with Footnotes and Explanations in the text by Rudolf Steiner
CW 2	Outlines of an Epistemology of the Goethean World View, with Special Consideration of Schiller
CW 3	Truth and Science
CW 4	The Philosophy of Freedom
CW 4a	Documents to "The Philosophy of Freedom"
CW 5	Friedrich Nietzsche, A Fighter against His Own Time
CW 6	Goethe's Worldview
CW 6a	*[Now in CW 30]*
CW 7	Mysticism at the Dawn of Modern Spiritual Life and Its Relationship with Modern Worldviews
CW 8	Christianity as Mystical Fact and the Mysteries of Antiquity
CW 9	Theosophy: An Introduction into Supersensible World Knowledge and Human Purpose
CW 10	How Does One Attain Knowledge of Higher Worlds?
CW 11	From the Akasha-Chronicle
CW 12	Levels of Higher Knowledge
CW 13	Occult Science in Outline
CW 14	Four Mystery Dramas

CW 15	The Spiritual Guidance of the Individual and Humanity
CW 16	A Way to Human Self-Knowledge: Eight Meditations
CW 17	The Threshold of the Spiritual World. Aphoristic Comments
CW 18	The Riddles of Philosophy in Their History, Presented as an Outline
CW 19	*[Contained in CW 24]*
CW 20	The Riddles of the Human Being: Articulated and Unarticulated in the Thinking, Views and Opinions of a Series of German and Austrian Personalities
CW 21	The Riddles of the Soul
CW 22	Goethe's Spiritual Nature and Its Revelation in "Faust" and through the "Fairy Tale of the Snake and the Lily"
CW 23	The Central Points of the Social Question in the Necessities of Life in the Present and the Future
CW 24	Essays Concerning the Threefold Division of the Social Organism and the Period 1915-1921
CW 25	Cosmology, Religion and Philosophy
CW 26	Anthroposophical Leading Thoughts
CW 27	Fundamentals for Expansion of the Art of Healing according to Spiritual-Scientific Insights
CW 28	The Course of My Life

II. Collected Essays

CW 29	Collected Essays on Dramaturgy, 1889-1900
CW 30	Methodical Foundations of Anthroposophy: Collected Essays on Philosophy, Natural Science, Aesthetics and Psychology, 1884-1901
CW 31	Collected Essays on Culture and Current Events, 1887-1901
CW 32	Collected Essays on Literature, 1884-1902
CW 33	Biographies and Biographical Sketches, 1894-1905
CW 34	Lucifer-Gnosis: Foundational Essays on Anthroposophy and Reports from the Periodicals "Lucifer" and "Lucifer-Gnosis," 1903-1908
CW 35	Philosophy and Anthroposophy: Collected Essays, 1904-1923
CW 36	The Goetheanum-Idea in the Middle of the Cultural Crisis of the Present: Collected Essays from the Periodical "Das Goetheanum," 1921-1925
CW 37	*[Now in CWs 251 and 260a]*

III. Publications from the Literary Estate

CW 38	Letters, Vol. 1: 1881-1890
CW 39	Letters, Vol. 2: 1890-1925
CW 40	Truth-Wrought Words
CW 40a	Sayings, Poems and Mantras; Supplementary Volume
CW 42	*[Now in CWs 264-266]*

CW 43	Stage Adaptations
CW 44	On the Four Mystery Dramas. Sketches, Fragments and Paralipomena on the Four Mystery Dramas
CW 45	Anthroposophy: A Fragment from the Year 1910

B. Lectures

I. Public Lectures

CW 51	On Philosophy, History and Literature
CW 52	Spiritual Teachings Concerning the Soul and Observation of the World
CW 53	The Origin and Goal of the Human Being
CW 54	The Riddles of the World and Anthroposophy
CW 55	Knowledge of the Supersensible in Our Times and Its Meaning for Life Today
CW 56	Knowledge of the Soul and of the Spirit
CW 57	Where and How Does One Find the Spirit?
CW 58	The Metamorphoses of the Soul Life. Paths of Soul Experiences: Part One
CW 59	The Metamorphoses of the Soul Life. Paths of Soul Experiences: Part Two
CW 60	The Answers of Spiritual Science to the Biggest Questions of Existence
CW 61	Human History in the Light of Spiritual Research
CW 62	Results of Spiritual Research
CW 63	Spiritual Science as a Treasure for Life
CW 64	Out of Destiny-Burdened Times
CW 65	Out of Central European Spiritual Life
CW 66	Spirit and Matter, Life and Death
CW 67	The Eternal in the Human Soul. Immortality and Freedom
CW 68	Public lectures in various cities, 1906-1918
CW 69	Public lectures in various cities, 1906-1918
CW 70	Public lectures in various cities, 1906-1918
CW 71	Public lectures in various cities, 1906-1918
CW 72	Freedom – Immortality – Social Life
CW 73	The Supplementing of the Modern Sciences through Anthroposophy
CW 73a	Specialized Fields of Knowledge and Anthroposophy
CW 74	The Philosophy of Thomas Aquinas
CW 75	Public lectures in various cities, 1906-1918
CW 76	The Fructifying Effect of Anthroposophy on Specialized Fields
CW 77a	The Task of Anthroposophy in Relation to Science and Life: The Darmstadt College Course

CW 77b	Art and Anthroposophy. The Goetheanum-Impulse
CW 78	Anthroposophy, Its Roots of Knowledge and Fruits for Life
CW 79	The Reality of the Higher Worlds
CW 80	Public lectures in various cities, 1922
CW 81	Renewal-Impulses for Culture and Science–Berlin College Course
CW 82	So that the Human Being Can Become a Complete Human Being
CW 83	Western and Eastern World-Contrast. Paths to Understanding It through Anthroposophy
CW 84	What Did the Goetheanum Intend and What Should Anthroposophy Do?

II. Lectures to the Members of the Anthroposophical Society

CW 88	Concerning the Astral World and Devachan
CW 89	Consciousness – Life – Form. Fundamental Principles of a Spiritual-Scientific Cosmology
CW 90	Participant Notes from the Lectures during the Years 1903-1905
CW 91	Participant Notes from the Lectures during the Years 1903-1905
CW 92	The Occult Truths of Ancient Myths and Sagas
CW 93	The Temple Legend and the Golden Legend
CW 93a	Fundamentals of Esotericism
CW 94	Cosmogony. Popular Occultism. The Gospel of John. The Theosophy in the Gospel of John
CW 95	At the Gates of Theosophy
CW 96	Origin-Impulses of Spiritual Science. Christian Esotericism in the Light of New Spirit-Knowledge
CW 97	The Christian Mystery
CW 98	Nature Beings and Spirit Beings – Their Effects in Our Visible World
CW 99	The Theosophy of the Rosicrucians
CW 100	Human Development and Christ-Knowledge
CW 101	Myths and Legends. Occult Signs and Symbols
CW 102	The Working into Human Beings by Spiritual Beings
CW 103	The Gospel of John
CW 104	The Apocalypse of John
CW 104a	From the Picture-Script of the Apocalypse of John
CW 105	Universe, Earth, the Human Being: Their Being and Development, as well as Their Reflection in the Connection between Egyptian Mythology and Modern Culture
CW 106	Egyptian Myths and Mysteries in Relation to the Active Spiritual Forces of the Present
CW 107	Spiritual-Scientific Knowledge of the Human Being
CW 108	Answering the Questions of Life and the World through Anthroposophy

CW 109 The Principle of Spiritual Economy in Connection with the Question of Reincarnation. An Aspect of the Spiritual Guidance of Humanity
CW 110 The Spiritual Hierarchies and Their Reflection in the Physical World. Zodiac, Planets and Cosmos
CW 111 *[Contained in CW 109]*
CW 112 The Gospel of John in Relation to the Three Other Gospels, Especially the Gospel of Luke
CW 113 The Orient in the Light of the Occident. The Children of Lucifer and the Brothers of Christ
CW 114 The Gospel of Luke
CW 115 Anthroposophy – Psychosophy – Pneumatosophy
CW 116 The Christ-Impulse and the Development of "I"- Consciousness
CW 117 The Deeper Secrets of the Development of Humanity in Light of the Gospels
CW 118 The Event of the Christ-Appearance in the Etheric World
CW 119 Macrocosm and Microcosm. The Large World and the Small World. Soul-Questions, Life-Questions, Spirit-Questions
CW 120 The Revelation of Karma
CW 121 The Mission of Individual Folk-Souls in Connection with Germanic-Nordic Mythology
CW 122 The Secrets of the Biblical Creation-Story. The Six-Day Work in the First Book of Moses
CW 123 The Gospel of Matthew
CW 124 Excursus in the Area of the Gospel of Mark
CW 125 Paths and Goals of the Spiritual Human Being. Life Questions in the Light of Spiritual Science
CW 126 Occult History. Esoteric Observations of the Karmic Relationships of Personalities and Events of World History
CW 127 The Mission of the New Spiritual Revelation. The Christ-Event as the Middle-Point of Earth Evolution
CW 128 An Occult Physiology
CW 129 Wonders of the World, Trials of the Soul, and Revelations of the Spirit
CW 130 Esoteric Christianity and the Spiritual Guidance of Humanity
CW 131 From Jesus to Christ
CW 132 Evolution from the View Point of the Truth
CW 133 The Earthly and the Cosmic Human Being
CW 134 The World of the Senses and the World of the Spirit
CW 135 Reincarnation and Karma and their Meaning for the Culture of the Present
CW 136 The Spiritual Beings in Celestial Bodies and the Realms of Nature
CW 137 The Human Being in the Light of Occultism, Theosophy and Philosophy

CW 138	On Initiation. On Eternity and the Passing Moment. On the Light of the Spirit and the Darkness of Life
CW 139	The Gospel of Mark
CW 140	Occult Investigation into the Life between Death and New Birth. The Living Interaction between Life and Death
CW 141	Life between Death and New Birth in Relationship to Cosmic Facts
CW 142	The Bhagavad Gita and the Letters of Paul
CW 143	Experiences of the Supersensible. Three Paths of the Soul to Christ
CW 144	The Mysteries of the East and of Christianity
CW 145	What Significance Does Occult Development of the Human Being Have for the Sheaths – Physical Body, Etheric Body, Astral Body, and Self?
CW 146	The Occult Foundations of the Bhagavad Gita
CW 147	The Secrets of the Threshold
CW 148	Out of Research in the Akasha: The Fifth Gospel
CW 149	Christ and the Spiritual World. Concerning the Search for the Holy Grail
CW 150	The World of the Spirit and Its Extension into Physical Existence; The Influence of the Dead in the World of the Living
CW 151	Human Thought and Cosmic Thought
CW 152	Preliminary Stages to the Mystery of Golgotha
CW 153	The Inner Being of the Human Being and Life Between Death and New Birth
CW 154	How does One Gain an Understanding of the Spiritual World? The Flowing in of Spiritual Impulses from out of the World of the Deceased
CW 155	Christ and the Human Soul. Concerning the Meaning of Life. Theosophical Morality. Anthroposophy and Christianity
CW 156	Occult Reading and Occult Hearing
CW 157	Human Destinies and the Destiny of Peoples
CW 157a	The Formation of Destiny and the Life after Death
CW 158	The Connection Between the Human Being and the Elemental World. Kalevala – Olaf Asteson – The Russian People – The World as the Result of the Influences of Equilibrium
CW 159	The Mystery of Death. The Nature and Significance of Middle Europe and the European Folk Spirits
CW 160	*[In CW 159]*
CW 161	Paths of Spiritual Knowledge and the Renewal of the Artistic Worldview
CW 162	Questions of Art and Life in Light of Spiritual Science
CW 163	Coincidence, Necessity and Providence. Imaginative Knowledge and the Processes after Death

CW 164	The Value of Thinking for a Knowledge That Satisfies the Human Being. The Relationship of Spiritual Science to Natural Science
CW 165	The Spiritual Unification of Humanity through the Christ-Impulse
CW 166	Necessity and Freedom in World Events and in Human Action
CW 167	The Present and the Past in the Human Spirit
CW 168	The Connection between the Living and the Dead
CW 169	World-being and Selfhood
CW 170	The Riddle of the Human Being. The Spiritual Background of Human History. Cosmic and Human History, Vol. 1
CW 171	Inner Development-Impulses of Humanity. Goethe and the Crisis of the 19th Century. Cosmic and Human History, Vol. 2
CW 172	The Karma of the Vocation of the Human Being in Connection with Goethe's Life. Cosmic and Human History, Vol. 3
CW 173	Contemporary-Historical Considerations: The Karma of Untruthfulness, Part One. Cosmic and Human History, Vol. 4
CW 174	Contemporary-Historical Considerations: The Karma of Untruthfulness, Part Two. Cosmic and Human History, Vol. 5
CW 174a	Middle Europe between East and West. Cosmic and Human History, Vol. 6
CW 174b	The Spiritual Background of the First World War. Cosmic and Human History, Vol. 7
CW 175	Building Stones for an Understanding of the Mystery of Golgotha. Cosmic and Human Metamorphoses
CW 176	Truths of Evolution of the Individual and Humanity. The Karma of Materialism
CW 177	The Spiritual Background of the Outer World. The Fall of the Spirits of Darkness. Spiritual Beings and Their Effects, Vol. 1
CW 178	Individual Spiritual Beings and their Influence in the Soul of the Human Being. Spiritual Beings and their Effects, Vol. 2
CW 179	Spiritual Beings and Their Effects. Historical Necessity and Freedom. The Influences on Destiny from out of the World of the Dead. Spiritual Beings and Their Effects, Vol. 3
CW 180	Mystery Truths and Christmas Impulses. Ancient Myths and their Meaning. Spiritual Beings and Their Effects, Vol. 4
CW 181	Earthly Death and Cosmic Life. Anthroposophical Gifts for Life. Necessities of Consciousness for the Present and the Future.
CW 182	Death as Transformation of Life
CW 183	The Science of the Development of the Human Being
CW 184	The Polarity of Duration and Development in Human Life. The Cosmic Pre-History of Humanity
CW 185	Historical Symptomology
CW 185a	Historical-Developmental Foundations for Forming a Social Judgment

CW 186	The Fundamental Social Demands of Our Time–In Changed Situations
CW 187	How Can Humanity Find the Christ Again? The Threefold Shadow-Existence of our Time and the New Christ-Light
CW 188	Goetheanism, a Transformation-Impulse and Resurrection-Thought. Science of the Human Being and Science of Sociology
CW 189	The Social Question as a Question of Consciousness. The Spiritual Background of the Social Question, Vol. 1
CW 190	Impulses of the Past and the Future in Social Occurrences. The Spiritual Background of the Social Question, Vol. 2
CW 191	Social Understanding from Spiritual-Scientific Cognition. The Spiritual Background of the Social Question, Vol. 3
CW 192	Spiritual-Scientific Treatment of Social and Pedagogical Questions
CW 193	The Inner Aspect of the Social Riddle. Luciferic Past and Ahrimanic Future
CW 194	The Mission of Michael. The Revelation of the Actual Mysteries of the Human Being
CW 195	Cosmic New Year and the New Year Idea
CW 196	Spiritual and Social Transformations in the Development of Humanity
CW 197	Polarities in the Development of Humanity: West and East Materialism and Mysticism Knowledge and Belief
CW 198	Healing Factors for the Social Organism
CW 199	Spiritual Science as Knowledge of the Foundational Impulses of Social Formation
CW 200	The New Spirituality and the Christ-Experience of the 20th Century
CW 201	The Correspondences Between Microcosm and Macrocosm. The Human Being – A Hieroglyph of the Universe. The Human Being in Relationship with the Cosmos: 1
CW 202	The Bridge between the World-Spirituality and the Physical Aspect of the Human Being. The Search for the New Isis, the Divine Sophia. The Human Being in Relationship with the Cosmos: 2
CW 203	The Responsibility of Human Beings for the Development of the World through their Spiritual Connection with the Planet Earth and the World of the Stars. The Human Being in Relationship with the Cosmos: 3
CW 204	Perspectives of the Development of Humanity. The Materialistic Knowledge-Impulse and the Task of Anthroposophy. The Human Being in Relationship with the Cosmos: 4
CW 205	Human Development, World-Soul, and World-Spirit. Part One: The Human Being as a Being of Body and Soul in Relationship to the World. The Human Being in Relationship with the Cosmos: 5

CW 206 Human Development, World-Soul, and World-Spirit. Part Two: The Human Being as a Spiritual Being in the Process of Historical Development. The Human Being in Relationship with the Cosmos: 6
CW 207 Anthroposophy as Cosmosophy. Part One: Characteristic Features of the Human Being in the Earthly and the Cosmic Realms. The Human Being in Relationship with the Cosmos: 7
CW 208 Anthroposophy as Cosmosophy. Part Two: The Forming of the Human Being as the Result of Cosmic Influence. The Human Being in Relationship with the Cosmos: 8
CW 209 Nordic and Central European Spiritual Impulses. The Festival of the Appearance of Christ. The Human Being in Relationship with the Cosmos: 9
CW 210 Old and New Methods of Initiation. Drama and Poetry in the Change of Consciousness in the Modern Age
CW 211 The Sun Mystery and the Mystery of Death and Resurrection. Exoteric and Esoteric Christianity
CW 212 Human Soul Life and Spiritual Striving in Connection with World and Earth Development
CW 213 Human Questions and World Answers
CW 214 The Mystery of the Trinity: The Human Being in Relationship with the Spiritual World in the Course of Time
CW 215 Philosophy, Cosmology, and Religion in Anthroposophy
CW 216 The Fundamental Impulses of the World-Historical Development of Humanity
CW 217 Spiritually Active Forces in the Coexistence of the Older and Younger Generations. Pedagogical Course for Youth
CW 217a Youth's Cognitive Task
CW 218 Spiritual Connections in the Forming of the Human Organism
CW 219 The Relationship of the World of the Stars to the Human Being, and of the Human Being to the World of the Stars. The Spiritual Communion of Humanity
CW 220 Living Knowledge of Nature. Intellectual Fall and Spiritual Redemption
CW 221 Earth-Knowing and Heaven-Insight
CW 222 The Imparting of Impulses to World-Historical Events through Spiritual Powers
CW 223 The Cycle of the Year as Breathing Process of the Earth and the Four Great Festival-Seasons. Anthroposophy and the Human Heart (*Gemüt*)
CW 224 The Human Soul and its Connection with Divine-Spiritual Individualities. The Internalization of the Festivals of the Year
CW 225 Three Perspectives of Anthroposophy. Cultural Phenomena observed from a Spiritual-Scientific Perspective
CW 226 Human Being, Human Destiny, and World Development

CW 227 Initiation-Knowledge
CW 228 Science of Initiation and Knowledge of the Stars. The Human Being in the Past, the Present, and the Future from the Viewpoint of the Development of Consciousness
CW 229 The Experiencing of the Course of the Year in Four Cosmic Imaginations
CW 230 The Human Being as Harmony of the Creative, Building, and Formative World-Word
CW 231 The Supersensible Human Being, Understood Anthroposophically
CW 232 The Forming of the Mysteries
CW 233 World History Illuminated by Anthroposophy and as the Foundation for Knowledge of the Human Spirit
CW 233a Mystery Sites of the Middle Ages: Rosicrucianism and the Modern Initiation-Principle. The Festival of Easter as Part of the History of the Mysteries of Humanity
CW 234 Anthroposophy. A Summary after 21 Years
CW 235 Esoteric Observations of Karmic Relationships in 6 Volumes, Vol. 1
CW 236 Esoteric Observations of Karmic Relationships in 6 Volumes, Vol. 2
CW 237 Esoteric Observations of Karmic Relationships in 6 Volumes, Vol. 3: The Karmic Relationships of the Anthroposophical Movement
CW 238 Esoteric Observations of Karmic Relationships in 6 Volumes, Vol. 4: The Spiritual Life of the Present in Relationship to the Anthroposophical Movement
CW 239 Esoteric Observations of Karmic Relationships in 6 Volumes, Vol. 5
CW 240 Esoteric Observations of Karmic Relationships in 6 Volumes, Vol. 6
CW 243 The Consciousness of the Initiate
CW 245 Instructions for an Esoteric Schooling
CW 250 The Building-Up of the Anthroposophical Society. From the Beginning to the Outbreak of the First World War
CW 251 The History of the Goetheanum Building-Association
CW 252 Life in the Anthroposophical Society from the First World War to the Burning of the First Goetheanum
CW 253 The Problems of Living Together in the Anthroposophical Society. On the Dornach Crisis of 1915. With Highlights on Swedenborg's Clairvoyance, the Views of Freudian Psychoanalysts, and the Concept of Love in Relation to Mysticism
CW 254 The Occult Movement in the 19th Century and Its Relationship to World Culture. Significant Points from the Exoteric Cultural Life around the Middle of the 19th Century
CW 255 Rudolf Steiner during the First World War
CW 255a Anthroposophy and the Reformation of Society. On the History of the Threefold Movement

CW 255b Anthroposophy and Its Opponents, 1919-1921
CW 256 How Can the Anthroposophical Movement Be Financed?
CW 256a Futurum, Inc. / International Laboratories, Inc.
CW 256b The Coming Day, Inc.
CW 257 Anthroposophical Community-Building
CW 258 The History of and Conditions for the Anthroposophical Movement in Relationship to the Anthroposophical Society. A Stimulus to Self-Contemplation
CW 259 The Year of Destiny 1923 in the History of the Anthroposophical Society. From the Burning of the Goetheanum to the Christmas Conference
CW 260 The Christmas Conference for the Founding of the General Anthroposophical Society
CW 260a The Constitution of the General Anthroposophical Society and the School for Spiritual Science. The Rebuilding of the Goetheanum
CW 261 Our Dead. Addresses, Words of Remembrance, and Meditative Verses, 1906-1924
CW 262 Rudolf Steiner and Marie Steiner-von Sivers: Correspondence and Documents, 1901-1925
CW 263/1 Rudolf Steiner and Edith Maryon: Correspondence: Letters, Verses, Sketches, 1912-1924
CW 264 On the History and the Contents of the First Section of the Esoteric School from 1904 to 1914. Letters, Newsletters, Documents, Lectures
CW 265 On the History and from the Contents of the Ritual-Knowledge Section of the Esoteric School from 1904 to 1914. Documents, and Lectures from the Years 1906 to 1914, as Well as on New Approaches to Ritual-Knowledge Work in the Years 1921-1924
CW 266/1 From the Contents of the Esoteric Lessons. Volume 1: 1904-1909. Notes from Memory of Participants. Meditation texts from the notes of Rudolf Steiner
CW 266/2 From the Contents of the Esoteric Lessons. Volume 2: 1910-1912. Notes from Memory of Participants
CW 266/3 From the Contents of the Esoteric Lessons. Volume 3: 1913, 1914 and 1920-1923. Notes from Memory of Participants. Meditation texts from the notes of Rudolf Steiner
CW 267 Soul-Exercises: Vol. 1: Exercises with Word and Image Meditations for the Methodological Development of Higher Powers of Knowledge, 1904-1924
CW 268 Soul-Exercises: Vol. 2: Mantric Verses, 1903-1925
CW 269 Ritual Texts for the Celebration of the Free Christian Religious Instruction. The Collected Verses for Teachers and Students of the Waldorf School
CW 270 Esoteric Instructions for the First Class of the School for Spiritual Science at the Goetheanum 1924, 4 Volumes

III. Lectures and Courses on Specific Realms of Life

Lectures on Art

CW 271 Art and Knowledge of Art. Foundations of a New Aesthetic
CW 272 Spiritual-Scientific Commentary on Goethe's "Faust" in Two Volumes. Vol. 1: Faust, the Striving Human Being
CW 273 Spiritual-Scientific Commentary on Goethe's "Faust" in Two Volumes. Vol. 2: The Faust-Problem
CW 274 Addresses for the Christmas Plays from the Old Folk Traditions
CW 275 Art in the Light of Mystery Wisdom
CW 276 The Artistic in Its Mission in the World. The Genius of Language. The World of Self-Revealing Radiant Appearances – Anthroposophy and Art. Anthroposophy and Poetry
CW 277 Eurythmy. The Revelation of the Speaking Soul
CW 277a The Origin and Development of Eurythmy
CW 278 Eurythmy as Visible Song
CW 279 Eurythmy as Visible Speech
CW 280 The Method and Nature of Speech Formation
CW 281 The Art of Recitation and Declamation
CW 282 Speech Formation and Dramatic Art
CW 283 The Nature of Things Musical and the Experience of Tone in the Human Being
CW 284/285 Images of Occult Seals and Pillars. The Munich Congress of Whitsun 1907 and Its Consequences
CW 286 Paths to a New Style of Architecture. "And the Building Becomes Human"
CW 287 The Building at Dornach as a Symbol of Historical Becoming and an Artistic Transformation Impulse
CW 288 Style-Forms in the Living Organic
CW 289 The Building-Idea of the Goetheanum: Lectures with Slides from the Years 1920-1921
CW 290 The Building-Idea of the Goetheanum: Lectures with Slides from the Years 1920-1921
CW 291 The Nature of Colors
CW 291a Knowledge of Colors. Supplementary Volume to "The Nature of Colors"
CW 292 Art History as Image of Inner Spiritual Impulses

Lectures on Education

CW 293 General Knowledge of the Human Being as the Foundation of Pedagogy
CW 294 The Art of Education, Methodology and Didactics
CW 295 The Art of Education: Seminar Discussions and Lectures on Lesson Planning

CW 296 The Question of Education as a Social Question
CW 297 The Idea and Practice of the Waldorf School
CW 297a Education for Life: Self-Education and the Practice of Pedagogy
CW 298 Rudolf Steiner in the Waldorf School
CW 299 Spiritual-Scientific Observations on Speech
CW 300a Conferences with the Teachers of the Free Waldorf School in Stuttgart, 1919 to 1924, in 3 Volumes, Vol. 1
CW 300b Conferences with the Teachers of the Free Waldorf School in Stuttgart, 1919 to 1924, in 3 Volumes, Vol. 2
CW 300c Conferences with the Teachers of the Free Waldorf School in Stuttgart, 1919 to 1924, in 3 Volumes, Vol. 3
CW 301 The Renewal of Pedagogical-Didactical Art through Spiritual Science
CW 302 Knowledge of the Human Being and the Forming of Class Lessons
CW 302a Education and Teaching from a Knowledge of the Human Being
CW 303 The Healthy Development of the Human Being
CW 304 Methods of Education and Teaching Based on Anthroposophy
CW 304a Anthroposophical Knowledge of the Human Being and Pedagogy
CW 305 The Soul-Spiritual Foundational Forces of the Art of Education. Spiritual Values in Education and Social Life
CW 306 Pedagogical Praxis from the Viewpoint of a Spiritual-Scientific Knowledge of the Human Being. The Education of the Child and Young Human Beings
CW 307 The Spiritual Life of the Present and Education
CW 308 The Method of Teaching and the Life-Requirements for Teaching
CW 309 Anthroposophical Pedagogy and Its Prerequisites
CW 310 The Pedagogical Value of a Knowledge of the Human Being and the Cultural Value of Pedagogy
CW 311 The Art of Education from an Understanding of the Being of Humanity

Lectures on Medicine

CW 312 Spiritual Science and Medicine
CW 313 Spiritual-Scientific Viewpoints on Therapy
CW 314 Physiology and Therapy Based on Spiritual Science
CW 315 Curative Eurythmy
CW 316 Meditative Observations and Instructions for a Deepening of the Art of Healing
CW 317 The Curative Education Course
CW 318 The Working Together of Doctors and Pastors
CW 319 Anthroposophical Knowledge of the Human Being and Medicine

Lectures on Natural Science

CW 320 Spiritual-Scientific Impulses for the Development of Physics 1: The First Natural-Scientific Course: Light, Color, Tone, Mass, Electricity, Magnetism

CW 321 Spiritual-Scientific Impulses for the Development of Physics 2: The Second Natural-Scientific Course: Warmth at the Border of Positive and Negative Materiality

CW 322 The Borders of the Knowledge of Nature

CW 323 The Relationship of the various Natural-Scientific Fields to Astronomy

CW 324 Nature Observation, Mathematics, and Scientific Experimentation and Results from the Viewpoint of Anthroposophy

CW 324a The Fourth Dimension in Mathematics and Reality

CW 325 Natural Science and the World-Historical Development of Humanity since Ancient Times

CW 326 The Moment of the Coming Into Being of Natural Science in World History and Its Development Since Then

CW 327 Spiritual-Scientific Foundations for Success in Farming. The Agricultural Course

Lectures on Social Life and the Threefold Arrangement of the Social Organism

CW 328 The Social Question

CW 329 The Liberation of the Human Being as the Foundation for a New Social Form

CW 330 The Renewal of the Social Organism

CW 331 Work-Council and Socialization

CW 332 The Alliance for Threefolding and the Total Reform of Society. The Council on Culture and the Liberation of the Spiritual Life

CW 332a The Social Future

CW 333 Freedom of Thought and Social Forces

CW 334 From the Unified State to the Threefold Social Organism

CW 335 The Crisis of the Present and the Path to Healthy Thinking

CW 336 The Great Questions of the Times and Anthroposophical Spiritual Knowledge

CW 337a Social Ideas, Social Reality, Social Practice, Vol. 1: Question-and-Answer Evenings and Study Evenings of the Alliance for the Threefold Social Organism in Stuttgart, 1919-1920

CW 337b Social Ideas, Social Realities, Social Practice, Vol. 2: Discussion Evenings of the Swiss Alliance for the Threefold Social Organism

CW 338 How Does One Work on Behalf of the Impulse for the Threefold Social Organism?

CW 339 Anthroposophy, Threefold Social Organism, and the Art of Public Speaking

CW 340 The National-Economics Course. The Tasks of a New Science of Economics, Volume 1

CW 341 The National-Economics Seminar. The Tasks of a New Science of Economics, Volume 2

Lectures and Courses on Christian Religious Work

CW 342 Lectures and Courses on Christian Religious Work, Vol. 1: Anthroposophical Foundations for a Renewed Christian Religious Working

CW 343 Lectures and Courses on Christian Religious Work, Vol. 2: Spiritual Knowledge – Religious Feeling – Cultic Doing

CW 344 Lectures and Courses on Christian Religious Work, Vol. 3: Lectures at the Founding of the Christian Community

CW 345 Lectures and Courses on Christian Religious Work, Vol. 4: Concerning the Nature of the Working Word

CW 346 Lectures and Courses on Christian Religious Work, Vol. 5: The Apocalypse and the Work of the Priest

Lectures for Workers at the Goetheanum

CW 347 The Knowledge of the Nature of the Human Being According to Body, Soul and Spirit. On Earlier Conditions of the Earth

CW 348 On Health and Illness. Foundations of a Spiritual-Scientific Doctrine of the Senses

CW 349 On the Life of the Human Being and of the Earth. On the Nature of Christianity

CW 350 Rhythms in the Cosmos and in the Human Being. How Does One Come To See the Spiritual World?

CW 351 The Human Being and the World. The Influence of the Spirit in Nature. On the Nature of Bees

CW 352 Nature and the Human Being Observed Spiritual-Scientifically

CW 353 The History of Humanity and the World-Views of the Folk Cultures

CW 354 The Creation of the World and the Human Being. Life on Earth and the Influence of the Stars

SIGNIFICANT EVENTS IN THE LIFE OF RUDOLF STEINER

1829: June 23: birth of Johann Steiner (1829-1910)—Rudolf Steiner's father—in Geras, Lower Austria.

1834: May 8: birth of Franciska Blie (1834-1918)—Rudolf Steiner's mother—in Horn, Lower Austria. "My father and mother were both children of the glorious Lower Austrian forest district north of the Danube."

1860: May 16: marriage of Johann Steiner and Franciska Blie.

1861: February 25: birth of *Rudolf Joseph Lorenz Steiner* in Kraljevec, Croatia, near the border with Hungary, where Johann Steiner works as a telegrapher for the South Austria Railroad. Rudolf Steiner is baptized two days later, February 27, the date usually given as his birthday.

1862: Summer: the family moves to Mödling, Lower Austria.

1863: The family moves to Pottschach, Lower Austria, near the Styrian border, where Johann Steiner becomes stationmaster. "The view stretched to the mountains...majestic peaks in the distance and the sweet charm of nature in the immediate surroundings."

1864: November 15: birth of Rudolf Steiner's sister, Leopoldine (d. November 1, 1927). She will become a seamstress and live with her parents for the rest of her life.

1866: July 28: birth of Rudolf Steiner's deaf-mute brother, Gustav (d. May 1, 1941).

1867: Rudolf Steiner enters the village school. Following a disagreement between his father and the schoolmaster, whose wife falsely accused the boy of causing a commotion, Rudolf Steiner is taken out of school and taught at home.

1868: A critical experience. Unknown to the family, an aunt dies in a distant town. Sitting in the station waiting room, Rudolf Steiner sees her "form," which speaks to him, asking for help. "Beginning with this experience, a new soul life began in the boy, one in which not only the outer trees and mountains spoke to him, but also the worlds that lay behind them. From this moment on, the boy began to live with the spirits of nature...."

1869: The family moves to the peaceful, rural village of Neudorfl, near Wiener-Neustadt in present-day Austria. Rudolf Steiner attends the village school. Because of the "unorthodoxy" of his writing and spelling, he has to do "extra lessons."

1870: Through a book lent to him by his tutor, he discovers geometry: "To grasp something purely in the spirit brought me inner happiness. I know that I first learned happiness through geometry." The same tutor allows him to draw, while other students still struggle with their reading and writing. "An artistic element" thus enters his education.

1871: Though his parents are not religious, Rudolf Steiner becomes a "church child," a favorite of the priest, who was "an exceptional character." "Up to the age of ten or eleven, among those I came to know, he was far and away the most significant." Among other things, he introduces Steiner to Copernican, heliocentric cosmology. As an altar boy, Rudolf Steiner serves at Masses, funerals, and Corpus Christi processions. At year's end, after an incident in which he escapes a thrashing, his father forbids him to go to church.

1872: Rudolf Steiner transfers to grammar school in Wiener-Neustadt, a five-mile walk from home, which must be done in all weathers.

1873-75: Through his teachers and on his own, Rudolf Steiner has many wonderful experiences with science and mathematics. Outside school, he teaches himself analytic geometry, trigonometry, differential equations, and calculus.

1876: Rudolf Steiner begins tutoring other students. He learns bookbinding from his father. He also teaches himself stenography.

1877: Rudolf Steiner discovers Kant's *Critique of Pure Reason*, which he reads and rereads. He also discovers and reads von Rotteck's *World History*.

1878: He studies extensively in contemporary psychology and philosophy.

1879: Rudolf Steiner graduates from high school with honors. His father is transferred to Inzersdorf, near Vienna. He uses his first visit to Vienna "to purchase a great number of philosophy books"—Kant, Fichte, Schelling, and Hegel, as well as numerous histories of philosophy. His aim: to find a path from the "I" to nature.

October 1879-1883: Rudolf Steiner attends the Technical College in Vienna—to study mathematics, chemistry, physics, mineralogy, botany, zoology, biology, geology, and mechanics—with a scholarship. He also attends lectures in history and literature, while avidly reading philosophy on his own. His two favorite professors are Karl Julius Schröer (German language and literature) and Edmund Reitlinger (physics). He also audits lectures by Robert Zimmerman on aesthetics and Franz Brentano on philosophy. During this year he begins his friendship with Moritz Zitter (1861-1921), who will help support him financially when he is in Berlin.

1880: Rudolf Steiner attends lectures on Schiller and Goethe by Karl Julius Schröer, who becomes his mentor. Also "through a remarkable combination of circumstances," he meets Felix Koguzki, an "herb gatherer" and healer, who could "see deeply into the secrets of nature." Rudolf Steiner will meet and study with this "emissary of the Master" throughout his time in Vienna.

1881: January: "... I didn't sleep a wink. I was busy with philosophical problems until about 12:30 a.m. Then, finally, I threw myself down on my couch. All my striving during the previous year had been to research whether the following statement by Schelling was true or not: *Within everyone dwells a secret, marvelous capacity to draw back from the stream of time—out of the self clothed in all that comes to us from outside—into our innermost being and there, in the immutable form of the Eternal, to look into ourselves.* I believe, and I am still quite certain of it, that I discovered this capacity in myself; I had long had an inkling of it. Now the whole of idealist philosophy stood before me in modified form. What's a sleepless night compared to that!"

Rudolf Steiner begins communicating with leading thinkers of the day, who send him books in return, which he reads eagerly.

July: "I am not one of those who dives into the day like an animal in human form. I pursue a quite specific goal, an idealistic aim—knowledge of the truth! This cannot be done offhandedly. It requires the greatest striving in the world, free of all egotism, and equally of all resignation."

August: Steiner puts down on paper for the first time thoughts for a "Philosophy of Freedom." "The striving for the absolute: this human yearning is freedom." He also seeks to outline a "peasant philosophy," describing what the worldview of a "peasant"—one who lives close to the earth and the old ways—really is.

1881-1882: Felix Koguzki, the herb gatherer, reveals himself to be the envoy of another, higher initiatory personality, who instructs Rudolf Steiner to penetrate Fichte's philosophy and to master modern scientific thinking as a preparation for right entry into the spirit. This "Master" also teaches him the double (evolutionary and involutionary) nature of time.

1882: Through the offices of Karl Julius Schröer, Rudolf Steiner is asked by Joseph Kurschner to edit Goethe's scientific works for the *Deutschen National-Literatur* edition. He writes "A Possible Critique of Atomistic Concepts" and sends it to Friedrich Theodore Vischer.

1883: Rudolf Steiner completes his college studies and begins work on the Goethe project.

1884: First volume of Goethe's *Scientific Writings* (CW 1) appears (March). He lectures on Goethe and Lessing, and Goethe's approach to science. In July, he enters the household of Ladislaus and Pauline Specht as tutor to the four Specht boys. He will live there until 1890. At this time, he meets Josef Breuer (1842-1925), the coauthor with Sigmund Freud of *Studies in Hysteria*, who is the Specht family doctor.

1885: While continuing to edit Goethe's writings, Rudolf Steiner reads deeply in contemporary philosophy (Edouard von Hartmann, Johannes Volkelt, and Richard Wahle, among others).

1886: May: Rudolf Steiner sends Kurschner the manuscript of *Outlines of Goethe's Theory of Knowledge* (CW 2), which appears in October, and which he sends out widely. He also meets the poet Marie Eugenie Delle Grazie and writes "Nature and Our Ideals" for her. He attends her salon, where he meets many priests, theologians, and philosophers, who will become his friends. Meanwhile, the director of the Goethe Archive in Weimar requests his collaboration with the *Sophien* edition of Goethe's works, particularly the writings on color.

1887: At the beginning of the year, Rudolf Steiner is very sick. As the year progresses and his health improves, he becomes increasingly "a man of letters," lecturing, writing essays, and taking part in Austrian cultural life. In August-September, the second volume of Goethe's *Scientific Writings* appears.

1888: January-July: Rudolf Steiner assumes editorship of the "German Weekly" (*Deutsche Wochenschrift*). He begins lecturing more intensively, giving, for example, a lecture titled "Goethe as Father of a New Aesthetics." He meets and becomes soul friends with Friedrich Eckstein (1861-1939), a vegetarian, philosopher of symbolism, alchemist, and musician, who will introduce him to various spiritual currents (including Theosophy) and with whom he will meditate and interpret esoteric and alchemical texts.

1889: Rudolf Steiner first reads Nietzsche (*Beyond Good and Evil*). He encounters Theosophy again and learns of Madame Blavatsky in the Theosophical circle around Marie Lang (1858-1934). Here he also meets well-known figures of Austrian life, as well as esoteric figures like the occultist Franz Hartman and Karl Leinigen-Billigen (translator of C.G. Harrison's *The Transcendental Universe*.) During this period, Steiner first reads A.P. Sinnett's *Esoteric Buddhism* and Mabel Collins's *Light on the Path*. He also begins traveling, visiting Budapest, Weimar, and Berlin (where he meets philosopher Edouard von Hartman).

1890: Rudolf Steiner finishes volume 3 of Goethe's scientific writings. He begins his doctoral dissertation, which will become *Truth and Science* (CW 3). He also meets the poet and feminist Rosa Mayreder (1858-1938), with whom he can exchange his most intimate thoughts. In September, Rudolf Steiner moves to Weimar to work in the Goethe-Schiller Archive.

1891: Volume 3 of the Kurschner edition of Goethe appears. Meanwhile, Rudolf Steiner edits Goethe's studies in mineralogy and scientific writings for the *Sophien* edition. He meets Ludwig Laistner of the Cotta Publishing Company, who asks for a book on the basic question of metaphysics. From this will result, ultimately, *The Philosophy of Freedom* (CW 4), which will be published not by Cotta but by Emil Felber. In October, Rudolf Steiner takes the oral exam for a doctorate in philosophy, mathematics, and mechanics at Rostock University, receiving his doctorate on the twenty-sixth. In November, he gives his first lecture on Goethe's "Fairy Tale" in Vienna.

1892: Rudolf Steiner continues work at the Goethe-Schiller Archive and on his *Philosophy of Freedom*. *Truth and Science*, his doctoral dissertation, is published. Steiner undertakes to write introductions to books on Schopenhauer and Jean Paul for Cotta. At year's end, he finds lodging with Anna Eunike, née Schulz (1853-1911), a widow with four daughters and a son. He also develops a friendship with Otto Erich Hartleben (1864-1905) with whom he shares literary interests.

1893: Rudolf Steiner begins his habit of producing many reviews and articles. In March, he gives a lecture titled "Hypnotism, with Reference to Spiritism." In September, volume 4 of the Kurschner edition is completed. In November, *The Philosophy of Freedom* appears. This year, too, he meets John Henry Mackay (1864-1933), the anarchist, and Max Stirner, a scholar and biographer.

1894: Rudolf Steiner meets Elisabeth Förster Nietzsche, the philosopher's sister, and begins to read Nietzsche in earnest, beginning with the as yet unpublished *Antichrist*. He also meets Ernst Haeckel (1834-1919). In the fall, he begins to write *Nietzsche, A Fighter against His Time* (CW 5).

1895: May, *Nietzsche, A Fighter against His Time* appears.

1896: January 22: Rudolf Steiner sees Friedrich Nietzsche for the first and only time. Moves between the Nietzsche and the Goethe-Schiller Archives, where he completes his work before year's end. He falls out with Elisabeth Förster Nietzsche, thus ending his association with the Nietzsche Archive.

1897: Rudolf Steiner finishes the manuscript of *Goethe's Worldview* (CW 6). He moves to Berlin with Anna Eunike and begins editorship of the *Magazin fur Literatur*. From now on, Steiner will write countless reviews, literary and philosophical articles, and so on. He begins lecturing at the "Free Literary Society." In September, he attends the Zionist Congress in Basel. He sides with Dreyfus in the Dreyfus affair.

1898: Rudolf Steiner is very active as an editor in the political, artistic, and theatrical life of Berlin. He becomes friendly with John Henry Mackay and poet Ludwig Jacobowski (1868-1900). He joins Jacobowski's circle of writers, artists, and scientists—"The Coming Ones" (*Die Kommenden*)—and contributes lectures to the group until 1903. He also lectures at the "League for College Pedagogy." He writes an article for Goethe's sesquicentennial, "Goethe's Secret Revelation," on the "Fairy Tale of the Green Snake and the Beautiful Lily."

1898-99: "This was a trying time for my soul as I looked at Christianity.... I was able to progress only by contemplating, by means of spiritual perception, the evolution of Christianity .... Conscious knowledge of real Christianity began to dawn in me around the turn of the century. This seed continued to develop. My soul trial occurred shortly before the beginning of the twentieth century. It was decisive for my soul's development that I stood spiritually before the Mystery of Golgotha in a deep and solemn celebration of knowledge."

1899: Rudolf Steiner begins teaching and giving lectures and lecture cycles at the Workers' College, founded by Wilhelm Liebknecht (1826-1900). He will continue to do so until 1904. Writes: *Literature and Spiritual Life in the Nineteenth Century; Individualism in Philosophy; Haeckel and His Opponents; Poetry in the Present;* and begins what will become (fifteen years later). *The Riddles of Philosophy* (CW 18). He also meets many artists and writers, including Käthe Kollwitz, Stefan

Zweig, and Rainer Maria Rilke. On October 31, he marries Anna Eunike.

1900: "I thought that the turn of the century must bring humanity a new light. It seemed to me that the separation of human thinking and willing from the spirit had peaked. A turn or reversal of direction in human evolution seemed to me a necessity." Rudolf Steiner finishes *World and Life Views in the Nineteenth Century* (the second part of what will become *The Riddles of Philosophy*) and dedicates it to Ernst Haeckel. It is published in March. He continues lecturing at *Die Kommenden*, whose leadership he assumes after the death of Jacobowski. Also, he gives the Gutenberg Jubilee lecture before 7,000 typesetters and printers. In September, Rudolf Steiner is invited by Count and Countess Brockdorff to lecture in the Theosophical Library. His first lecture is on Nietzsche. His second lecture is titled "Goethe's Secret Revelation." October 6, he begins a lecture cycle on the mystics that will become *Mystics after Modernism* (CW 7). November-December: "Marie von Sivers appears in the audience...." Also in November, Steiner gives his first lecture at the Giordano Bruno Bund (where he will continue to lecture until May, 1905). He speaks on Bruno and modern Rome, focusing on the importance of the philosophy of Thomas Aquinas as monism.

1901: In continual financial straits, Rudolf Steiner's early friends Moritz Zitter and Rosa Mayreder help support him. In October, he begins the lecture cycle *Christianity as Mystical Fact* (CW 8) at the Theosophical Library. In November, he gives his first "Theosophical lecture" on Goethe's "Fairy Tale" in Hamburg at the invitation of Wilhelm Hubbe-Schleiden. He also attends a tea to celebrate the founding of the Theosophical Society at Count and Countess Brockdorff's. He gives a lecture cycle, "From Buddha to Christ," for the circle of the *Kommenden*. November 17, Marie von Sivers asks Rudolf Steiner if Theosophy does not need a Western-Christian spiritual movement (to complement Theosophy's Eastern emphasis). "The question was posed. Now, following spiritual laws, I could begin to give an answer...." In December, Rudolf Steiner writes his first article for a Theosophical publication. At year's end, the Brockdorffs and possibly Wilhelm Hubbe-Schleiden ask Rudolf Steiner to join the Theosophical Society and undertake the leadership of the German section. Rudolf Steiner agrees, on the condition that Marie von Sivers (then in Italy) work with him.

1902: Beginning in January, Rudolf Steiner attends the opening of the Workers' School in Spandau with Rosa Luxemberg (1870-1919). January 17, Rudolf Steiner joins the Theosophical Society. In April, he is asked to become general secretary of the German Section of the Theosophical Society, and works on preparations for its founding. In July, he visits London for a Theosophical congress. He meets Bertram

Keightly, G.R.S. Mead, A.P. Sinnett, and Annie Besant, among others. In September, *Christianity as Mystical Fact* appears. In October, Rudolf Steiner gives his first public lecture on Theosophy ("Monism and Theosophy") to about three hundred people at the Giordano Bruno Bund. On October 19-21, the German Section of the Theosophical Society has its first meeting; Rudolf Steiner is the general secretary, and Annie Besant attends. Steiner lectures on practical karma studies. On October 23, Annie Besant inducts Rudolf Steiner into the Esoteric School of the Theosophical Society. On October 25, Steiner begins a weekly series of lectures: "The Field of Theosophy." During this year, Rudolf Steiner also first meets Ita Wegman (1876-1943), who will become his close collaborator in his final years.

1903: Rudolf Steiner holds about 300 lectures and seminars. In May, the first issue of the periodical *Luzifer* appears. In June, Rudolf Steiner visits London for the first meeting of the Federation of the European Sections of the Theosophical Society, where he meets Colonel Olcott. He begins to write *Theosophy* (CW 9).

1904: Rudolf Steiner continues lecturing at the Workers' College and elsewhere (about 90 lectures), while lecturing intensively all over Germany among Theosophists (about a 140 lectures). In February, he meets Carl Unger (1878-1929), who will become a member of the board of the Anthroposophical Society (1913). In March, he meets Michael Bauer (1871-1929), a Christian mystic, who will also be on the board. In May, *Theosophy* appears, with the dedication: "To the spirit of Giordano Bruno." Rudolf Steiner and Marie von Sivers visit London for meetings with Annie Besant. June: Rudolf Steiner and Marie von Sivers attend the meeting of the Federation of European Sections of the Theosophical Society in Amsterdam. In July, Steiner begins the articles in *Luzifer-Gnosis* that will become *How to Know Higher Worlds* (CW 10) and *Cosmic Memory* (CW 11). In September, Annie Besant visits Germany. In December, Steiner lectures on Freemasonry. He mentions the High Grade Masonry derived from John Yarker and represented by Theodore Reuss and Karl Kellner as a blank slate "into which a good image could be placed."

1905: This year, Steiner ends his non-Theosophical lecturing activity. Supported by Marie von Sivers, his Theosophical lecturing—both in public and in the Theosophical Society—increases significantly: "The German Theosophical Movement is of exceptional importance." Steiner recommends reading, among others, Fichte, Jacob Boehme, and Angelus Silesius. He begins to introduce Christian themes into Theosophy. He also begins to work with doctors (Felix Peipers and Ludwig Noll). In July, he is in London for the Federation of European Sections, where he attends a lecture by Annie Besant: "I have seldom seen Mrs. Besant speak in so inward and heartfelt a manner...." "Through Mrs. Besant I have found the way to H.P. Blavatsky."

September to October, he gives a course of thirty-one lectures for a small group of esoteric students. In October, the annual meeting of the German Section of the Theosophical Society, which still remains very small, takes place. Rudolf Steiner reports membership has risen from 121 to 377 members. In November, seeking to establish esoteric "continuity," Rudolf Steiner and Marie von Sivers participate in a "Memphis-Misraim" Masonic ceremony. They pay forty-five marks for membership. "Yesterday, you saw how little remains of former esoteric institutions." "We are dealing only with a 'framework'... for the present, nothing lies behind it. The occult powers have completely withdrawn."

1906: Expansion of Theosophical work. Rudolf Steiner gives about 245 lectures, only 44 of which take place in Berlin. Cycles are given in Paris, Leipzig, Stuttgart, and Munich. Esoteric work also intensifies. Rudolf Steiner begins writing *An Outline of Esoteric Science* (CW 13). In January, Rudolf Steiner receives permission (a patent) from the Great Orient of the Scottish A & A Thirty-Three Degree Rite of the Order of the Ancient Freemasons of the Memphis-Misraim Rite to direct a chapter under the name "Mystica Aeterna." This will become the "Cognitive Cultic Section" (also called "Misraim Service") of the Esoteric School. (See: *From the History and Contents of the Cognitive Cultic Section* (CW 264). During this time, Steiner also meets Albert Schweitzer. In May, he is in Paris, where he visits Edouard Schuré. Many Russians attend his lectures (including Konstantin Balmont, Dimitri Mereszkovski, Zinaida Hippius, and Maximilian Woloshin). He attends the General Meeting of the European Federation of the Theosophical Society, at which Col. Olcott is present for the last time. He spends the year's end in Venice and Rome, where he writes and works on his translation of H.P. Blavatsky's *Key to Theosophy*.

1907: Further expansion of the German Theosophical Movement according to the Rosicrucian directive to "introduce spirit into the world"—in education, in social questions, in art, and in science. In February, Col. Olcott dies in Adyar. Before he dies, Olcott indicates that "the Masters" wish Annie Besant to succeed him: much politicking ensues. Rudolf Steiner supports Besant's candidacy. April-May: preparations for the Congress of the Federation of European Sections of the Theosophical Society—the great, watershed Whitsun "Munich Congress," attended by Annie Besant and others. Steiner decides to separate Eastern and Western (Christian-Rosicrucian) esoteric schools. He takes his esoteric school out of the Theosophical Society (Besant and Rudolf Steiner are "in harmony" on this). Steiner makes his first lecture tours to Austria and Hungary. That summer, he is in Italy. In September, he visits Edouard Schuré, who will write the introduction to the French edition of *Christianity as Mystical Fact* in Barr, Alsace. Rudolf Steiner writes the autobiographical statement known as the "Barr Document." In *Luzifer–Gnosis*, "The Education of the Child" appears.

1908: The movement grows (membership: 1150). Lecturing expands. Steiner makes his first extended lecture tour to Holland and Scandinavia, as well as visits to Naples and Sicily. Themes: St. John's Gospel, the Apocalypse, Egypt, science, philosophy, and logic. *Luzifer-Gnosis* ceases publication. In Berlin, Marie von Sivers (with Johanna Mücke (1864-1949) forms the *Philosophisch-Theosophisch* (after 1915 *Philosophisch-Anthroposophisch) Verlag* to publish Steiner's work. Steiner gives lecture cycles titled *The Gospel of St. John* (CW 103) and *The Apocalypse* (104).

1909: *An Outline of Esoteric Science* appears. Lecturing and travel continues. Rudolf Steiner's spiritual research expands to include the polarity of Lucifer and Ahriman; the work of great individualities in history; the Maitreya Buddha and the Bodhisattvas; spiritual economy (CW 109); the work of the spiritual hierarchies in heaven and on Earth (CW 110). He also deepens and intensifies his research into the Gospels, giving lectures on the Gospel of St. Luke (CW 114) with the first mention of two Jesus children. Meets and becomes friends with Christian Morgenstern (1871-1914). In April, he lays the foundation stone for the Malsch model—the building that will lead to the first Goetheanum. In May, the International Congress of the Federation of European Sections of the Theosophical Society takes place in Budapest. Rudolf Steiner receives the Subba Row medal for *How to Know Higher Worlds*. During this time, Charles W. Leadbeater discovers Jiddu Krishnamurti (1895-1986) and proclaims him the future "world teacher," the bearer of the Maitreya Buddha and the "reappearing Christ." In October, Steiner delivers seminal lectures on "anthroposophy," which he will try, unsuccessfully, to rework over the next years into the unfinished work, *Anthroposophy (A Fragment)* (CW 45).

1910: New themes: *The Reappearance of Christ in the Etheric* (CW 118); *The Fifth Gospel; The Mission of Folk Souls* (CW 121); *Occult History* (CW 126); the evolving development of etheric cognitive capacities. Rudolf Steiner continues his Gospel research with *The Gospel of St. Matthew* (CW 123). In January, his father dies. In April, he takes a month-long trip to Italy, including Rome, Monte Cassino, and Sicily. He also visits Scandinavia again. July-August, he writes the first mystery drama, *The Portal of Initiation* (CW 14). In November, he gives "psychosophy" lectures. In December, he submits "On the Psychological Foundations and Epistemological Framework of Theosophy" to the International Philosophical Congress in Bologna.

1911: The crisis in the Theosophical Society deepens. In January, "The Order of the Rising Sun," which will soon become "The Order of the Star in the East," is founded for the coming world teacher, Krishnamurti. At the same time, Marie von Sivers, Rudolf Steiner's coworker, falls ill. Fewer lectures are given, but important new ground is broken. In Prague, in March, Steiner meets Franz Kafka (1883-1924) and Hugo Bergmann (1883-1975). In April, he delivers his paper to the

Philosophical Congress. He writes the second mystery drama, *The Soul's Probation* (CW 14). Also, while Marie von Sivers is convalescing, Rudolf Steiner begins work on *Calendar 1912/1913*, which will contain the "Calendar of the Soul" meditations. On March 19, Anna (Eunike) Steiner dies. In September, Rudolf Steiner visits Einsiedeln, birthplace of Paracelsus. In December, Friedrich Rittelmeyer, future founder of the Christian Community, meets Rudolf Steiner. The *Johannes-Bauverein*, the "building committee," which would lead to the first Goetheanum (first planned for Munich), is also founded, and a preliminary committee for the founding of an independent association is created that, in the following year, will become the Anthroposophical Society. Important lecture cycles include *Occult Physiology* (CW 128); *Wonders of the World* (CW 129); *From Jesus to Christ* (CW 131). Other themes: esoteric Christianity; Christian Rosenkreutz; the spiritual guidance of humanity; the sense world and the world of the spirit.

1912: Despite the ongoing, now increasing crisis in the Theosophical Society, much is accomplished: *Calendar 1912/1913* is published; eurythmy is created; both the third mystery drama, *The Guardian of the Threshold* (CW 14) and *A Way of Self-Knowledge* (CW 16) are written. New (or renewed) themes included life between death and rebirth and karma and reincarnation. Other lecture cycles: *Spiritual Beings in the Heavenly Bodies and the Kingdoms of Nature* (CW 136); *The Human Being in the Light of Occultism, Theosophy, and Philosophy* (CW 137); *The Gospel of St. Mark* (CW 139); and *The Bhagavad Gita and the Epistles of Paul* (CW 142). On May 8, Rudolf Steiner celebrates White Lotus Day, H.P. Blavatsky's death day, which he had faithfully observed for the past decade, for the last time. In August, Rudolf Steiner suggests the "independent association" be called the "Anthroposophical Society." In September, the first eurythmy course takes place. In October, Rudolf Steiner declines recognition of a Theosophical Society lodge dedicated to the Star of the East and decides to expel all Theosophical Society members belonging to the order. Also, with Marie von Sivers, he first visits Dornach, near Basel, Switzerland, and they stand on the hill where the Goetheanum will be. In November, a Theosophical Society lodge is opened by direct mandate from Adyar (Annie Besant). In December, a meeting of the German section occurs at which it is decided that belonging to the Order of the Star of the East is incompatible with membership in the Theosophical Society. December 28: informal founding of the Anthroposophical Society in Berlin.

1913: Expulsion of the German section from the Theosophical Society. February 2-3: Foundation meeting of the Anthroposophical Society. Board members include: Marie von Sivers, Michael Bauer, and Carl Unger. September 20: Laying of the foundation stone for the *Johannes Bau* (Goetheanum) in Dornach. Building begins immediately. The third mystery drama, *The Soul's Awakening* (CW 14), is completed.

Also: *The Threshold of the Spiritual World* (CW 147). Lecture cycles include: *The Bhagavad Gita and the Epistles of Paul* and *The Esoteric Meaning of the Bhagavad Gita* (CW 146), which the Russian philosopher Nikolai Berdyaev attends; *The Mysteries of the East and of Christianity* (CW 144); *The Effects of Esoteric Development* (CW 145); and *The Fifth Gospel* (CW 148). In May, Rudolf Steiner is in London and Paris, where anthroposophic work continues.

1914: Building continues on the *Johannes Bau* (Goetheanum) in Dornach, with artists and coworkers from seventeen nations. The general assembly of the Anthroposophical Society takes place. In May, Rudolf Steiner visits Paris, as well as Chartres Cathedral. June 28: assassination in Sarajevo ("Now the catastrophe has happened!"). August 1: War is declared. Rudolf Steiner returns to Germany from Dornach—he will travel back and forth. He writes the last chapter of *The Riddles of Philosophy*. Lecture cycles include: *Human and Cosmic Thought* (CW 151); *Inner Being of Humanity between Death and a New Birth* (CW 153); *Occult Reading and Occult Hearing* (CW 156). December 24: marriage of Rudolf Steiner and Marie von Sivers.

1915: Building continues. Life after death becomes a major theme, also art. Writes: *Thoughts during a Time of War* (CW 24). Lectures include: *The Secret of Death* (CW 159); *The Uniting of Humanity through the Christ Impulse* (CW 165).

1916: Rudolf Steiner begins work with Edith Maryon (1872-1924) on the sculpture "The Representative of Humanity" ("The Group"—Christ, Lucifer, and Ahriman). He also works with the alchemist Alexander von Bernus on the quarterly *Das Reich*. He writes *The Riddle of Humanity* (CW 20). Lectures include: *Necessity and Freedom in World History and Human Action* (CW 166); *Past and Present in the Human Spirit* (CW 167); *The Karma of Vocation* (CW 172); *The Karma of Untruthfulness* (CW 173).

1917: Russian Revolution. The U.S. enters the war. Building continues. Rudolf Steiner delineates the idea of the "threefold nature of the human being" (in a public lecture March 15) and the "threefold nature of the social organism" (hammered out in May-June with the help of Otto von Lerchenfeld and Ludwig Polzer-Hoditz in the form of two documents titled *Memoranda*, which were distributed in high places). August-September: Rudolf Steiner writes *The Riddles of the Soul* (CW 20). Also: commentary on "The Chemical Wedding of Christian Rosenkreutz" for Alexander Bernus (*Das Reich*). Lectures include: *The Karma of Materialism* (CW 176); *The Spiritual Background of the Outer World: The Fall of the Spirits of Darkness* (CW 177).

1918: March 18: peace treaty of Brest-Litovsk—"Now everything will truly enter chaos! What is needed is cultural renewal." June: Rudolf Steiner visits Karlstein (Grail) Castle outside Prague. Lecture cycle: *From Symptom to Reality in Modern History* (CW 185). In mid-November,

Emil Molt, of the Waldorf-Astoria Cigarette Company, has the idea of founding a school for his workers' children.

1919: Focus on the threefold social organism: tireless travel, countless lectures, meetings, and publications. At the same time, a new public stage of Anthroposophy emerges as cultural renewal begins. The coming years will see initiatives in pedagogy, medicine, pharmacology, and agriculture. January 27: threefold meeting: " We must first of all, with the money we have, found free schools that can bring people what they need." February: first public eurythmy performance in Zurich. Also: "Appeal to the German People" (CW 24), circulated March 6 as a newspaper insert. In April, *Toward Social Renewal* (CW 23)—"perhaps the most widely read of all books on politics appearing since the war"—appears. Rudolf Steiner is asked to undertake the "direction and leadership" of the school founded by the Waldorf-Astoria Company. Rudolf Steiner begins to talk about the "renewal" of education. May 30: a building is selected and purchased for the future Waldorf School. August-September, Rudolf Steiner gives a lecture course for Waldorf teachers, *The Foundations of Human Experience (Study of Man)* (CW 293). September 7: Opening of the first Waldorf School. December (into January): first science course, the *Light Course* (CW 320).

1920: The Waldorf School flourishes. New threefold initiatives. Founding of limited companies *Der Kommenden Tag* and *Futurum A.G.* to infuse spiritual values into the economic realm. Rudolf Steiner also focuses on the sciences. Lectures: *Introducing Anthroposophical Medicine* (CW 312); *The Warmth Course* (CW 321); *The Boundaries of Natural Science* (CW 322); *The Redemption of Thinking* (CW 74). February: Johannes Werner Klein—later a cofounder of the Christian Community—asks Rudolf Steiner about the possibility of a "religious renewal," a "Johannine church." In March, Rudolf Steiner gives the first course for doctors and medical students. In April, a divinity student asks Rudolf Steiner a second time about the possibility of religious renewal. September 27-October 16: anthroposophic "college course." December: lectures titled *The Search for the New Isis* (CW 202).

1921: Rudolf Steiner continues his intensive work on cultural renewal, including the uphill battle for the threefold social order. "College" arts, scientific, theological, and medical courses include: *The Astronomy Course* (CW 323); *Observation, Mathematics, and Scientific Experiment* (CW 324); the *Second Medical Course* (CW 313); *Color*. In June and September-October, Rudolf Steiner also gives the first two "priests' courses" (CW 342 and 343). The "youth movement" gains momentum. Magazines are founded: *Die Drei* (January), and—under the editorship of Albert Steffen (1884-1963)—the weekly, *Das Goetheanum* (August). In February-March, Rudolf Steiner takes his first trip outside Germany since the war (Holland). On April 7, Steiner receives a letter regarding "religious renewal," and May 22-23, he agrees to address the question in a practical way. In June, the Klinical-Therapeutic Institute opens in Arlesheim under the direction of Dr. Ita Wegman. In August, the Chemical-Pharmaceutical Laboratory opens in Arlesheim (Oskar Schmiedel and Ita Wegman, directors). The Clinical Therapeutic Institute is inaugurated in Stuttgart (Dr. Ludwig Noll, director); also the Research Laboratory in Dornach (Ehrenfried Pfeiffer and Gunther Wachsmuth, directors). In November-December, Rudolf Steiner visits Norway.

1922: The first half of the year involves very active public lecturing (thousands attend); in the second half, Rudolf Steiner begins to withdraw and turn toward the Society—"The Society is asleep." It is "too weak" to do what is asked of it. The businesses—*Die Kommenden Tag* and *Futura A.G.*—fail. In January, with the help of an agent, Steiner undertakes a twelve-city German tour, accompanied by eurythmy performances. In two weeks he speaks to more than 2,000 people. In April, he gives a "college course" in The Hague. He also visits England. In June, he is in Vienna for the East-West Congress. In August-September, he is back in England for the Oxford Conference on Education. Returning to Dornach, he gives the lectures *Philosophy, Cosmology, and Religion* (CW 215), and gives the third priest's course (CW 344). On September 16, The Christian Community is founded. In October-November, Steiner is in Holland and England. He also speaks to the youth: *The Youth Course* (CW 217). In December, Steiner gives lectures titled *The Origins of Natural Science* (CW 326), and *Humanity and the World of Stars: The Spiritual Communion of Humanity* (CW 219). December 31: Fire at the Goetheanum, which is destroyed.

1923: Despite the fire, Rudolf Steiner continues his work unabated. A very hard year. Internal dispersion, dissension, and apathy abound. There is conflict—between old and new visions—within the society. A wake-up call is needed, and Rudolf Steiner responds with renewed lecturing vitality. His focus: the spiritual context of human life; initiation science; the course of the year; and community building. As a foundation for an artistic school, he creates a series of pastel sketches. Lecture cycles: *The Anthroposophical Movement; Initiation Science* (CW 227) (in England at the Penmaenmawr Summer School); *The Four Seasons and the Archangels* (CW 229); *Harmony of the Creative Word* (CW 230); *The Supersensible Human* (CW 231), given in Holland for the founding of the Dutch society. On November 10, in response to the failed Hitler-Ludendorf putsch in Munich, Steiner closes his Berlin residence and moves the *Philosophisch-Anthroposophisch Verlag* (Press) to Dornach. On December 9, Steiner begins the serialization of his *Autobiography: The Course of My Life* (CW 28) in *Das Goetheanum*. It will continue to appear weekly, without a break, until his death. Late December-early January: Rudolf Steiner refounds the Anthroposophical Society (about 12,000 members internationally) and takes over its leadership. The new board members are: Marie Steiner, Ita Wegman, Albert Steffen, Elizabeth Vreede, and Guenther Wachsmuth. (See *The Christmas Meeting for the Founding of the General Anthroposophical Society* (CW 260). Accompanying lectures: *Mystery Knowledge and Mystery Centers* (CW 232); *World History in the Light of Anthroposophy* (CW 233). December 25: the Foundation Stone is laid (in the hearts of members) in the form of the "Foundation Stone Meditation."

1924: January 1: having founded the Anthroposophical Society and taken over its leadership, Rudolf Steiner has the task of "reforming" it. The process begins with a weekly newssheet ("What's Happening in the Anthroposophical Society") in which Rudolf Steiner's "Letters to Members" and "Anthroposophical Leading Thoughts" appear (CW 26). The next step is the creation of a new esoteric class, the "first class" of the "College of Spiritual Science" (which was to have been followed, had Rudolf Steiner lived longer, by two more advanced classes). Then comes a new language for Anthroposophy—practical, phenomenological, and direct; and Rudolf Steiner creates the model for the second Goetheanum. He begins the series of extensive "karma" lectures (CW 235-40); and finally, responding to needs, he creates two new initiatives: biodynamic agriculture and curative education. After the middle of the year, rumors begin to circulate regarding Steiner's health. Lectures: January-February, *Anthroposophy* (CW 234); February: *Tone Eurythmy* (CW 278); June: *The Agriculture Course* (CW 327); June-July: Speech [?] Eurythmy (CW 279); *Curative Education* (CW 317); August: (England, "Second International Summer School"), *Initiation Consciousness: True and False Paths in Spiritual Investigation* (CW 243); September: *Pastoral Medicine* (CW 318). On September 26, for the first time, Rudolf Steiner cancels a lecture. On September 28, he gives his last lecture. On September 29, he withdraws to his studio in the carpenter's shop; now he is definitively ill. Cared for by Ita Wegman, he continues working, however, and writing the weekly installments of his *Autobiography* and *Letters to the Members/Leading Thoughts* (CW 26).

1925: Rudolf Steiner, while continuing to work, continues to weaken. He finishes *Extending Practical Medicine* (CW 27) with Ita Wegman.

On March 30, around ten in the morning, Rudolf Steiner dies.

INDEX